The Camorra

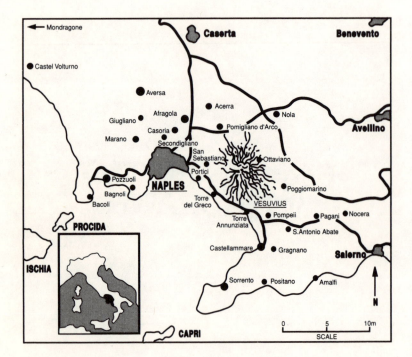

Campania

The Camorra

Tom Behan

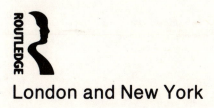

London and New York

First published 1996
by Routledge
11 New Fetter Lane, London EC4P 4EE

Simultaneously published in the USA and Canada
by Routledge
29 West 35th Street, New York, NY 10001

Typeset in Monophoto Bembo by
Datix International Limited, Bungay, Suffolk

Printed and bound in Great Britain by
Redwood Books, Trowbridge, Wiltshire

British Library Cataloguing in Publication Data
A catalogue record for this book is available from the British Library

Library of Congress Cataloguing in Publication Data
A catalogue record for this book has been requested

ISBN 0-415-09987-0

Contents

Acknowledgements

As the Italians say, this book *parte da lontano* – it comes from a long way back. In many ways it is the result of visiting and often living in Naples over a fifteen-year period, and to thank all the people who have helped me to understand a city characterised by such an uneven and combined development would simply be impossible.

It is far easier to thank those who have helped me to find material and who have commented on the work in draft. Apart from the individuals who agreed to be interviewed, specific thanks should go to the following: Percy Allum for widespread guidance over the years, Anna Rosa Gualtieri for help during the main period of composition, Debbie Kunda for the map, and Anne Webber for her initial suggestion and help at various stages. Tess Lee Ack deserves special mention for detailed comments on the draft, although Tom Orsag and Steve Wright also provided useful advice. Another precious advantage down the years has been my brother Max and his work.

Two institutions and their staff also deserve a mention: Tiziana Vernola and Eugenio Zambrano at the *Osservatorio sulla Camorra* and Andrea Cinquegrani and Maria Rosaria Sacco at *La Voce della Campania*.

Introduction

No, it was not a paradise on Earth because there were always slum dwellers and poverty.

— Raffaele La Capria

Never perhaps has the reality of modern parliamentary democracy been so accurately exposed as in Italy during the early 1990s: a reality of wall-to-wall corruption.

In less than two years, five ministers and four party leaders were forced to resign due to their alleged illegal activities, and the level of public anger and dissatisfaction was such that all political parties, including some with over a hundred years' history, either split or changed their name and policies. But even that was not enough to placate public anger; in the March 1994 elections the centre parties which had ruled Italy for nearly fifty years all but disappeared.

Even respected commentators, such as one of Italy's premier academics, Ernesto Galli della Loggia, writing in Italy's equivalent of *The Times*, the *Corriere della Sera*, reflected:

> One case of corruption is one case of corruption, ten cases of corruption are ten cases of corruption, but a hundred cases of corruption is a system of corruption.
>
> *Tangentopoli* ['bribe city', the name given to the series of scandals which first emerged in Milan in 1992] has revealed this system, which in turn is divided up into a multiplicity of subsystems. The system of written laws had been replaced by a system of implicit regulations, which were nearly always in conflict with the law of the land.
>
> Italian capitalism was and is part of that system. The

stubborn denial of this, the idea that only individual capitalists were involved and not capitalism, means to deny that there was a system, and at this point, almost deny the light of day . . .

Yet the responsibility for a system can not be individual, it must be collective.[1]

In electoral terms Italians have collectively punished the parties which managed this system. This has led to the growth of parties such as the Northern League – from non-existence ten years ago to being the largest party in the north of the country – as well as voting in media magnate Silvio Berlusconi's Forza Italia as the country's largest party in the 1994 election.

The extent of illegality has been simply bewildering, and the public's anger and indignation have been equally deep-seated. There can be no other country in the world where one of the most popular television programmes of 1993 was a two-hour transmission showing edited highlights of politicians squirming and wriggling their way around a prosecuting magistrate's questions. Such was the show's popularity that at one point two of the state television channels were arguing over which had the right to broadcast the hearings.

Although most ordinary Italians had been aware that corruption was widespread, nobody imagined it was so huge and all-encompassing. Yet there was one section of the population which had always been acutely and accurately aware of the situation: the business community. In a recent survey among 800 members of the Confindustria, Italy's major employers' association, 85 per cent of the respondents admitted that bribes were paid to get public sector contracts before the bubble burst in 1992.[2] In other words, those who preached the values of a 'free market' were doing anything but practising it, given that bribes were often paid to shut out a competing firm.

The main political party initially to benefit from all this was Umberto Bossi's Northern League, which leapt from having one MP and 1.3 per cent of the vote in the 1987 elections to fifty-five MPs and 8.7 per cent of the vote in 1992, largely repeating its 1992 performance in the 1994 general election. The League had two things going for it: it was new and consequently outside the system and therefore not corrupt; and its leader Umberto Bossi delighted many northern Italians with his crude but accurate insults against the politicians down in Rome and their alliances with organised crime even further south.

Yet just two years after his 1992 triumph, Bossi had been tamed and humbled. In January 1994 he followed the politicians he had been bellowing against into court, in what had by then become a highly conventional and pedestrian appearance, to explain why a $160,000[3] donation from a private company was given to the League's treasurer in a paper bag in a street in Rome. The 'Lion of Pontida', as Bossi was known, meekly and pathetically defined the money as a 'gift' rather than a bribe given in exchange for future political favours, although both Bossi and his treasurer are now facing trial accused of unlawful appropriation. Even though it was the crudest of parties, representing a gut hatred of the corrupt politicians who had ruled Italy for decades, it had effectively taken the Northern League less than five years to fall into step with the dominant ethos of Italian political life. And in May 1994 it completed its 'revolution' of the Italian political system and took up control of five ministries in Berlusconi's government.[4]

The day after Bossi's embarrassing court appearance, it emerged that the national police commissioner, Vincenzo Parisi, had been under investigation for two months concerning the use of slush funds belonging to the secret service, an organisation he had previously been in charge of. When the accusations were first made Parisi declared that the $2,400 per month he received from these funds were 'an annuity established in law'. Parisi is also facing more serious accusations, and the important point in this case is that such a senior figure has wide powers to destroy evidence and blackmail witnesses. Yet despite the fact that the investigations concerning Parisi were known to the President of the Republic, the Prime Minister and the Minister of the Interior, he had never been asked to resign.

These two events are just the major examples of the illegality that emerged over two days selected at random, yet revelations concerning the corruption of politicians, financial wheeler-dealers and government bureaucrats have been emerging at this kind of rate since *Tangentopoli* first began in March 1992. The new government elected in March 1994 has continued in the same tradition: first with the arrest of Paolo Berlusconi for corruption, and later with Prime Minister Silvio's embroilment in corruption accusations later in the year.

These details are important because they show that it is from this political, financial and bureaucratic cesspool that organised crime manages to find protection and to make deals. What has clearly emerged from the *Tangentopoli* scandal is that the most powerful criminal organisation in the country is Parliament: over 30 per cent of deputies in the 1992–4 Parliament are either facing trial or under investigation. If 30 per cent of workers in a factory were all facing similar charges, or alternatively 30 per cent of workers in a social security office, most people would draw the inevitable conclusion that there had been an organised conspiracy. People would start to wonder, 'surely it is impossible that only those who have been caught knew about it?' And if the accusations facing the MPs of the five parties of the ruling government coalition are collated, three out of four MPs are facing serious charges. The whole institution had become nothing but a criminal conspiracy; indeed a recent study has revealed a real crime wave amongst the MPs of recent Parliaments, with crime levels estimated at twenty times the national average.[5]

Although the extreme economic and social problems in the South are the immediate causes of organised crime, before these can be eradicated the elected politicians and unelected big businessmen and bureaucrats have to be taken on as the first stage in the fight against organised crime. The solution to organised crime in the South cannot come from these institutions; it has to come from those ordinary people who suffer the consequences of organised crime.

Indeed, the existence of large criminal organisations in the South has historically been looked upon favourably by major southern politicians. In the postwar period a backward-looking ruling class, raised on traditions of nepotism and string-pulling, has transformed southern political life into a bureaucratic nightmare in which any public service or project is viewed as a favour, not an automatic right, and even then the service or project in question is normally only provided if there is some kind of bribe or trade-off.

The trade-off between politicians and professional criminals is quite simple: the criminals mobilise their considerable electorate around specific candidates, invest large parts of their illegal profits in legal activities which create desperately needed jobs, and create a climate of fear and intimidation, keeping the lid on a society that often resembles a pressure cooker. The politician repays the favour in three ways: by awarding public sector contracts to companies controlled by professional criminals; guaranteeing a considerable amount of legal protection through applying specific pressure within the judiciary and the police force; and often allowing gang leaders to control the allocation of resources and personal favours to ordinary people.

THE STRENGTH OF THE CAMORRA

The Camorra predates the Mafia by several decades. But its history has been less linear than that of its Sicilian counterpart, as at various points in its history it has been declared completely extinct or close to extinction: the first pronouncement of the Camorra's death occurred following a major trial in 1912; then during the interwar period the fascists claimed to have eradicated it through widespread repression, while the historian Eric Hobsbawm declared that it was approaching extinction in his 1959 book *Primitive Rebels*.

The reality, though, is that, like the Mafia, the Camorra has had its ups and downs; and the 1980s were a decade of unprecedented growth. While the number of murders committed in Sicily between 1981 and 1990 was 2,905, in Campania the number was almost identical: 2,621, or 21 per cent of the national total.[6]

The political connections of the Camorra are of even greater concern: while nineteen councils in Sicily have been disbanded under suspicion of criminal infiltration since the passing of a law in 1992, Campania has had thirty-two councils disbanded, the most among Italy's twenty regions. Since 1990 twenty-six Sicilian councillors have been removed for having committed illegal acts; in Campania the number is sixty-four, another national record.[7] The same pattern applies to MPs and senators facing trial for criminal association: three in Sicily compared with eight in Campania.[8] But the disbanding of these councils is not the result of just a few individuals wielding an unacceptable level of influence. In a report published in late 1993, the Parliamentary Anti-Mafia Commission (a permanent government committee established to investigate organised crime and make recommendations to Parliament) stated: 'In the disbanded councils of Campania, rather than speaking of the Camorra's infiltration, penetration or conditioning, one can speak of the Camorra's merging with local administration.'[9]

It is not only politicians who have committed misdeeds at the top level of society, the judiciary have also played their role. In Sicily three magistrates are facing charges of favouring organised crime; Campania again has the national record of sixteen.[10]

Assets seized by investigators in recent years are a good, although not infallible, indicator of wealth generated outside the law. According to a recent report various Mafia bosses have had $105 million of assets seized, while Camorra bosses lost double that amount – $210 million.[11]

While many people may have heard of Totò Riina and Tommaso Buscetta, very few people outside Italy have heard of Carmine Alfieri or Pasquale Galasso. Yet in the Anti-Mafia Commission report mentioned above, Alfieri's gang is described as 'a phenomenon that has taken on a stronger form of oppression and corruption than the Mafia', and when Alfieri was arrested in September 1992 his personal assets were estimated at $1,200 million, making him the richest criminal in Italy.

Alfieri's gang is not based in Sicily but in the town of Nola, 15 miles north-east of Naples, and became the most powerful Camorra gang of the 1980s. In terms of violence, while the Mafia often engages in spectacular assassinations, the Camorra is perhaps an even more efficient killing machine, as proved by the recent admission of Carmine Alfieri's main hit man, Domenico Cuomo, who confessed to 'about' ninety murders in the 1983–93 period. Indeed the police estimate that Alfieri's killers alone may have been responsible for 500 murders.[12]

Outside Italy, even the British *Sun* had heard of the Camorra over ten years ago, referring to it in typically lurid but inaccurate tones as 'the Camorra, the Mafia's most evil branch'.[13] A few years ago, without making any distinction between the Camorra and the Mafia, the *Daily Mail* published a list of Italy's top ten organised crime bosses – the top two were Carmine Alfieri and Lorenzo Nuvoletta, both members of the Camorra.[14]

In recent years, however, reporting in the more serious newspapers has become more accurate, particularly thanks to the *Guardian*'s former Italian correspondent Ed Vulliamy, who once gave this vivid picture of the city:

Naples is a Third World city with Third World politics, its

super-rich surrounded by a miserable hinterland sprawling back from the volcano and the bay, a dilapidated jungle of violence, half-finished buildings, motorways that lead nowhere, cocaine, primitive Catholicism and stinking, dumped rubbish.

Its legal economy is based only on lavish state aid, money procured by its political leaders and distributed at their discretion and pleasure . . .

There is vast private wealth in the city – at night the downtown streets are crammed with new cars, mobile phones and fur coats – but this is illegal wealth, the result of the most important ingredient of the Neapolitan scandal: the Camorra . . .

Hundreds of thousands of people in Naples owe their jobs and livelihoods to either Byzantine political patronage or to the Camorra – or both. In southern Italy there are no rights – only privileges – and for those you pay a politician, either in cash or with your vote – or both.[15]

It is perhaps not surprising to learn that in a recent opinion poll amongst young people the Camorra received an approval rating of 14.6 per cent and political parties just 13.7 per cent.[16]

But how has the growth of the Camorra occurred? Even though it has disappeared for long periods since its first appearance at the beginning of the last century, it is perhaps the only urban criminal organisation based on unemployed or under-employed workers that has managed to become part of the local political class. The important point to grasp here is that this has only happened over the last twenty years; the Camorra is anything but the continuing expression of an urban environment based on feudal relations. Rather, it has grown to its present strength and structure in a late twentieth-century economic and political environment.

Indeed the Camorra has changed far more than the Mafia over the decades, and in many senses this makes it more dangerous. Membership is less family-based than in the Mafia and therefore harder to trace and predict; the territory it controls is urban and therefore more difficult to monitor; and its growth has occurred very recently, i.e. under fully 'modern' conditions.[17]

As the Anti-Mafia report describes:

The lack of specific criteria of selection for entry into a Camorra group, the general absence of rituals (which are essential in the Mafia and the 'Ndrangheta), the centuries-old state of illegality in which the poorer stratas of the population live, the willingness to use young boys as drug dealers and couriers, or to transport weapons, lead one to believe that the criminal labour force which can be mobilised by Camorra organisations – given the current social conditions in Campania, and especially in Naples and its hinterland – may be greater [than the Mafia].[18]

While much media and government attention, both nationally and internationally, has been concentrated on Sicily and the Mafia, a separate and distinct organisation, arguably even more difficult to eradicate, has been consolidating itself in the shadow of Vesuvius.

Chapter 1

The origins of the Camorra and the Mafia

Death is only a possibility, but hunger is certain.

— Victor Serge

THE ORIGINS OF THE CAMORRA

The origins of a Neapolitan criminal organisation called the Camorra are far from clear. Some writers have claimed a history which goes back as far as the sixteenth century, arguing that it is the direct descendant of a Spanish secret society, the Garduna, founded in 1417 and subsequently introduced by officials of the Spanish monarchy to Naples.[1]

Another possibility is that the members of a criminal organisation called Camorra were a new type of *lazzaroni*, a word used to describe a very poor common thief. But as Naples grew both in size and wealth criminality began to change. The *lazzaroni* were individuals, whereas *camorristi* were part of an organisation.

A far more likely explanation is that the Camorra grew out of Neapolitan society during the period of the French Revolution between the end of the eighteenth century and the beginning of the nineteenth century.

What is beyond doubt is that throughout the centuries there is evidence of small criminal gangs operating in Naples. All of these gangs arose amongst the city's poor — people who never kept written records due to their illiteracy; hence the difficulty in establishing any categorical evidence about what kind of organisation, if any, the Camorra grew out of.

It is therefore not surprising that there are also differing opinions on the origin of the word itself. The first official use of the word occurred in 1735, when a royal circular authorised the establishment of eight gaming-houses in Naples, including the 'Camorra avanti palazzo' (the 'Camorra in front of the Palace'), the Royal Palace in today's Piazza del Plebiscito, where a gaming-house had existed for many centuries. In this instance, the word is almost certainly an amalgamation of *capo* (boss) and the Neapolitan street game, the *morra*. The *morra* is still one of Italy's more popular games, in which two players open their fists varying the numbers of fingers on display. The player who guesses the right number, which they must shout out as the fists are opened, is the winner.[2]

Alternatively, it was the word used to describe the rake-off earned by *camorristi* from goods being delivered or transported around the city; in other words, it was a word used to describe extortion.

Despite the disputes surrounding the precise origins of the Camorra, what is certainly beyond doubt is the following:

> When the Camorra emerges into the life of Naples it does not seem a totally new fact, it is rather the point of arrival, or the result, of the city's long history, and it almost seems the most natural expression of the history of the Neapolitan popular classes.[3]

This is not to say that ordinary Neapolitans had some inbuilt biological instinct which led them to create a large criminal organisation; rather, a combination of political ignorance and autocratic repression probably left them incapable of creating any other form of organisation.

Indeed it is the history of Naples itself which explains why such an organisation arose here and not elsewhere, and why organised crime has remained such a dominant feature of the city during the last two hundred years.

The city of Naples had been Europe's third largest city for three hundred years, from around 1500 to the early 1800s; with a population of approximately 350,000 throughout the sixteenth century, it often vied with Paris for the title of Europe's second largest city.

But towards the end of the seventeenth century it began to experience economic difficulties due to a fall in its exports of silk, wheat, oil and wine, caused in turn by an international economic recession and the rise of new competitors. Furthermore, the plague of 1656 led to 60 per cent of the city's population either dying or leaving the city.

Despite such calamities, throughout this period many thousands of people migrated from the countryside to Naples because the city offered the possibility of work; furthermore, the ruling aristocracy had decreed that taxes were not to be paid within the city walls. Work, however, was often scarce, so for the ruling aristocracy the city's key problem was the existence of masses of impoverished and unemployed people desperate for money and some kind of solution to their misery. The authorities needed a repressive network able to control an unpredictable population which could suddenly break out into violent revolt, such as the popular rebellion led by Masaniello in 1647–8.

Three-quarters of southern Italian trade passed through Naples, with large numbers being employed in the port, the warehouses and in the distribution of commodities; the servicing of the aristocracy and the middle classes also employed many people. As the eighteenth century came to an end, the rest of Europe and northern Italy were experiencing huge economic expansion during the industrial revolution, while Naples was stuck in a virtually feudal system, run by a monarchy terrified of any innovation. The city's role as a capital also meant it had a large number of non-productive inhabitants: it has been estimated that in 1792 over a third of the entire population was made up of clerics, aristocrats and the bourgeoisie.[4]

As the decades and centuries progressed it became clear that population growth was not being matched by an increase in production. Indeed, by 1871 35,000 people, out of an active population of 220,000, were still employed as cooks, chambermaids and gardeners, the same percentage as in the first half of the seventeenth century.[5]

Another related problem which affected the city at the time, and which is arguably still important today, was the absence of a dynamic entrepreneurial spirit amongst the middle classes. Up until the French Revolution, Naples had been a residential centre for the ruling classes of the South, as well as a bureaucratic and administrative capital. Most of the middle classes lived off government monopolies and the production of commodities such as tobacco, silk and linen, which were protected by tariff barriers, and therefore had no interest in innovation. Although only 1,356 'merchants' were recorded in the 1845 census (out of a population of 400,000), most of these were shopowners. Very few were engaged in investment and manufacture; and most decisions were made within the immediate family circle.[6]

It is likely that the Camorra emerged in this period as a result of the failure of the Neapolitan Republic, proclaimed in 1799 on the wave of the French Revolution. If the Masaniello revolt 150 years earlier had been a revolution made by the people without leaders, the 1799 revolt was carried through by liberal leaders without the people. This allowed the whole experiment to be quickly destroyed by an alliance of the Bourbons, the Church and the British navy under Horatio Nelson. Although the Bourbon dynasty was not fully restored until 1815, the Camorra first emerged during the chaotic vacuum of power in the years between 1799 and 1815.

In the following period, the middle classes organised themselves into secret societies such as the Freemasons and the Carbonaria, and negotiated with the Bourbons. But for the vast majority of Neapolitans the Camorra became their only voice, the only way in which their presence was felt: 'in this fashion the Camorra was a class-based mass phenomenon, one of the most popular illegal manifestations of nineteenth-century European history.'[7]

At this time economic development was completely different in northern Italy and the rest of Europe: trade was blossoming between states and with overseas territories, industrialisation had begun, along with the widespread building of railways. Yet in the early part of the nineteenth century the only railways built in southern Italy linked up the three royal palaces.

In many areas of his kingdom, Ferdinand II was known as 'King Bomba', because during the 1848 revolutions he ordered the bombardment of Palermo and Messina. He reigned for thirty years (1830–59) as a total autocrat and was highly distrustful of any innovations, at one point even banning the introduction of the first cameras into the city. Marco Monnier, a Swiss academic living in Naples during this period, described the king's attitude towards ordinary people thus:

He never considered for a moment raising the people up from their level of degradation; on the contrary, he wanted to keep them there until the end of time as he knew very well that, given the nature of the period we live in, an absolute monarchy is only possible if it rules over a degraded and exhausted populace.[8]

The first official news of the Camorra as an organisation dates from 1820, when police records detail a disciplinary meeting of the Camorra. Such an event indicates a qualitative change: the Camorra and *camorristi* were no longer simply local gangs living off theft and extortion; they now had a fixed structure and some kind of hierarchy. The first written statute of a Camorra organisation was also discovered in 1820, once again indicating a stable organisational structure amongst the underworld, and the second statute was discovered in 1842.[9] There were initiation rites, and funds set aside for the families of those imprisoned.

In the early part of the nineteenth century, Naples was both economically and politically stagnant. The general level of poverty is illustrated by the outbreak of cholera – a water-borne disease primarily caused by impure water and lack of public and personal hygiene – in 1836–7, which killed 20,000 people.[10] This mass poverty, together with the lack of any political outlet, made for a chaotic and ungovernable city, and under these conditions the capacity to unleash a widespread reign of terror is an important consideration for those in power. The control of the impoverished and alienated masses was a service which the Camorra could offer local rulers. And for many of the Neapolitan poor, the use of violence was the only way out of their miserable existence; the static economic climate blocked any other solution.

One of the Camorra's first strongholds developed within the prison system. This is how Marco Monnier described an inmate's relationship with the Camorra:

> he wasn't allowed to eat, drink, smoke or gamble without a *camorrista*'s permission. He had to give him a tenth of all the money he was sent, and had to pay for the right to buy and sell, as well as paying for both essential and superfluous things. He even paid to get legal advice, as if he were granted a privilege: he even paid when he was poorer and more naked than the walls of his cell, he was forced to deprive himself of everything. Those who refused to accept such impositions ran the risk of being clubbed to death.[11]

Camorristi also took money from the prison authorities, as they effectively guaranteed order. Interestingly, however, they generally left the few aristocratic and middle-class prisoners alone;

even though some *camorristi* had considerable wealth, they still felt some deference towards those in a higher social position.

The revolution of 1848 appeared to offer new political hope to the city, with Ferdinand II initially granting a liberal constitution. But the key weakness of the revolt was its lack of mass popular support, as the same writer noted a few years afterwards:

> that revolution, if it can be called such, took the form of a simple demonstration of gentlemen, without even one sword being drawn. The common people supported the absolute monarchy. In the insurrection of 15 May the barricades were defended by heroic young men, who were all from good families.[12]

Conscious that ordinary people 'cared little about whether they were a citizen or a subject',[13] the king was soon able to clamp down again, suspending the new constitution and imprisoning leading liberals. But he was not only spurred on by the inherent weakness of the Neapolitan revolt, he was also worried because liberals had taken power in cities such as Milan and Venice. Both Ferdinand and the Pope were strongly opposed to liberalism; indeed the Pope sheltered in Naples during the Roman republic of 1848–9, and Neapolitan forces contributed to the overthrow of the Roman republic led by Garibaldi and Mazzini.

Hopes of any immediate change were dashed, and communication with the outside world became very difficult:

> You found yourself living among people who were isolated from the rest of Europe, extraneous to all the issues which interested the two Worlds, imprisoned in their beautiful cell, where neither ideas, beliefs, or the material discoveries of our century could penetrate ... Foreign newspapers could only be obtained through foreign legations, booksellers hid forbidden books under their beds and then sold them at exorbitant prices: people then dug out holes in the walls of their rooms to hide their illicit and forbidden fruits.[14]

This repression not only affected liberals and the educated middle classes, it also conditioned people in the business world, both Neapolitan and foreign: 'I have seen highly respected foreign merchants and industrialists buying portraits, chalk busts, or little bronze and terracotta statues of the King and Queen. They then placed them around their premises so they wouldn't be suspected of liberalism.'[15]

The effect on ordinary people, and the consequences, were even more serious:

> any social, political or religious links had been destroyed through terror. As with the intelligentsia, the healthy forces in the country are directionless and worn out because they are too isolated and dispersed. No cohesion whatsoever was possible: the authorities even banned groups of people who met to play chess ... What emerges from this is that in all the popular classes no association could be created to counteract the dominance of the wicked.[16]

Despite the liberals' ineptitude, their lack of popular support and the strict rule of Ferdinand II, demands for change continued throughout the 1850s. The southern economy continued to grow slowly, with the vast majority of goods passing through Naples. Between 1838 and 1852 grain exports increased sixfold, with fruit exports also doubling from 1832 to 1859. Naples' dock was now handling a huge amount in trade; in 1855–9 alone the port doubled its activity.[17]

The Camorra was involved in all these activities. Not only was it earning money from gambling and theft, it also earned rake-offs from goods which arrived at the port and passed through the city's gates; indeed the amount they took could often reach 10 per cent of the value of the goods themselves.

Alongside this economic growth, the Camorra may have also enjoyed a degree of political protection. In some circumstances they effectively took the place of the police: 'The police had no need to intervene in those dangerous places; they entrusted the members of the sect [the Camorra], which was then tolerated.'[18]

Not only had trade increased, a degree of industrialisation had also started; for example, the Naples cigarette factory was probably the largest in the entire South, employing 1,220 women.

Yet most of this was taking place *despite* the King and his administration; most of the capital invested came from Germany, France or Switzerland. Tariff barriers discouraged new investment and new methods of production; and many members of the middle class depended on the old system for jobs within the administration.

Throughout Ferdinand II's reign Neapolitan society was highly unstable: the poor masses were forced to eke out a living doing whatever came to hand, which obviously included criminal activities, while the middle classes were frustrated by economic and political restrictions. This situation might well have continued for the rest of the century. What changed matters was Giuseppe Garibaldi's landing in Sicily in May 1860 and the beginning of the campaign to unite Italy.

The other catalyst was the liberals' coming to an agreement with the Camorra. Following their defeat in 1848, members of the liberal opposition had realised that they needed the support of the masses to overthrow the King. And it is an indication of the Camorra's strength that the liberals turned to them, and paid them, in order to build links with ordinary people.

A meeting was arranged behind the Albergo de' Poveri, during which the *camorristi*

> told them off for their gentlemanly revolution in 1848. They told them what I had already noted, that this revolt had not broken out amongst the people, and neither was it for the people: the well-dressed and educated middle classes had only thought of themselves, leaving the poor people aside. If any changes were to occur the rabble did not intend to give all the advantages to those who already had money; at the end of the day, the art of launching an uprising needed money, lots of money, and to start with, every local leader, that is every Camorra boss, demanded payment of ten thousand ducats.[19]

The liberals had few alternatives; Ferdinand II's ferocious repression had meant that the masses had no organisation but the Camorra —(in reality the *camorristi* were the leaders of the city's poor.) The Camorra had clearly come a long way in just a few decades, effectively becoming power brokers. It is important to note, however, that their attitude was mercenary; there is no evidence of the organisation consistently expressing any kind of political belief or following a strategy of its own independently of others.

So as Garibaldi defeated the Bourbons in Sicily and crossed over onto the Italian mainland, the old regime was about to come to an end.

'NA BESTEMMIA PE' 'STA LIBERTÀ:[20]
UNIFICATION AND THE STABILISATION OF
THE CAMORRA

As Garibaldi's expeditionary force advanced up the peninsula from Sicily, the government of Piedmont, which had organised his trip without the intention of uniting the whole of Italy, became severely alarmed. The Prime Minister, Cavour, tried to engineer a conservative revolt in Naples in favour of Victor Emmanuel, the King of Piedmont and future King of Italy, but it failed due to an almost total lack of support.

On 24 June 1860 Francis II, the new King, was obliged to finally institute the constitution agreed upon in 1848; he also released many *camorristi* who had been arrested the previous year accused of spying for the liberals. Francis was desperately trying to head off the enthusiasm for Garibaldi's victories in Sicily and success in Calabria, as he feared that the revolutionary enthusiasm of poor peasants would jeopardise his own rule. But he had moved far too late: two days later attacks began on police patrols and on numerous police barracks, probably the work of *camorristi* taking revenge for their imprisonment. The old order was rapidly collapsing; the police soon began taking off their uniforms and melting into the crowds, while senior members of the old regime tried to convert their banknotes into gold, aware that the old regime could quickly be completely overthrown. Finally, on the evening of the 26th, a state of siege was declared.

Italian Unification, following the Italian Marxist Antonio Gramsci, can be seen as a 'passive revolution', with little involvement of the masses. In effect the change of government in Naples was the result of *trasformismo* – the incorporation of the opposition into the ruling circle – with ordinary people barred from any important or long-term role.

In the chaos of a disintegrating dynasty a new prefect of police had been appointed, Liborio Romano, who turned to the Camorra to maintain 'law and order'. This attitude of managing the level of illegality is still a characteristic of the Neapolitan ruling class, and it is therefore worth quoting from his memoirs at length:

> How could the city be saved in the midst of so many disruptive elements and imminent dangers? Amongst all the

possibilities which passed through my anxious mind, rendered such by the seriousness of the situation, only one appeared to me to offer probable, although not certain success, so I tried it. I thought of making use of the evil skills of *camorristi*, offering the most influential leaders a means to rehabilitate themselves. It appeared to me that this would drag them away from the mob, and at least paralyse their most evil intentions, it also meant that there would be no attempt to repress or contain them, as this was a moment in which I lacked any kind of strength . . .

It was my intention to draw a veil over their past and ask the best of them to join a new police force, which would no longer be made up of wicked assassins and vile spies, but of honest people who, well paid for their important services, would have soon gained the respect of their fellow citizens.

The man [a Camorra leader invited to Romano's house], who initially appeared to be doubtful and uncertain, after I had spoken threw away all suspicion and wanted to kiss my hand; he also promised more than I had asked for and added that he would return in an hour to see me at the Prefettura. Even before the hour was up he had returned with a colleague, and they assured me that they had passed on my instructions to their friends, and that they would lay down their lives for me.[21]

The fact that one of the Camorra leaders who ran this new police force, Salvatore De Crescenzo, had already been convicted on six separate occasions, once for murder, did not seem to concern the Prefect of Police. The most important thing was the maintenance of 'order', or in other words, stopping the masses from taking control; any considerations of a moral or legal nature came a very poor second.

Romano's manoeuvres worked. The King withdrew from Naples on September 6 and Garibaldi arrived by train from Salerno the following day.[22] The changeover was so smooth that Garibaldi arrived with just thirty companions to take over the running of a city of half a million people, the largest city in the new state.

The need, first for the liberals and then for Romano, to make an alliance with the Camorra was a clear indication of the organisation's strength. However, Romano's account also illustrates that *camorristi* were very easily manipulated. In effect, the Camorra had become mercenaries within the city, acting as secret policemen in the last year of Ferdinand II's reign, as liberal oppositionists during the last year of Bourbon rule and then as official policemen in the first few months following Unification. The Camorra had played all of these roles for money; there is no evidence of *camorristi* having had any consistent political opinions.

But the fact that leading *camorristi* were now moving quite regularly in the corridors of power obviously increased their political awareness and self-confidence. Their position as policemen naturally gave them greater freedom to manoeuvre and they quickly moved into the contraband industry, not only extorting money from those already smuggling goods, but also obliging shopkeepers and merchants to take smuggled instead of official goods. Once they had paid off the Camorra, traders found that they were still paying far less than the official price.

This clearly meant a huge drop in revenue for the new administration. But traders were very unwilling to change their habits:

> They chose the lesser of two evils. If they paid a tax to the sect [the Camorra] they only ran the risk of being discovered by tax inspectors and suffering a minor conviction; but if they paid the tax inspectors then they were certain of being caught by *camorristi* and given a good beating. So they paid a tax to the sect.[23]

The new administration had soon realised that its income was being severely reduced, and that using the Camorra as a police force had created a whole range of problems. So they set up a new police force, brought soldiers in from outside Naples and in December 1860 turned on the Camorra, arresting ninety people. The Camorra responded with demonstrations against the new Chief of Police, Silvio Spaventa, and with attacks on both his house and office.

Marco Monnier commented on the growing power and self-confidence of some Camorra leaders:

> All those swaggering men from the market squares of Naples were no longer satisfied with stealing small amounts from ordinary people: they had become politicians. During the

elections they prohibited certain candidates, comforting the conscience and the beliefs of voters with their weapons.[24]

However, it is important not to exaggerate this tendency towards some kind of intervention in politics. Although some Camorra leaders began to make statements in favour of the deposed Bourbon regime, these were never part of any independent political ideology or strategy. Such manoeuvres were limited in scope and were probably aimed at conditioning politicians over a small number of specific issues. For example, in the first years of Unification, if (in the Camorra's eyes) a deputy had behaved badly at the new Parliament in Turin, demonstrations were organised in front of his house – but the Camorra never tried to put forward its own candidates.

In effect the Camorra could only apply pressure under certain circumstances as it did not have either the ability or the know-how to enter its own candidates. Economically it still lived mostly on extortion, so the ruling authorities did not rely on its investments to keep the economy ticking over.

These political and economic weaknesses made it possible to curb the Camorra's growth, but it was too strong to be totally destroyed. A state of siege was declared in July 1862, and in the next three months 500 camorristi were rounded up. The special legislation passed to defeat the banditry which was sweeping remote southern areas and required the deployment of 100,000 northern troops throughout the South was also applied to Naples, with the Camorra being defined as 'urban banditry'. In this period the authorities clearly re-established their dominance, as 1,200 convicted camorristi were sentenced to house arrest in 1863–4.[25]

Nevertheless the post-Unification period constitutes the Camorra's second phase, which lasted until about the turn of the century – and is characterised by the Camorra's steady advance into many areas of Neapolitan society.

Most economic indicators for this period show that Naples and the South began to fall even further behind the rest of Italy. The highest tariff barriers in Europe (80 per cent), set up to contain competition from France and Britain, were swiftly removed; the sudden influx of cheap foreign goods devastated local producers whose goods were priced artificially high. Taxation also doubled; but the majority of the taxes collected and the capital accumulated were destined for investment in the mush-rooming industry of the North.[26] Poverty remained widespread and surfaced in a particular virulent form in another outbreak of cholera in 1884. (Cholera is endemic to the city, which last suffered an outbreak in 1973).

The Camorra began to enter new economic areas, becoming directly involved in commerce for the first time through the buying and selling of bran and horses. The city's economy became increasingly dominated by council contracts and the rebuilding of many of the city's oldest areas.

The change in the Camorra's manner of dress also indicated some kind of transformation. In the period from their emergence up until 1860, it was important for them to be recognised as *camorristi* so as to be able to intimidate people. So many of them adopted a kind of uniform, which included tight jackets and wide trousers, often with a beret, tattoos and several rings on their fingers. But as some now aspired to enter the middle classes, their dress became more respectable and inconspicuous.

The extension in suffrage in 1882 and 1889 also led them to gain more influence in politics for the very same reason as thirty years before: the liberal politicians had very little contact with the vast majority of the population and were therefore obliged to look to the Camorra to guarantee them votes. It is in this period that the Camorra began to gain political protection, and in exchange it led street protests in 1893 against the massacre of Italian workers at Aigues-Mortes in France. It also organised the demonstrations in support of the liberal politician Francesco Crispi's prime ministerial election campaign.

The Camorra's predominantly mercenary attitude towards politics emerged once again when an eleven-year-old boy was killed by the police during a demonstration. Tram and carriage drivers went on strike in protest, and following the precedent set during the 1860 crisis, the prefect asked Ciccio Cappuccio, leader of the Camorra at that time, to bring the strike to an end, which was swiftly done.

Even the limited democracy which existed provided the space for challenges to be made against the collusion between the local political system and the Camorra. In 1879 the Republican Party made the following accusation in its newspaper (although its distribution was banned by the Questura, the Police Headquarters):

We have heard that Questura policemen are being subsidised by gaming-houses, and that the average daily amount is the tidy sum of ten lire! One could say that the Camorra are always around, all that changes is the uniform of the lazy bourgeois and that of the idle police official.[27]

This political dispute was one of the first signs of various changes which were soon to take effect, leading to the long-term decline of the Camorra, a decline which was to last until about 1970.

DOWN BUT NOT OUT: THE LONG-TERM DECLINE OF THE CAMORRA

The next major street demonstrations occurred in 1898, in protest against a massacre of workers in Milan. One contemporary account described the events:

Ordinary people left their work and started to move through the streets where large factories were, calling their brothers out. As the crowd got bigger, it moved to the richer areas where the government building was, and kept on chanting: 'Long live the Republic, long live socialism, long live our brothers in Milan.'[28]

The fact that Neapolitans were demonstrating in solidarity with people in a faraway northern city was an important event in itself; the provincialism of Neapolitan society, nurtured under the Bourbons, was being whittled away.

The people behind the demonstration were members of the Socialist Party (PSI) and trade unionists; the gradual industrialisation of the city meant that ordinary people finally had a new ideology of a better future, that of socialism. Although most people were still highly religious they had remained indifferent to the liberals; the socialists were offering a new society in which working people would finally be able to take control of their own lives. The socialist tradition in Naples goes back as far as December 1868, when a branch of Karl Marx's First International was founded, with a reported membership in August 1872 of 800–1,000 members.[29]

The Camorra was absent from these demonstrations; their lack of political understanding meant that they had lost control of the streets and the working masses for the first time. The socialists also began to attack the collusion between the city council and the Camorra, a campaign which led to the conviction of a councillor for corruption and eventually to the resignation of the entire council in November 1900. Campaigns such as this made the whole country aware of the links between politicians and the Camorra, and led to a huge public inquiry conducted by Giuseppe Saredo, instituted in November 1900 and eventually reporting with 2,000 pages of evidence in September 1901.

Saredo's conclusions deserve to be quoted at length because they constitute a damning indictment of Neapolitan society in the forty years since Unification. Politicians had been more concerned with jockeying for position in order to maintain power than with solving any of the city's problems. The result of their lack of mass support and the desperation engendered by mass poverty was that the Camorra had thrived:

> Together with the original 'low level' Camorra, which had ruled over the poor people with diverse forms of bullying in periods of abjection and servitude, a 'high level' Camorra has arisen, which is made up of the more audacious and cunning members of the bourgeoisie. These people, taking advantage of the indolence of their own class and its lack of resolve, which was mainly caused by economic difficulties, also imposed masses of ignorant and violent people upon their former colleagues. They managed to feed off commerce and council contracts, as well as public demonstrations, clubs and the press ... With the development of the Camorra, there also arose a new electoral organisation based on patronage; services were exchanged and rendered in return for votes, and took the form of protection, help, advice, recommendation; which also permitted the growth of a strata of intermediaries and fixers, who in the period before 1860 were already an essential element in the business cycle ... The addition of electoral corruption not only rendered all this possible, but even made the presence of an intermediary essential in all corners of general social and administrative practice ...
>
> From the rich industrialist who wants a clear road into politics or administration to the small shopowner who wants to ask for a reduction in his taxes; from the businessman

trying to win a contract to a worker looking for a job in a factory; from a professional who wants more clients or greater recognition to somebody looking for an office job; from somebody from the Provinces who has come to Naples to buy some goods to somebody who wants to emigrate to America; they all find somebody stepping into their path, and nearly all make use of them.[30]

Although such a picture is clearly alarming, the Camorra was nevertheless already entering a period of decline. Its influence did not disappear overnight. In 1904 the Camorra, led by a priest named Vito Vittozzi, managed to stop the election of socialist deputy Ettore Ciccotti in the Vicaria area. A few years later Ciccotti wrote that the campaign: 'had a clear aim . . . that of breaking the working-class movement and the Trades Council in Naples.'[31]

Not only did the Saredo enquiry make a great impact, a mass trial in 1911–12, investigating the murder of a *camorrista* named Gennaro Cuocolo a few years earlier, led to the conviction of twenty-seven leading gangsters for a whole range of crimes.

Mass migration also destabilised the Camorra's power base, the urban poor. Only 3,165 Neapolitans emigrated from the city in 1876, yet this figure rose to 76,000 in 1901 and 90,000 in 1906.[32] This obviously meant that large numbers of the poor actually left the city, but at the same time many areas were also transformed as a result of an urban renewal policy.

Those who did remain were living in far worse conditions than their northern counterparts; forty years of national unity had done nothing to solve the perennial 'Southern question' of Italian politics; indeed, in many ways things had become worse. Statistics from the 1901 census show that 42 per cent of Neapolitan adults were illiterate, compared with 18 per cent in Genoa, 11 per cent in Turin and 4 per cent in Milan.[33]

Nevertheless the western and eastern outskirts of the city were now industrialised to quite a significant extent, and there had also been considerable growth of small industries throughout the city. The increase in stable employment, and the consequent rise in trade union and socialist party membership, meant that the Camorra's power to attract the city's poor to a life of crime was for the moment eclipsed. The masses could now find a different voice from that of their traditional spontaneous rebellion.

This is not to say that contemporary lessons cannot be drawn from the first fifty years of Unification in Naples. In short, a small secret society of illiterate working-class criminals had managed to penetrate the highest levels of Neapolitan society – often as a result of direct encouragement by ruling politicians. A hundred years later the Camorra would not only be more experienced and educated, it would also have far greater economic power, and so in the 1980s it would prove impossible to deprive it of power and influence.

By the outbreak of the First World War, however, the word 'Camorra' had all but disappeared from normal usage. For example, the new songs about the Neapolitan underworld began to talk about *guappi*, or *guapparia*, which is more to do with individual attitude than membership of an organisation.[34]

The advent of Fascism in 1922 brought a virtual end to the Camorra within Naples, although small gangs still existed in the countryside. A totalitarian regime such as Mussolini's could not tolerate organised illegal activities and clamped down hard wherever they were suspected. Following in the traditions of *trasformismo*, some members of the Camorra were simply invited to join the Fascist Party, often becoming leading members in the more outlying areas of the city. Many ex-*camorristi* found themselves supervising fruit and vegetable markets, the manufacture of tobacco, or trading in the port. In other words, the few remaining *camorristi* were largely incorporated within the Fascist system of power.

In the countryside surrounding the city a more 'Sicilian' situation was allowed to exist. Fascism used the small Camorra gangs to intimidate those peasants who managed to maintain a small degree of organised opposition to the regime. However, any mention of Sicily in this context obviously brings the Mafia to mind, so it is useful at this point to examine the similarities and differences between the Camorra and its Sicilian counterpart.

THE DIFFERENCES BETWEEN THE MAFIA AND THE CAMORRA

The origins of the Camorra lie in the urban poor of Naples at the beginning of the last century. The Mafia has completely different origins – it appeared later and its origins are rural.

This is not to say that the two organisations had no

connections whatsoever in the last century. In its early period the Camorra used the Sicilian word *picciotto* to describe an apprentice member. The same word is still used today to describe a common foot-soldier of the Mafia; in this case the common use probably derives from the fact that *camorristi* and *mafiosi* were held together in the same jails.

Even the early use of the word 'Mafia' reveals another difference, as it was normally used to describe an attitude, whereas the word 'Camorra' originally related to an activity and to an organisation.

The first known use of the word 'Mafia' was recorded in 1862, over a hundred years after the first use of the word 'Camorra' in Naples, and the first police reference to the Mafia occurred in 1865, forty-five years after the first police report on the Camorra.[35]

Although the fact that the Camorra and the Mafia arose in different periods may be interesting in itself, their diverse social origins are far more important in explaining the very real differences which still exist between them.

The predecessor of the Mafioso was the *gabellotto* of the Sicilian countryside at the beginning of the last century.[36] *Gabellotti* were employed by absentee landowners to supervise the correct functioning of short-term contracts, known as *gabella*, between the landlord and the local peasantry; in other words, the *gabellotto* played a key role in checking peasant revolt.

When disputes occurred the landlord often ordered that his interpretation of the contract be enforced violently. (So, as with the Camorra, violent intimidation as a service was an important first element in the Mafia's growth.)

Violence was very frequent in the Sicilian countryside during this period and had two main sources: of these banditry was the more common one, and *gabellotti* were often sworn in as irregular policemen by the Bourbon authorities to fight the bandits. The other source of violence was the continuing resentment of Sicilian peasants towards landowners. The peasants were acutely aware that previously common lands had been effectively stolen from them; in the case of peasant disturbances the *gabellotto* was often the private policeman of large landowners.

Furthermore, in the early part of the nineteenth century many *gabellotti* were already 'upwardly mobile' peasants, in that they often managed *masserie*, or large farms. These farms, which were often dozens of hectares in size, were the result of th splitting up of the old feudal landed estates in an effort to increase production. This meant that the *gabellotti* were quite adept at rudimentary administration, using agricultural machinery and dealing with large amounts of cash – all key differences in comparison with the *camorristi*. They also played another important role: ensuring the safe passage of agricultural produce through the countryside to ports on the coast, and in an area without any kind of modern communication, they often were a vital source of information concerning events in the outside world. The *gabellotti* therefore developed a broad range of communication skills and friendships, an important contrast to the early *camorristi*.

Another vital difference between Sicily and Naples is the weakness of the government, whether it be the Bourbon government or the new Italian state. The remoteness of the island and the hostility of its population towards any foreign domination meant that the emerging Mafia sometimes acted as a crude form of government.

In the two decades preceding and following Unification in 1860, the *gabellotto*, or Mafioso, began to take over from the absentee landowners. This was done either legally, through buying the land in question, or through threats and violence – and the landlords, who had often lived off the rent for these areas for generations, had no real means of opposing this change.

Some Mafiosi also began to practise extortion on the land; 'either the owner or the tenant have to pay the Mafioso if they want to get something useful out of their land, and not see it return to being "a desert".'[37] The landowner also felt obliged to pay because he was normally aware of the collusion between the police and the Mafia; the peasant paid for similar reasons.

The emerging Mafia put this cash to good use, becoming money lenders in the countryside: 'The *mafioso gabellotto* was the only person to have cash and lent it whenever he wanted to; for a wedding, a funeral, an illness, emigration.'[38] The peasant obviously had to pay interest, and if he failed to pay, his goods and animals were seized, or he was killed. Given the disintegration of the old feudal system and the weakness of absentee landowners, the Mafia quickly diversified into other economic areas, for example the lease and purchase of sulphur mines or salt banks; as a result, it very quickly began to engage in legal activities.

Not only did the Mafia accumulate capital and move into legal economic activities, it also entered politics – two very stark differences from the early Camorra. The Mafia already had a certain sophistication, moving quite adeptly amongst peasants, aristocratic landowners, state officials and the first businessmen. Not surprisingly, it took very little time to gain entry into important areas of the local political system. Whether it be landowners, politicians or businessmen, they all needed the Mafia, and the Mafia needed political protection.

By 1874 the prefect of Palermo could write to Rome: 'up until now there is an opinion that has become firmly established in these Provinces ... that without the Mafia a good police force cannot exist either in the towns or the countryside'.[39] By the end of the century many Sicilian towns had Mafia mayors.

Furthermore, the Sicilian countryside continued to be characterised by far more radical traditions than the rural areas surrounding Naples. During the First World War many southern peasants had been promised land on their return home – a promise Sicilian peasants transformed into reality during a series of land occupations between 1918 and 1920. Sicily also had a strong socialist tradition; in the 1922 parliament, twenty of the island's fifty-two deputies were socialists. Faced with such a situation, both government and landowners continued to feel the need for a force that could terrorise the peasantry, and thus employed the Mafia.

As in Naples, there were both public inquiries and the resignation or conviction of politicians. Sicily also experienced many of the changes that occurred in Naples around the turn of the century: mass migration, the growth of socialism and a campaign for 'public morality'. But the key difference is that the Mafia had already consolidated itself; it had diversified economically and gained control of legal activities, and it had sent its own men into politics, or was at least strongly conditioning the behaviour of other local politicians.

Mafiosi had become power brokers – seen as people who got good deals for a local area, as well as being in a position to award favours to those who accepted their authority. To some extent even today membership of the Mafia involves some association with an honourable way of behaving, a concept totally lacking from popular conceptions of the Camorra in Naples.

Due to their different development, the two organisations have historically behaved in very distinctive ways, and Neapolitans' attitude towards the Camorra differs from Sicilians' attitude towards the Mafia. Because the Camorra has generally been an urban mass phenomenon, it initially felt the need to 'flaunt' itself by wearing a recognisable uniform. The Mafia, in contrast, still retains many traditionally rural characteristics: total territorial control, discretion, the myth of 'honour' and a close-knit family structure normally absent from the Camorra. Camorra gangs are usually 'open' organisations, while the Mafia cosche are generally based on a family structure.[40]

And, as we have already seen, the political behaviour of the two organisations has been very different. The Mafia sent its own men into politics as soon as possible, whereas it was not until around 1980 that the Camorra began to penetrate the local political system. The Mafia has always been almost totalitarian in its desire for complete control over its own territory, a desire that will often lead it to kill any politicians who get in its way; political assassinations are much rarer with the Camorra.

The advent of Fascism saw these two organisations suffer similar but not identical fates. In Sicily there were several major trials against the Mafia, but as Mafiosi were by now property owners in both the towns and the countryside, and involved in local politics, the regime integrated Mafiosi into the Fascist Party in significant numbers.

A crucial development for the Mafia was mass emigration to the United States, which took place both before and during the early period of Fascism, a move which was partly prompted by the fact that the Fascists had effectively taken over the role of the Mafia in many areas. In the 1920s the American Mafia became very powerful through its dealings in illicit alcohol, later moving into gambling and prostitution.

The link with the United States paid huge dividends for the Mafia in 1943, when American forces landed in Sicily. Due to Fascism's twenty-year reign, the Allies were to an extent unaware of any pro-Fascist or anti-Fascist structure on the island and tended to rely on Italo-American Mafiosi. Many of these men immediately became mayors of major towns and quickly made massive use of the Allied presence, often controlling the black market and the sale of stolen Allied goods.

These men were politically convenient individuals because they could not be accused of direct association with Fascism, and furthermore they were willing to repress any signs of peasant radicalism. This murderous knowhow was quickly grafted onto the Mafia's relationship with the new Italian government and culminated in the massacre of twelve peasants at a May Day celebration in Portella delle Ginestre in 1947.

In the immediate postwar period both the Camorra and the Mafia were revitalised: the Allies' presence in Naples not only meant the end of Fascism, it also provided new criminal opportunities, which were encouraged by the presence of notorious Mafiosi such as Lucky Luciano in Naples.

The contraband and black market industries which revolved around the port of Naples were one of the key growth areas of the Mafia in the postwar period and were to constitute the springboard for the Camorra a few decades later.

Chapter 2

The postwar development of the Camorra

Ours is a state founded on labour and theft.

— Dario Fo

In the period preceding Fascism certain differences between the north and south of Italy had already become pronounced. Although there had been a degree of industrialisation and urbanisation in the South, these processes had occurred to a far greater extent in the northern cities, particularly in Turin, Milan and Genoa.

This had led to the growth of mass trade unions and a large socialist party. Many peasant organisations in rural areas of northern and central Italy had also arisen, partly in response to increased farm mechanisation. Yet the South remained far more rural, and feudal remnants such as large landowners and religious dominance of village life persisted.

Fascism maintained this political and social gap. In the North Fascism received finance from major industrialists in return for government contracts and favourable policies; in the South the Fascists maintained protectionist policies on agricultural produce, banned peasants from leaving the countryside to look for work and suppressed any signs of rural discontent.

The way in which Fascism collapsed perpetuated a fundamental difference between the two ends of the peninsula. Northern Italy experienced a virtual civil war in the years between 1943 and 1945. By the end of the war in April 1945, the resistance movement controlled a partisan army of 300,000, which sometimes governed mountain valley communities for several months and successfully organised carefully planned insurrections in northern cities shortly before the arrival of the Allied forces.

Events were very different in the South: the Allies arrived by and large before society became polarised between Fascists, reactionaries and conservatives on one hand, and communists, socialists and liberals on the other.

The city of Naples suffered far more damage and hardship during the war than its northern counterparts. The area around the port was devastated as a result of over a hundred Allied bombing raids, which left 200,000 people homeless. The Germans had also briefly occupied the city in September 1943, following the signing of an armistice between the Italian government and the Allies. They immediately demanded that young men report for compulsory labour service, and when they refused, the Germans began to round men up indiscriminately, sparking off the 'Four Days' of revolt, which lasted from 28 September to 1 October and forced the Germans to withdraw from the city.[1]

This was a spontaneous uprising, lacking the political organisation and objectives that were to predominate in the northern cities. This lack of a developed political consciousness was to continue after the war, prompting one historian to note:

> the contradictory terms of the clearly fierce insurgency of the 'Four Days' and the moderate outcome as witnessed in the 1946 elections. Between one event and the other, there is the negative effect of the lack of a generalised campaign of resistance, and the presence of Allied troops of occupation.[2]

While, at a national level, a small majority of Italians voted against the King and created a republic in a referendum held in 1946, in Naples support for the monarchy reached 80 per cent.

If the Unification of 1860 had been a kind of 'passive revolution' throughout the country, then the 'second war of national liberation' of 1943–5 (or the 'second Risorgimento', as it was sometimes called) was almost exclusively a northern affair. The traditions of *trasformismo* surfaced once again in the South, with the vast majority of southerners playing no significant or longterm role in their liberation from Fascism.[3]

The legacy of this tradition can often be seen today during national elections. In the five elections between 1948 and 1968 the Monarchist Party vote fluctuated between 26.3 per cent and 9.2 per cent in Naples, compared with a national vote of between 6.9 per cent and 1.4 per cent. And in the five elections since 1972 the neofascist MSI has polled between 26.3 per cent and 11.2 per cent, compared with a national average of between 8.7 per cent and 5.1 per cent. Although votes for the Communist Party have largely followed the national average, until recently the Socialist Party vote has normally been significantly below national trends.[4]

(To a far greater extent than the North, Naples and southern society witnessed the reappearance) of old politicians and old attitudes; political corruption and patronage)quickly reasserted themselves as fundamental elements of southern political life.

THE ALLIES RESURRECT THE MAFIA

The Allied invasion of continental Europe began in Sicily on 9 July 1943. In strategic terms it might well have been easier to start the invasion of Italy by attacking Sardinia, which was not as strongly defended as Sicily and only slightly further from the Allies' North African bases. One tactical explanation is that the Americans had close links with Italo-American 'advisers', in other words Sicilian Mafiosi, who provided them with two vital services: military information about Sicily itself and the ability to guarantee social order once Fascism had collapsed.

In the early months of 1943 several American and English secret agents left Allied headquarters in Algiers and arrived clandestinely in Sicily. They included people such as the British writer Gavin Maxwell and Colonel Charles Poletti, an American businessman of Italian background, who was to become the senior Allied administrator in occupied Italy. Not only did they gather military information, they also encouraged acts of sabotage and met individuals who would later take control of the island.[5]

It is commonly acknowledged that these agents were able to make contact with 'pro-Allied anti-Fascists' through Lucky Luciano, one of America's major gangsters, then serving a 30-year sentence in America for running a prostitution ring. Before the Allied invasion many Italo-American Mafiosi had named Luciano as being indispensable for making the right contacts in Sicily, and there is clear evidence of collaboration between Luciano and US authorities.[6]

(Even before the fall of Fascism the Mafia was being consciously resurrected by those responsible for governing postwar

Italy. As the veteran anti-Mafia campaigner Michele Pantaleone commented:

> it was no secret that Charles Poletti, governor of Sicily after the occupation, had slipped into Palermo on the quiet at least a year before the end of the war, and had stayed for some time in the villa belonging to a Mafia lawyer.[7]

Poletti went on to use his position as head of Allied administration first in Palermo, then in Naples and all the way up to Milan, 'to trade in foodstuffs with Vito Genovese and Damiano Lumia in Sicily, who was a nephew of Calogero Vizzini, and with Jimmy Hoffa of the Teamsters Union in New York'.[8] The company run by Poletti in Italy collapsed into bankruptcy soon after the Allies' withdrawal, suggesting that his business lifeline was the creaming off of Allied goods for sale on the highly profitable black market. Poletti was also a member of the Freemasons, a highly secretive organisation in Italy, whose shady dealings were dramatically exposed during the discovery of the P2 Lodge in 1981.[9]

The question of public order was the Allies' primary concern in enlisting Mafiosi. The British, under Winston Churchill, were particularly hostile towards communists and socialists. Churchill had first displayed his virulent hatred of trade unionists and socialists as British Home Secretary during the great labour 'unrest' of 1910–14, when he ordered troops to open fire in several towns halted by strike activity. And he even went as far as declaring support for Mussolini during a visit to Rome in 1927:

> I could not help being charmed, like so many other people have been, by Signor Mussolini's gentle and simple bearing and by his calm, detached pose, in spite of so many burdens and dangers . . . Anyone could see that he thought of nothing but the lasting good, as he understood it, of the Italian people, and that no lesser interest was of the slightest consequence to him.
>
> If I had been an Italian, I am sure that I should have been wholeheartedly with you from start to finish in your triumphant struggle against the bestial appetites and passions of Leninism.[10]

Churchill also supported the Italian monarchists, and throughout the period from 1943 to 1946 he fought a running battle against the Americans, who were more agnostic on the question. But what united both Allied camps was the desire to see Italy transformed from a hostile country seeking to create a self-sufficient economy into a politically compliant free-market nation, highly dependent on foreign investment, imports and technology. They were willing to enlist any kind of help to ensure that this transformation took place, including the Mafia.

The political legacy of Fascism to Sicilian society was that very little middle ground existed. The Democrazia Cristiana (DC), the Italian Christian Democrat party, had not even been formed, so the Allies enlisted the help of elderly politicians who had been pushed aside by Fascism. These men had enjoyed very little popular support before Fascism, and gained even less now. In other cases, the Allies simply appointed known Mafiosi mayors of several important Sicilian towns. All the Mafiosi had to do was to proclaim their 'anti-Fascism', and the Allies thereby acquired trusted partners who were able to police society very effectively. For both the Americans and the British, the thought of encouraging socialists and communists was completely abhorrent, and so Mafiosi quickly became part of the Allies' administrative machinery.

As Raimondo Catanzaro, a leading Italian academic, has noted:

As mayors the mafiosi resumed their time-honoured functions as brokers between the Allied government and the population. But it was not only this position through which the mafiosi once again began to exercise their traditional function. They acted as interpreters at the military command posts; they held (as Vito Genovese did at Nola) important jobs and performed important tasks that once again gave them the opportunity to place themselves at critical junctures of the relations between political authorities and the population.[11]

Genovese had fled from New York in 1936 to escape several charges of murder. In Italy he was praised by Mussolini in an official meeting in 1937, where his 'Italian work carried out in Brooklyn' was recognised with the award of the highest civilian decoration; furthermore he was given important banking responsibilities.[12] Genovese later returned the favour by giving $290,000 towards the construction of a Fascist Party headquarters.[13]

Despite such a record, Genovese was employed as Colonel Poletti's personal interpreter, but the relationship was far from that of a senior officer giving orders to his lowly batman. Poletti would often drive about in a 1938 Packard, which the FBI later discovered had been a gift from Genovese.[14]

It is therefore beyond doubt that the Allies occupied southern Italy with the help of the Mafia, and in early October 1943, three months after their landing in Sicily, the Allies reached Naples and its highly prized port.

THE MAFIA RESURRECTS THE CAMORRA

A major command post was set up in the town of Nola, to the east of Naples, where both Charles Poletti and Vito Genovese were based; for Genovese it was a return to the town where he had been born in 1897. Looting, particularly from American stores, was already widespread; the Mafia also began to siphon off the Allies' supplies of Italian foodstuffs. Some studies estimate that 60 per cent of the merchandise unloaded in Naples during this period ended up on the black market.[15]

Theft on such a scale quickly led to investigations, and the following is a typical case. In the summer of 1944, Naples police searched a railway wagon at Nola. It had been sent from Villalba in Sicily, a town run by the head of the Sicilian Mafia, Don Calogero Vizzini, and was supposed to be full of broad beans and lentils. But police discovered that of the three hundred 50-kilo sacks in the wagon, sixty were full of salt.[16]

Genovese and his men were clearly moving fast and making huge profits: grain legally bought from official sources at between $1.60 and $2 a ton was being sold on the black market for up to $12.[17]

Genovese's greed, however, finally led to his demise. The FBI had already reached the conclusion that he stole trucks full of sugar, oil, flour and other highly prized goods from the American army and then went on to sell them in the markets of nearby towns.[18] In the summer of 1944 American police stopped Canadian soldiers driving two trucks full of oil on their way from the port of Naples to Nola. Under interrogation the soldiers admitted that the trucks had been stolen from the port and would be destroyed once their load had been disposed of at Nola – indeed at the rendezvous investigators found the remains of twenty burnt-out trucks. Genovese was subsequently arrested on 27 August, charged with both theft and passing on military information, and eventually sent back to the US.[19]

Yet individuals like Genovese were just the tip of a very large iceberg. Once he was removed, there were many other Mafiosi more than willing to take his place, and it quickly became 'business as usual' again.

With the Allies stuck south of Rome in the winter and spring of 1943–4, the port of Naples remained of vital strategic importance. Goods for the Allied forces, as well as those destined for the much larger civilian population, continued to pour ashore. The fact that the Mafia enjoyed a monopoly of Allied 'protection' meant that it was able to consolidate its position in the coming years, and it obviously had no interest in favouring the creation of a rival organisation. As Michele Pantaleone perceptively commented as far back as 1962:

> From 1943 to 1946 the entire Sicilian mafia dedicated itself to this black market traffic which made large fortunes for its chiefs. And during the same years the foundations were laid for the drug traffic which, as we shall see, had one of its major distribution centres in Sicily.[20]

Even though there was as yet no real Camorra in the city of Naples itself, the seeds were being sown. Large sums of money could be made working for the Mafia, which needed a wide variety of skills and services.

Both the Allied administration and the Italian police had become aware of the Mafia's resurgence, and so they often put known leaders under observation, concentrating on Sicily itself. Naples meanwhile became a convenient staging post for Mafia activities, and while the contraband trade disappeared from other areas of Italy soon after 1945, it became rooted in Naples, constituting one of the city's principal economic activities: during the war food dominated the trade, followed by various Allied goods, then clothes and textiles, then cigarettes and electrical appliances, and finally hard drugs from the 1970s onwards.

The gap left by Vito Genovese's departure was partly filled by Lucky Luciano two years later. In 1946 the head of the American Navy's secret service wrote that Luciano 'had been a great help to the armed forces', a testimonial which spurred his release on parole from a 30-year minimum jail sentence handed down in 1936. As he had never taken American citizenship, he could conveniently be deported. He arrived in Naples in the summer of 1946 and was to live there until his death in 1962.[21]

Luciano was arguably one of the Mafia's most influential bosses during the late 1940s and 50s. The intelligence chief of the New York Police publicly admitted after his death: 'There is no question that [Luciano's] power was so great that even in Europe he could exercise it.' Biographers of Luciano have also written that 'No important decision that might affect the future of organised crime in the United States . . . was made without his consultation and advice.'[22]

Although it is impossible to verify the accuracy of these statements, what is beyond doubt is that Luciano decided to base his operations in Naples. Luciano's notoriety in the United States meant that Naples became a port of call for Mafiosi in transit. The veteran American journalist Claire Sterling has estimated that there were 'some five hundred Italian-born racketeers, dope traffickers, and all-purpose mobsters shipped back from New York in the wake of Senator Kefauver's 1951 hearings. Half of them were in Naples, desperate and broke.'[23] And according to Luciano, many of them would come to him for help.

The contraband industry was not the work of a few dozen modern-day pirates. Large amounts of money were needed to keep it running, and considerable investments in transport and wages were required. The Mafia employed Neapolitans very much as junior partners, but over a period of many years those Neapolitans who were later to become Camorra leaders progressed from activities such as casual thefts of Allied goods to working in a highly organised, professional operation involving large amounts of money. Organised crime was starting to evolve from small-time extortion and racketeering into international business syndicates, and the Camorra was eventually to follow the Mafia's lead.

Two Neapolitan groups slowly began to emerge within the Mafia-run contraband industry. The main one centred around the town of Giugliano, to the north of the city, and extended up to Mondragone and as far as the Garigliano river. This was initially led by Alfredo Maisto, with Luigi Sciorio, Raffaele Ferrara and the Nuvoletta brothers all joining later. The other was based to the south of the city, in the towns of San Giovanni a Teduccio and Portici.

Top Mafiosi were active in Naples throughout the 1950s; Tommaso Buscetta has admitted to working with Lucky Luciano immediately after the war, and Tommaso Spadaro was amongst many Mafiosi sent into 'internal exile' in Naples.[24] Many of them happily continued their activities, including Spadaro, who went to live in Via Pallonetto a Santa Lucia, the heart of the contraband industry.[25]

At the same time as the Mafia was consolidating its position in Naples and nurturing a new generation of Neapolitan criminals, separate developments were taking place in Campania, the region surrounding Naples. Over a period of two decades these developments would lead to the rise of Camorra groups totally distinct from the Mafia.

THE RURAL CAMORRA IN THE PROVINCES

In the aftermath of the Second World War, most areas of the southern Italian countryside experienced a wave of land occupations by peasants. In many cases the peasants were taking advantage of government indecision concerning the return of common lands stolen from them in the last century.

But Campania was different. Under Fascism it had lacked an organised and sustained resistance movement, and now land occupations were similarly scarce. Consequently, its social structure remained largely unchanged. The main reason for this was that Campania had fewer large estates than other Italian regions, with only 12.4 per cent of the land belonging to estates larger than 100 hectares, compared with a national average of 26 per cent.[26] Despite the fact that it contained 4.5 per cent of the nation's cultivated land, only 2.2 per cent of Campania's arable land was redistributed as a result of postwar agricultural reforms. This low level of land redistribution, and the relatively minor degree of concomitant dislocation, may have been the main reason why Campania again reached pre-war levels of agricultural production by 1949–51, one of the few Italian regions to achieve this.[27]

This is not to say that there was no industry in Campania; according to the 1911 census the region was fifth out of twenty in terms of industrial development. But as Table 1 shows, it was mainly concentrated in Naples:

Table 1: Sectoral employment in Campania, 1911[28]

Province	Agriculture and fishing	Industry
Avellino	161,209	8,466
Benevento	108,270	6,363
Caserta	260,073	26,674
Naples	109,277	91,389
Salerno	178,154	25,227
Total	816,983	158,119

Coastal towns and towns with easy access to the coast had been industrialised to a significant extent, whereas the more mountainous areas of the interior remained predominantly agricultural.

Evidence of Camorra activity in the provinces of Campania is scarce; in any case virtually all criminal activity was likely to be the work of isolated local gangs rather than an urban organisation as in Naples. Nevertheless, it appears that in the period preceding the First World War local provincial criminals had played a key role in getting politicians elected:

> The Terra di Lavoro – which was still huge at this time, extending from Nola to Sora – was characterised, especially in the Aversa area, by the clear domination of the Camorra. They were physically represented by a deputy called Peppuccio Romano, a strong Giolitti supporter and undisputed head of the local underworld, who was first the great elector of [Pietro] Romano, one of Giolitti's personal friends and ministers, and later of [Carlo] Schanzer, general director of the civilian branch of the Ministry of the Interior, who later also became a minister, although after the war he became a follower of Nitti. This huge expanse of territory – which today comes under the Provinces of Caserta, Frosinone, Latina and Naples – also facilitated the growth of a diversity of activities.[29]

In the twenty years of Fascist rule social relations remained largely static; local criminal gangs were probably tolerated to some extent as they could occasionally be employed as convenient shock troops against peasant unrest, or as assassins of individual political enemies, but by and large nothing much changed in these areas between 1922 and 1943.

The end of Fascism and the arrival of the Allies, and particularly of individuals such as Vito Genovese in Nola, meant that both social relations and the local economy suddenly experienced rapid changes.

With the withdrawal of the Allies the main activity of local gangs became control over agricultural produce. Their influence was particularly strong in rural areas to the north and east of Naples, particularly in the rich cattle area around Nola. Sometimes gangs would shoot it out for dominance in a given market; for example, sixty-one murders were committed in the Nola area from 1954 to 1956.[30] They also intimidated farmers who refused to pay for their services or protection, normally by burning their crops.

Although Nola itself was not a large town, the *camorristi* acted as parasitical mediators between cattle farmers and butchers because the town was the main centre for sending meat to Naples, a market of a million people. Compared with the entire city of Naples, in a town such as Nola the Camorra gangs must have been far stronger and enjoyed greater political protection, which in turn enabled them to take a cut of any meat sales.

However, there was no reason to stop at meat, so the Camorra quickly moved on to other areas of agricultural produce. And by the mid-1950s,

> in the fruit and vegetables sector, the underworld exercises control above all over the San Giuseppe Vesuviano market, but in all cases it always makes its presence felt before goods reach Naples; as for milk, the supervising of inspections and all other concerns has been moved from the Central Dairy in Naples to the Castellammare Consortiums, which are controlled by camorristi.[31]

Just as there was no reason for *camorristi* to limit themselves to control over the meat market, there was also no reason for them to physically limit themselves to small agricultural towns. A third of all Italian fruit exports passed through Naples in this period, amounting to $23 million of produce annually, and from the early 1950s many rural gangsters moved to the city to supervise this trade. The prices between buyers and sellers, according to one trader, were 'not imposed through violence, but through convincing arguments', with the *guappi* then taking a percentage of the sale price.[32]

This was a business carried out without offices, in the open air, and based only on verbal agreements. The Camorra, both in the provinces and within Naples, was therefore still characterised by rather small-scale intimidation and extortion. *Camorristi* had yet to amass enough money to think about where to invest it; their horizons were limited and decisions therefore remained tactical rather than strategic. This is a crucial difference from Palermo, where the Mafia's activities already involved widespread participation in postwar property speculation and control over council contracts, a process which led to the intermeshing of criminal and political power in the Sicilian capital.

Nevertheless the Camorra's operations were already sizeable and, as in the last century, they could not have developed without some political protection. A good example of this was the funeral in 1955 of a major Camorra leader, Pascalone 'e Nola, to which twelve deputies sent wreaths.

One of these MPs was Giovanni Leone, who began his career as a lawyer and Christian Democrat politician in the town of Pomigliano and later had to resign as President of Italy in 1978 as a result of his involvement in a corruption scandal concerning the Lockheed aircraft corporation. Leone defended many people accused of belonging to Camorra gangs throughout the 1950s, including later Pascalone 'e Nola, who dictated prices at the main fruit and vegetable market. Indeed, their relationship had been so close that Leone had been best man at Pascalone 'e Nola's marriage to Pupetta Maresca in 1955. Yet there was a political as well as a personal element to their association: Pascalone was also the Christian Democrat deputy mayor of Nola, and he managed to do his lawyer a good turn by getting 2,000 first-preference votes for Leone at every election during this period.[33]

As early as 1957 one observer began to outline the reasons behind the failure of the police to stop Camorra activity in Nola: 'it is not difficult to work out the reasons for the police's difficulties: they lie in the political protection which is normally granted out of electoral interests, and which allows the underworld to prosper and to impede the fight against crime.'[34] In other words, local politicians, who were either too cynical or too fearful to seek genuine mass support, turned to the Camorra to guarantee their election.

A similar complaint was made in 1961:

the work of people whose responsibility it was to apply the law was being hindered by the political protection provided by those who personally benefit from certain ramifications of the Camorra, in exchange for the electoral preferences which the Camorra is able to ensure.[35]

Although the Camorra was slowly gaining in power and influence in the provinces during this period, it was in Naples and Campania's coastal towns, i.e. in the Mafia-dominated contraband industry, that Camorra gangs were to make their next major step forward.

THE CONTRABAND INDUSTRY

Throughout the 1950s several important Mafiosi had been sent into internal exile in Naples and the surrounding area. The main activity of the Mafia during this period was cigarette smuggling, which in the Mediterranean region centred on the free port of Tangiers. The profit margins involved were enormous: in 1959 a case of Chesterfield, Camel or Pall Mall could be bought for $23 and sold on the streets of Europe for $170.

Most of this trade was run by a Corsican named Paolo Molinelli, who also carried morphine base from the Lebanon to Marseilles, where it was refined into heroin and sent to Sicily for forwarding to the United States.[36] Both the scale of cigarette smuggling and the profits to be made from heroin meant that Italian police were keeping the Sicilian coastline under very close observation.

The free port of Tangiers was closed in 1961, and the warehouses of companies selling cigarettes moved to the Yugoslavian and Albanian coast. This move was to transform Naples into the cigarette smuggling capital of the world. Not only did the Mafia increase its activity in the port and along the Campania coast, the Neapolitans began to carve out a niche for themselves too. One writer commented on this transformation: 'it gave a reason to firm up those business relationships that had been sporadic and connected with personal situations before; they now had to become complex linkages of an associational and commercial nature.'[37]

Delivery was no longer made in ports, but outside territorial waters on the high seas. The terms of trade were also modified;

suppliers now wanted to be paid 50 per cent upon placement of the order, and 50 per cent when the speedboats came to pick up the goods. The need for capital and for large investments in transport necessitated a big commitment on the part of the Mafia to both smuggling and the use of Naples as a base. This also meant that some Neapolitans had to be taken on as equal members of the Mafia:

> if a Mafia organisation severely exposed itself in terms of capital expenditure (in foreign currency) and taking on great risks, in exchange it had to be sure that it was operating with a cast-iron structure, in which every member carried out their duty blindly.[38]

Given that Naples' contraband industry was undoubtedly enjoying rapid expansion throughout the 1960s, we shall shortly return to this argument. However, in social terms the internal regions of Campania were undergoing huge and traumatic changes, which were subsequently to give rise to a new type of Camorra, different from the previously dominant rural model.

THE URBANISATION OF THE PROVINCES AND THE GROWTH OF THE PUBLIC SECTOR

The whole of Italy was on the move during the 1950s and 60s. Most of the movement was from the South to the North, from the southern countryside to either the industrial cities of Genoa, Milan and Turin or even further north to Germany or Belgium.

Although the population born in the South rose by 5 million from 1951 to 1971, emigration took 4.1 million away, leaving an effective increase of 900,000. The key change within the South itself was urbanisation, as people moved from the countryside to large towns and cities. During the same 20-year period, the number of people living in towns and cities of over 100,000 increased by about 1 million. This was due to towns' growing high local birth rates, or internal migration within the South.

In any case, the changes were very rapid, particularly after the war. While at the start of the century only 12 per cent of southerners lived in towns of 100,000, this figure rose to 16 per cent in 1951 and 23.4 per cent in 1971.[39]

Yet in the city of Naples in the period between 1950 and 1980 the populationy rose by only 1 per cent, with three-quarters of this increase taking place in the 1950s alone. Compared to Naples' stagnation, most towns in Campania recorded huge population increases during this 30-year period. Small towns close to Naples registered a population increase of between 60 per cent (Torre del Greco) and 200 per cent (San Giorgio a Cremano). The area around Vesuvius too saw increases ranging from a minimum of 60 per cent (Grumo Nevano) to a maximum of 150 per cent (San Sebastiano). And to the north of the city, the lowest increase was recorded in Frattamaggiore (60 per cent) and the highest in Casoria, with over 200 per cent.[40]

In a slightly later period, the towns closest to Naples showed even more remarkable trends. Between the end of the 1950s and the start of the 1970s Arzano, Casandrino, Cercola, Mugnano, Portici, Pozzuoli and Volla all doubled their population, while Casavatore, Casoria, Marano, Quarto and San Giorgio a Cremano saw their population rise by an incredible 300 per cent.

These population increases had two main reasons: industrialisation and its concomitant increase in employment and the overcrowding of Naples, which forced people to live outside the city and commute in for work. One of the consequences was the creation of an urban sprawl, with the towns closest to Naples effectively becoming part of the city.

While Naples had first experienced industrial expansion soon after Unification, one of the first major industrial developments in the provinces was the arrival of the aeronautical industry in Pomigliano d'Arco during the 1930s. Pozzuoli had a significant engineering industry, which increased in size between the wars, while at nearby Baia a torpedo factory was built.[41]

Most of these industries were linked to war production. After their reconstruction and conversion in the immediate postwar period, industrialisation began anew in the second half of the 1950s, when both Olivetti and Pirelli built factories in Pozzuoli. The first new factories in the inland were set up in Casoria, where Rhodiatrice produced synthetic fibres and Resia synthetic resins.[42] Development mainly occurred in towns to the north of Naples, such as Afragola, Arzano and Casavatore. Most of this expansion took place in the period between 1955 and 1965 and usually involved small and medium-sized factories owned by engineering, chemical, wood, rubber and soft drinks companies.

Until the mid-1960s the population increase in the province of Naples was clearly differentiated:

> For the towns situated to the north and west of Naples, demographic increases could mainly be linked to the establishment of . . . new productive activities . . . while for the towns at the foot of Vesuvius, the increase derived from becoming a residential appendix of the provincial capital.[43]

These developments – population increase, urbanisation, industrialisation – all led to a change in the characteristics of organised crime. Although agricultural produce continued to be important for Camorra gangs, whole new areas were beginning to open up: extortion from small and medium-sized firms as well as from local shopowners, and the awarding of local public sector contracts and development grants. Agricultural products may still have been important, but people and therefore money were moving away from the land; in 1951 46 per cent of Campania's active population worked in agriculture; by 1971 this figure had fallen to 24 per cent.[44]

One of the main reasons for this was government intervention in the South. It is widely accepted that this intervention has gone through three main phases: 1950–7, 1957–73 and from 1974 to today. The first phase involved the creation of a basic infrastructure rather than real industrialisation. During the second period, when public enterprises were obliged to invest at least 40 per cent of their profits in the South, problems began to arise. Local authority consortia were set up in an attempt to create 'poles of development', but politicians were more concerned with guaranteeing their re-election through the clientelist use of public funds and jobs, and so more often than not *cattedrali nel deserto*, 'cathedrals in the desert', were built. The most famous example of this is the Alfa Romeo factory in Pomigliano d'Arco, 'a cathedral' whose construction was intended to lead to the development of a local component industry centred around the factory. This project failed abysmally, and the area consequently retained many aspects of a 'desert'.

A grasp of political concepts such as patronage and *clientela* is essential for understanding not only local politics, but also how these mechanisms favour the influence and entrance of organised crime. As the political scientist Percy Allum noted in 1973:

The key to a successful parliamentary career in Naples is having a following or a *clientela*. The building of a *clientela* requires economic resources or patronage. In consequence, the politician with parliamentary ambitions is obliged to join an organisation to win resources.[45]

Through control over public expenditure and the favours which can be granted, a politician will slowly build up 'clients' who will then return the favour granted, usually in the form of votes.

Although political patronage exists throughout Italy and in most other advanced countries, in Naples it was grafted onto an already weak tradition of democracy and political honesty. In addition, owing to the endemic poverty of the region the problem has become far more entrenched and widespread than elsewhere:

> Where Naples differs from the North is in the placing of people in strategic positions at the middle and lower levels of society ... In Naples, patronage appointment has been extended to all levels of society. The reasons are simple: Naples is a society of limited resources and unemployment is still rife. In these circumstances, the state provides the chief source of employment, not only through the extension of the public administration, but also through the introduction of modern industry ... The intelligentsia aspire 'for a job in the municipality' or 'for stable employment with the chance of a career ... probably in the public administration', while the workers dream of 'a job with a regular income'.[46]

This tradition encourages Camorra influence within the political system, as its members can often act either as brokers for people looking for jobs or as election agents for politicians seeking election. As for economic development, the patronage system produced a public sector dominated by corruption, and as a result any development remained haphazard and uncoordinated.

The economic crisis of the 1970s and 80s changed this situation considerably. In the private sector the crisis hit Campania just as hard as other areas, and by the end of the 1970s one of the two new companies set up in Casoria had closed down, and the second one had moved eleswhere.

The public sector tended to maintain its existing

commitments, but there was no longer any strategy for growth; local authorities were later to be transformed by their management of funds for reconstruction after the 1980 earthquake.

Due to the rapid, chaotic and often illegal nature of economic development, almost half of the houses registered in Campania were, according to the 1971 census, built after 1951.[47] Many towns had been thrown up within fifteen or twenty years, and planners had been either unable or unwilling to create any sense of social cohesion. Since the war Campania has suffered the highest population density in Italy, with an average of 422 people per km² in 1988. This figure rises to far higher levels within individual provinces such as the Salerno plain, which has an average of 810 people per km², the Neapolitan plain with 1,318, the Avellino hill areas with 2,629 and the hills of the Province of Naples with 3,065, one of the highest population densities in Europe.[48]

There had been a severe shortage of public transport, schools, street lighting and cultural amenities throughout the years of development; and public hygiene is still so bad that many towns suffer outbreaks of contagious hepatitis during the summer, while the city of Naples even faced a small outbreak of cholera in 1973.

By the mid-1970s economic development in Campania had largely come to a halt. The rise in industrial unemployment, however, was largely camouflaged by the use of government-financed redundancy schemes, which guaranteed 75 per cent of wages to those laid off. For example, the total amount of lay-off hours financed in Campania rose from 7 million in 1972 to 20 million in 1980 and 63 million in 1982.[49]

Until the advent of this economic crisis, many people had been willing to accept high levels of unemployment and low levels of public services, as they had generally believed that there would be some future economic development. With the onset of a long-term and seemingly intractable economic crisis, 'a life of crime' became more appealing.

The new Camorra gangs that sprang up in the 1970s did not need to assert their predominance over the old Camorra through violence. The huge economic changes ushered in by state and local authority activities, and the effects of urbanisation and emigration had severely, if not terminally, affected the pre-war and postwar gangs. The predominance of urban areas over rural areas, of industry and the tertiary sector over agriculture, led to their rapid and painless demise. However, it is now time to turn our attention away from the towns of the hinterland and examine further changes within the contraband industry.

CONTRABAND: FROM CIGARETTES TO DRUGS

Until the late 1960s the European contraband trade was run by a complex mixture of Corsicans, Genoese, Marseillaise and Sicilians. Naples was the centre of the cigarette trade, and mainly provided the manpower for the unloading and transportation of goods, although the urban area of Naples and Campania also constituted a large market in itself. The fact that port costs as a whole were reportedly inflated by 35 per cent due to gangs demanding protection money also indicates a high level of lawlessness.[50]

George Bush was not the first American President to declare 'war on drugs'. Soon after his inauguration in 1969, Richard Nixon promised a war on drug traffickers, setting up 'Task Force One' under Henry Kissinger. Its only real success was the smashing of the 'French Connection' run by the Marseillaise and Corsicans in France's second city. Not only did France close down eight heroin refineries, probably the world's biggest, the Corsicans' operations in Brazil were also stopped.[51]

But the problem simply moved on, partially to Naples but also to Sicily and elsewhere; the gangs from Marseille decided to diversify more into tobacco contraband and saw Naples as an excellent territory to move into. In the meantime the Mafia had been reorganising its activities, sending top Mafioso Gerlando Alberti to the town of San Sebastiano al Vesuvio at the beginning of 1971. He set to work organising the contraband industry on a far greater scale, but his work was interrupted by his arrest in December 1971.

At the same time the Marseillaise were trying to move into the port and were enticing local *camorristi* into becoming their partners by loaning them some of their boats. The French were well organised, with their own container ship and fast motorboats, compared with the Neapolitans' slow fishing vessels. However, the French also limited their offers of integration as they did not fully trust the Neapolitans, believing them to be far too close to the Mafia.[52]

Estimates of the number of people directly involved in contraband rose from 3,420 in 1970 to 4,672 in 1971 and 4,885 in 1973; by then roughly 50,000 people depended on smuggling to survive.[53] By 1975 40 per cent of arrests for contraband in Italy were made in the Campania region alone, and in the following year more than 528 tonnes of foreign cigarettes were seized by police in Campania.[54]

The growth in the drug trade inevitably increased the tension amongst the emerging criminal gangs. One notorious example was the killing of Gennaro Ferrigno by Antonio Spavone in 1971; Ferrigno was a drug trafficker importing cocaine from Peru while Spavone was a major Camorra boss of the postwar period who had received a presidential pardon from a life sentence four years earlier. The following year a major Mafia summit, also involving Camorra gangs, was broken up by the police at the Hotel Commodore in Naples. A bloody gang war between the Sicilians and the Marseillaise followed, with the defeated French leaving the port in 1973–4. The Camorra was still weak, playing a very minor role in the gang warfare between the Mafia and the Marseillaise, but the huge profits to be made from drugs soon led to a swift growth in its importance.

According to estimates of the Italian Customs and Excise Police, 1 per cent of contraband cigarette cargoes in 1970 were in fact made up of hashish; a percentage which rose to between 5 and 10 per cent by 1975.[55] Because neither politicians nor police yet perceived the Camorra as a serious threat in Naples, and because Sicily and the Mafia attracted a significant degree of police attention, the quantity of hard drugs coming into Naples under Camorra control also increased sharply.

By 1979 a total of 400 speedboats had been seized by customs police, and it is estimated that 105 were in operation throughout that year alone. With the price per boat at around $24,000–$29,000, a total of approximately $13.5 million had been invested in the primary means of transport alone.[56]

Michele Zaza was one of the first *camorristi* to emerge as a powerful figure in the contraband industry. The son of a fisherman from Procida (the smallest of the three islands in the Gulf of Naples), Zaza was known as *Michele 'o pazzo*, or Mad Mike, for

his outspoken and improbable public pronouncements. His rise
to power, however, was achieved through his connections with
the Mafia rather than his supposedly unbalanced mind. He was
first arrested for criminal association in 1974, along with top
Mafiosi Gerardo Alberti, Stefano Bontate and Rosario Ric-
cobono. Soon after that he was arrested in Palermo with Alfredo
Bono for illegal possession of firearms. According to the Mafia
'supergrass' Tommaso Buscetta, from the mid-1970s Zaza, along
with the Nuvoletta and Bardellino gangs, belonged already to
Michele Greco's *cupola*, the supreme body of the Sicilian Mafia.

Twice in 1977 Zaza was discovered in the company of top
Mafiosi, first at a restaurant with Vincenzo Spadaro and Filippo
Messina, and again at a Social Democrat Party branch in Naples,
with Domenico Camarda and Francesco Messina.[57]

Zaza is prepared to admit that he made large amounts of
money smuggling cigarettes. This is how he once described his
activities during questioning by an investigating magistrate:

> First I'd sell five cases of Philip Morris, then ten, then a
> thousand, then three thousand, then I bought myself six or
> seven ships that you took away from me . . .
>
> I used to load fifty thousand cases a month . . . I could load
> a hundred thousand cases, $10 million on trust, all I had to do
> was make a phone call . . .
>
> I'd buy $24 million worth of Philip Morris in three months,
> my lawyer will show you the receipts. I'm proud of that –
> $24 million![58]

It would appear that Zaza's success was due to the fact that he
was less interested in traditional activities such as extortion –
concentrating far more on smuggling first cigarettes and then
drugs. From there he quickly moved to investing in more
'legitimate' areas such as real estate, construction companies and
restaurants, but as most of these developments were part of the
'new Camorra' which emerged in the late 1970s, they will be
explained in detail in a subsequent chapter.

However, this is not to say that the Mafia totally controlled
the emergence of the 'new Camorra'; indeed the strongest
Camorra organisation for most of the 1970s was distinctly
hostile to the Mafia.

THE 'MASS CAMORRA' OF RAFFAELE CUTOLO'S *NUOVA CAMORRA ORGANIZZATA*

The origins of Raffaele Cutolo's *nuova camorra organizzata* (i.e. New Organised Camorra, or NCO) in some ways recall the Camorra of the last century.

Apart from eighteen months on the run, Cutolo has lived inside maximum security jails or psychiatric prisons since 1963, and it was from there that he built up his organisation. He began by befriending young inmates unfamiliar with jail, giving them a sense of identity and worth, so much so that when they were released they would send Cutolo 'flowers' (i.e. money), which enabled him to increase his network.[59]

Another more direct method was to help poorer prisoners by buying food for them from the jail store, or arranging for food to be sent in from outside. In such ways Cutolo created many 'debts' or 'rain cheques' which he would cash at the opportune moment.[60] As his following grew, he also began to exercise a monopoly of violence within a number of prisons, thus increasing his power. Another key bond Cutolo created was regular payments to the families of NCO members sent to prison, thereby guaranteeing the allegiance of both prisoners and their families.[61]

What is unusual about Cutolo is that he has a kind of ideology, another factor which appealed to rootless and badly educated youths. He founded the NCO in his home town of Ottaviano on 24 October 1970, the day of Cutolo's patron saint, San Raffaele; and the organisation deliberately used a statute and rules, often purely notional, but deliberately harking back to the Camorra of the last century.

The NCO's strongholds were the towns to the east of Naples, such as Ottaviano, and Cutolo appealed to a Campanian rather than Neapolitan sense of identity, perhaps a result of his poor peasant background: 'The day when the people of Campania understand that it is better to eat a slice of bread as a free man than to eat a steak as a slave is the day that Campania will win.'[62]

This approach naturally made the NCO hostile to the Sicilian Mafia and its Neapolitan allies, and Cutolo consequently developed an alliance with Calabrian gangs, who had no designs on Naples or Campania whatsoever.[63]

Through his book of 'thoughts and poems', *Poesie e pensieri*, and his many interviews with journalists, Cutolo was able to create a strong sense of identity amongst his members. Even though his book was impounded by magistrates within days of its publication, many prisoners, alienated from society both 'inside' and 'outside' jail, wrote to Cutolo and other NCO leaders asking for a copy.[64]

Cutolo's organisation was unique in the history of the Camorra in that it was highly centralised and possessed a rudimentary form of ideology. For example, he publicly declared that children were not to be kidnapped or mistreated and allegedly arranged the assassination of at least one kidnapper.

Perhaps the most potent ideological weapon was the cult of violence, which sometimes bordered on a kind of death wish, as Cutolo once wrote:

> the value of a life doesn't consist of its length but in the use made of it; often people live a long time without living very much. Consider this, my friends, as long as you are on this earth everything depends on your will-power, not on the number of years you have lived.[65]

Although such opinions would appear bizarre to most people, they found an audience amongst considerable numbers of young people – a depressing but accurate testimony to the lack of future or purpose which so many young people feel in these towns. This is how one NCO member once looked back on how he got involved:

> I was in Novara prison, and my relatives had come to see me ... when I went back to my cell and sat down on my bed, I got to think how everything I'd ever done in my life seemed wrong 'cause I never did anything I myself cared about personally. Every single thing I've done was someone else's idea. I haven't done a thing in my entire life. I was a farmer, and in 1978 they got me for extortion by mistake, but I was innocent. I went to the old Avellino jail, and there I got to know a few *camorristi*. I used to think that the Camorra was just, was only ... at most, I thought, I'd break into houses or rob a bank, that sort of stuff.[66]

In order to understand this fully one needs to analyse the wider context of poverty and alienation that is experienced in these towns. It is no coincidence that the strength of organised crime in Italy largely corresponds to levels of poverty) For example, government statistics from 1978 show that Campania, out of Italy's twenty regions, had the second-lowest average share of wealth. Using the figure 100 as the average per capita share of gross national product, Calabria had the lowest share at 53.1, followed by Campania at 64.8 and Sicily with 65.3[67] – and it is no coincidence that these are the three Italian regions where organised crime is at its most powerful.

Official figures for unemployment amongst 14–24-year-olds in 1979 again illustrate why organised crime is so dominant in the South (see table 2).

Table 2: Unemployment among 14–24-year-olds in 1979[68]

Region	Unemployment (%)
Calabria	40.5
Campania	38.2
Lombardy	15.6
Piedmont	20.7
Sicily	33.6
Veneto	17.2

Statistics from the town of Secondigliano, just north of Naples, illustrate the same tendency on a smaller scale. One measure of its widely acknowledged poverty is that it has the highest percentage of council houses in Campania; it also holds the sad record of the highest percentage of murders committed using firearms. Before they even reach adulthood, 3 per cent of children from Secondigliano will have spent some time behind bars.[69]

In 1983 the journalist Luca Rossi recorded this tragic statement from a Secondigliano youth:

the life of a man is worth nothing here. I have seen enough in my twenty-three years and I already feel dead. Now I am living another year, and it feels like an extra life. If they want to kill me then let them go ahead, I've already seen enough.[70]

Of the 148 people killed by firearms in Naples and its province during 1980, and of the 235 victims in 1981 (80 per cent of which are estimated to be Camorra murders), almost half were

under 30, and a third were under 25.[71] The attention which
Cutolo paid to young inmates inside prison, and the sense of
identity which he attempted to give them on the outside, often
provided the only occasions when these youths felt valued and
cared for. However, people such as Cutolo can only prosper if
those who are responsible for providing employment, housing
and social services fail in their task.

The NCO spread like wildfire in the crisis-ridden Campanian
towns of the late 1970s, offering alienated youths an alternative
to a lifetime of unemployment or poorly paid jobs. Initially, the
main specialisation of NCO gangs was extorting money through
protection rackets from local businesses; they later moved on to
cocaine, partly because it was less subject to police investigation
than heroin, but also because the Mafia were less involved in the
cocaine trade.

Two different types of Camorra gangs were now beginning
to take shape: the NCO-type gangs which dealt mainly in
cocaine and protection rackets, preserving a strong regional
sense of identity, and the business-orientated gangs linked to the
Mafia, who dealt in cigarettes and heroin, but soon moved on to
invest in real estate and construction firms.

However, a brief comparison with the Mafia and its stronghold of Palermo shows that clear differences still remain. The
Mafia faces no external criminal competition in Sicily, and over
three decades has created a stable hierarchy and division of
spoils. The Camorra was resurrected largely thanks to the
Sicilian Mafia, which had its own agenda, and pursued its own
particular interests. Crucially, no hierarchy between Camorra
gangs or stable spheres of influence had been created, and no
gang leader was likely to agree to taking a back seat without
making a fight of it.

And this is what happened towards the end of 1979. The
previous year Michele Zaza had formed the 'honourable brother-
hood' in an attempt to get the Mafia-aligned Camorra gangs to
oppose Cutolo and his NCO, although without much success. It
was in this period, before the outbreak of the gang war and
during the NCO's highest point of expansion, that Michele
Zaza paid Cutolo's organisation $400,000 for the right to carry
on operating in contraband cigarettes.[72]

THE GANG WAR BETWEEN THE NCO AND THE 'NEW FAMILY'

The NCO was expanding rapidly during this period and moving into new territories and operations. The turning point came when the NCO took on the Giuliano gang, which has traditionally controlled the Forcella or 'casbah' area in the centre of Naples. Until the first half of 1979 Giuliano's men had been friendly with the *cutoliani* (members of Cutolo's NCO), indeed it appears that the Giuliano gang were on bad enough terms with Zaza to launch an attack against his nephew Pasquale in December 1979.[73]

Another gang leader named Luigi Vollaro had first raised the idea of an anti-Cutolo alliance with Luigi Giuliano in 1979, following Cutolo's demand to receive a cut from his illegal gambling centres and lottery system in his base of Portici.[74] A provisional 'death squad' was set up, which contributed to the dozens of gangland deaths in 1979, but this was on a small scale when one considers the resources of the various gangs that had mushroomed during the 1970s. Indeed, the fact that more than 1,500 people were murdered in the Campania region in the years between 1977 and 1983, and the fact that over 10,000 people were accused of membership of a Mafia-type organisation,[75] are clear evidence of the Camorra's growth.

The breaking point was reached when the *cutoliani* tried to move into the Giulianos' strongholds of Forcella, Piazza Mercato and Via Duomo, in the heart of the old city.[76] A few days before Christmas 1980 two *cutoliani* presented themselves at an unloading of contraband cigarettes at Santa Lucia and demanded immediate payment to their organisation of $400,000, as well as insisting on future payment of $25 for every crate of cigarettes brought ashore.[77] They then shot and wounded one of the men unloading the cigarettes, a member of the Giuliano gang. The pace then quickened; and on Christmas Eve, the gang's leader, Luigi Giuliano, was also wounded in an attack.

This clash, which had obviously occurred in a period of growing tension, led to the formation of the *nuova famiglia*, or New Family (NF), an alliance of all the major Camorra gangs against Cutolo's predominant NCO.

Attacks continued over the next month, until a summit meeting was called at the end of January 1981 in a top Roman hotel, under the mediation of Antonio Spavone.[78] A shaky peace was established, only to be broken on 14 February when, during the confusion provoked by a strong earth tremor, *cutoliani* in Naples' Poggioreale prison killed three adversaries.

A more serious incident occurred in May, when the NCO bombed houses in Portici owned by men working in the contraband cigarette trade for the Zaza brothers. Retaliation followed two weeks later: the two men who had tried to encroach on the Zazas' patch were shot, and a car bomb planted outside Cutolo's family home in Ottaviano.[79]

(The gang war) was far from being the result of individual psychological derailments which suddenly pushed the structure of organised crime off the tracks. In short, the war was caused by two main factors: the rapid growth of two distinct types of Camorra gangs and the profound political and financial instability created by the November 1980 earthquake.)

The war rapidly became a straightforward battle for power which was fuelled by the billions coming down from Rome for earthquake reconstruction. Table 3 illustrates the cycle of violence. The highest number of deaths occurred in 1981–2, when most reconstruction contracts were being assigned. Indeed, during this period some Neapolitans placed illegal and macabre bets, in a system run by the Camorra itself, on whether there would be more gangland murders than days over the coming year.

Table 3: Murders in Naples and the Province of Naples, 1975–92[80]

Year	Deaths	Year	Deaths	Year	Deaths
1975	49	1981	235	1987	134
1976	56	1982	265	1988	171
1977	51	1983	197	1989	231
1978	62	1984	160	1990	230
1979	85	1985	150	1991	233
1980	148	1986	106	1992	174

As regards the balance of forces between the two groups, not only was Cutolo more exposed in terms of notoriety, he had not expected such a strong reaction from his adversaries. His hostility to the Mafia also gave his opponents another tactical advantage as they were able to call on Sicilian help. Yet it was as a result of his intervention in the Cirillo kidnapping (see Chapter 5) that Cutolo was fundamentally weakened.

Cutolo's demise became starkly evident in the first of a series of 'maxi-blitzes' between 1983 and 1984. In the first round-up on 17 June 1983, for instance, 800 people were arrested in a single day of coordinated operations involving 8,000 police and *carabinieri*. Of those arrested in that series of raids, 300 were convicted very quickly and another 630 committed for trial.[81] Perhaps because of their youth and their fairly unsophisticated criminal activities, NCO members also had a tendency to kill fellow members they suspected of treachery, thus further reducing their numbers. Important NCO members such as Pasquale Barra and Giovanni Pandico began to cooperate with investigators, probably aware that the NCO was destined for defeat. Cutolo's influence was also reduced as a result of President Sandro Pertini's insistence that Cutolo be removed from a mainland jail to a maximum security prison on a small island near Sardinia.

Speculation about the importance of the Cirillo affair aside, Cutolo's defeat was clearly the result of several factors. The first was simply his impatience and arrogance, which provoked the formation of the NF; if he had moved at a slower pace and sought greater consensus he might have eventually succeeded in becoming the undisputed gang leader of the Naples area. The second factor was the youth and rawness of many of the NCO's 'foot-soldiers' compared with the more experienced members of the NF gangs; as one supergrass recalled: 'The *cutoliani* committed arrogant acts, killing people for no reason.'[82] The third factor was strategic: Cutolo had made a crucial error in concentrating on labour-intensive activities such as protection rackets and avoiding heroin trafficking almost entirely. As an investigating magistrate commented in 1985: 'one might say that most of the organisation's energies were employed in this sector [protection rackets], which is more demanding and less profitable than the former [drug trafficking].'[83] In other words, the financially more sophisticated organisations won the day.

Another key advantage was that the individual gangs of the NF alliance were less notorious than Cutolo's NCO; they were initially less affected by police operations and therefore able to carry the attack to the NCO, although the NF suffered its own 'maxi-blitz' in 1984.

But with Cutolo and his NCO out of the picture, the NF alliance quickly fell apart, with a war breaking out between the Bardellino and Nuvoletta gangs towards the end of 1983.[84] Once again we can see a (difference between the Mafia and the Camorra: the Mafia can often enjoy long periods of internal peace, but until 1984 Camorra gangs were unable to set aside their long-term rivalry and mistrust.)

These gang wars also had an important lasting effect on Naples and Campania: that of intimidating the local population. Until then the Camorra had been a fairly sporadic if worrying phenomenon in the eyes of the public, but the continual news of mass murders and shoot-outs obviously created a climate of fear and conditioned Neapolitans to accept permanently high levels of Camorra activity.

However, an event which has so far only been mentioned in passing came to dominate the Naples area in the 1980s: the earthquake of November 1980 and its consequences.

Chapter 3

The 'administrative economy' and the 1980 earthquake

The Christian Democrats were truly democratic, they divided power up. You could come to an arrangement, you could . . . cheat a lot more.
— Mafia supergrass Antonino Calderone

The San Carlo theatre clock showed 7.35 p.m. and I was in the Mayor's box with my wife and some friends. We were applauding the last piece that Gazzelloni had played and at that point I was obviously standing up. I had the sensation of feeling ill, it seemed like my head was spinning and I had the time to say 'I don't feel well, what's happening to me?' The entire theatre was moving in waves. Only after a few seconds did we realise what was happening.[1]

The earthquake struck at 7.35 in the evening of Sunday 23 November 1980. According to government figures, it caused 2,735 deaths, 8,848 injuries and made 300,000 people homeless. Many more people, however, found themselves living in buildings that were either unsafe or in serious need of repair. Commercial premises were also destroyed or damaged, as were public offices, telephones, electricity, gas and water supplies, as well as many major roads and railways.

A huge programme of reconstruction would clearly be needed, and the Camorra was already in a position to win major contracts and siphon off large amounts of money. Furthermore, reconstruction was to provide an excellent opportunity for gangs to diversify: moving away from drug trafficking and into the construction industry, as well as providing them with an area within which they could recycle their 'dirty money'.

Indeed, the earthquake represents a turning point in the development of the Camorra. Yet it is only if the surreptitious growth of the Camorra during the 1970s is born in mind that the qualitative and quantitative leap which the organisation took in the 1980s can be understood. As Isaia Sales – a local left-wing politician and author of probably the most comprehensive book on the Camorra – comments: 'Italy discovered the Camorra after the earthquake, but it is not the case that the earthquake signalled the beginning of the Camorra as a business phenomenon.'[2]

By 1980 the Camorra had already become a serious economic power, and as regards the earthquake bonanza, it is vital to analyse the advances they had already made towards obtaining public sector contracts and in conditioning local politicians.

LOCAL POLITICAL TRADITIONS

The changing climate within the ruling political class was personified in the decline of the Monarchist Party Mayor of Naples during most of the 1950s, Achille Lauro. His localised power base was slowly eroded by the emergence of nationally orientated politicians such as Silvio Gava and his son Antonio during the 1960s.

Silvio Gava was a Catholic activist under Fascism; after the war he soon became linked to the Catholic trade union association ACLI (Associazione Cattolica dei Lavoratori Italiani). His arrival on the national political stage did not stop him from developing a series of 'patron–client' relationships within the Naples area. His contacts were concentrated within parastatal economic organisations, such as ISVEIMER (Istituto per lo Sviluppo Economico dell'Italia Meridionale) and SMF (Società Meridionale Finanziaria), the control of which enabled him to slowly eat away at the basis of Lauro's political support and to persuade his backers to change their allegiance.[3]

The Gavas were new faces compared with many leading Christian Democrats of this period. Most DC politicians, in the South at least, were 'notables' – ex-landowners who had recently sold off their landed estates and were now investing in property speculation in major southern cities.

In other words, the old system of 'notables' was slowly being replaced by a series of technocratic managers, although this process only became significant at the end of the 1950s. The postwar period therefore saw a fundamental change in the ruling group of southern Italian society:

> in the South a new social bloc was taking shape; no longer based on the countryside and land ownership, it depended on the control of the huge flows of public expenditure that were channelled through the Southern Development Fund. The progressive emptying of the countryside and inland regions caused population increases in towns, especially along the coast, that were dominated by public administration and the service sector, i.e. by activities that were largely parasitical and speculative. So southern cities did not become modern urban centres of rationalist neocapitalism; in the 1960s they took on the form of nerve centres of a new social bloc based on the urban middle classes, largely unproductive and linked to a system of political control over the allocation of resources.[4]

Many of these changes were also the result of the policies instituted by the Christian Democrats' new Party Secretary, Amintore Fanfani, elected in 1954; faced with very efficient Communist competition in all walks of life, Fanfani galvanised his rather complacent party into creating more structures on the ground, as well as setting up better patronage networks.

However, over the postwar decades each Christian Democrat faction, reliant on its own local leader for national influence and resources, fought an increasingly bitter battle to defend its own position within the party's national pecking order, with the definition of victory being the control of ever greater financial resources and client networks. In the South, by the 1970s, these internal Christian Democrat battles became translated into public political slogans, such as the call for 'special intervention' or 'extraordinary intervention' in the South. The existence of real problems was constantly referred to in political debate, yet there was little serious commitment to providing solutions; indeed, to resolve the problems would have reduced the justification for resources and thus diminished the power base of the local ruling group.

Once the major economic crisis of the early 1970s began to make its presence felt, the whole gravy train was thrown into confusion and traditional southern politics entered into crisis. Disquiet began to spread within the DC, and the Gavas' predominance in Campania was challenged by Ciriaco De Mita in Avellino. Nominally on the left of the party, De Mita succeeded in forcing the Gavas to share power with him. Writing in 1973, the political scientist Percy Allum commented:

> the fall of the Gavas, when it comes, in no way implies the fall of the power system they incarnated. The De Mita group centred in the Province of Avellino is built substantially on the same clientelistic foundations, even if it has different ideological orientations.[5]

Much the same can be said twenty years later: the fall from grace of Antonio Gava, Ciriaco De Mita and other leading Neapolitan politicians in 1993 in no way implies the end of the clientelistic tradition of mainstream Neapolitan politics.

Indeed clientelism and illegality have become so ingrained in Neapolitan society that it can sometimes reach the level of the absurd. In an attempt to reduce the number of re-offenders, a scheme was established in the late 1970s to provide public sector jobs for those who had recently been released from prison. As a public sector job at that time was widely seen as a job for life, some unemployed created false criminal records for themselves in the hope of getting one of these jobs.[6]

With a relative reduction in funding as a result of economic crisis, many of the established notables could no longer guarantee favours and jobs, leading on the one hand to the growth of the left, epitomised in the election of a Communist Party council in Naples in 1975, and on the other to the rise of the illegal economy and organised crime.

The growth of illegality and the entrance of organised crime into positions of influence were generally overseen by a new generation of ambitious middle-ranking politicians. The administrative system was soon to be futher decentralised, giving local councils greater economic influence in the context of a 'deindustrialisation linked to the crisis of large industries and large cities, and the reindustrialisation of the region's whole area with a new industrial structure linked to small and medium-sized businesses and provincial centres'.[7] One historian has described this period in the following terms:

> a process involving the faster circulation and substitution of local political leaders in favour of younger and more ambitious

elements, who came from a more modest social background and who were less well-educated. There were small businessmen, shopowners and professional politicians, people who would be the protagonists of the breakup of the monopoly of political representation previously held by the liberal professions.[8]

Although these new groups were younger, more ambitious and technocratic than their predecessors, they nevertheless maintained and updated a system of patronage and clientilism which was enhanced by changes to local administration.

DECENTRALISATION AND PUBLIC SECTOR CONTRACTS

The creation of fifteen new regional units of government in 1970 played a crucial role in the development of the relationship between organised crime and the political structure.

From the following year the billions set aside for agricultural and industrial development in the South began to pass through a regional rather than a national government structure. And in 1975–7 the Socialist and Communist parties, in return for not voting against Giulio Andreotti's weak Christian Democrat government, insisted on even greater devolution of powers, so much so that by 1980 the regions were spending 18 per cent of the national budget.[9]

From the early 1970s and the creation of regional government the pendulum of political power began to swing back in favour of local politicians and their control of a local system of patronage. No major political party held back from developing a series of client networks which depended on them for the obtainment of influence and favours; Communist politicians were to invite senior trade unionists to play an important role in their administrations, while Christian Democrats tended to absorb local businessmen. Local councillors also nominated themselves to sit on the board of local health authorities, which controlled huge financial resources.

The onset of economic crisis in Italy in the early 1970s meant that the widespread industrial development planned earlier did not take place. The level of industrial development in the South, as a percentage of national figures, charts the decline in the

South's industrialisation. From a low point of 16 per cent in the 1950s, the South's share of national industrial investment rose to 37 per cent in the 1969–73 period, before falling back to 31 per cent in 1975 and 27 per cent in 1978.[10]

Local government therefore came to play a more and more important role as both private industry and national authorities scaled down their activities in the area. An official report has calculated that in the 1976–82 period local expenditure increased by 26 per cent, while inflation rose by an average of 16 per cent a year and GNP by 22 per cent a year.[11]

So in areas of low industrialisation such as Campania local authorities were often the only economic agent able to make large investments. Isaia Sales, who has termed this an 'administrative economy', writes: 'In this fashion political power becomes the absolute regulator of social and economic life.'[12] Although Sales may be guilty of ignoring a degree of investment by private industry and national government, as well as the service and tourism sectors, he nevertheless has a point. And in a wider context northern industrialists must also take their share of the blame for the closer relationship which developed between local politicians and organised crime, as their withdrawal from the area only exacerbated the dangers of this kind of development.

Nevertheless it is important to acknowledge the political consequences of decentralisation, given that it is still proposed as a solution:

> increased power and finance have not created greater democracy and popular participation in the South. On the contrary: all the power which has been delegated or transferred has become personal power, often secret and clandestine. Local political democracy emerged from this phase fundamentally transformed and reshaped.[13]

There is another important argument that reveals the failure of decentralisation (although it does not necessarily follow that centralisation, under the existing political system, would be any more successful): in economic terms southern administration is more inefficient. Once accountability is largely avoided and politics becomes a battle for the control of resources rather than the solution of common problems, the achievement of financial rigour becomes impossible.

For example, ticket revenue covers only 9.4 per cent of the

total cost of Naples' public transport, while the national average is 30 per cent.[14] Although the price structure of public transport may be similar to northern cities in terms of each mile travelled, investment policy and general planning are often vastly different.

The same thing can be seen in the maintenance of public parks and spaces: in the North, 2 lire are spent per m², while in the South the figure is 11 lire per m². Similarly, rubbish collection costs $11 per tonne in the North as against $16 in the South.[15]

Once organised crime takes hold in an area, then financial mismanagement becomes even more serious. A good example of this is the Marano council, the stronghold of the Nuvoletta gang discussed in the next chapter:

> the Marano council pays the Naples Water Board $4 million annually for its consumption, yet it only manages to obtain payment amounting to $1,840,000 because $2,160,000 worth of water is consumed by people who have made illegal connections to the water system.[16]

POLITICAL CORRUPTION

Although Camorra bosses had already obtained votes for Monarchist Party candidates during the 1950s, closer political contacts with criminals came into existence with the Christian Democrats at the end of the 1960s, when Camorra gangs first began to accumulate significant amounts of capital.

These 'modern' Camorra gangs now began to diversify alarmingly. They bought large tracts of land, supplied public authorities with fruit and vegetables, set up food processing plants, ran stud farms, set up construction companies and built residential areas, ran nightclubs and illegal gambling rings, and kept control of the drug trade. But

> despite the evolutionary process described here, despite the power and economic strength they had carved out for themselves, the Camorra, until the eve of the 1980 earthquake, had not yet surfaced in terms of national public opinion.[17]

Local politicians, however, became increasingly aware of the Camorra during the 1970s; and the nature of the political system itself meant that it was relatively easy prey for powerful criminal gangs.

By the mid-1970s politics in the Naples area had largely been a Christian Democrat fiefdom for over twenty years. The dividing line between the party and public administration had begun to merge – the decision-making process now revolved far more around meetings between party officials, their respective factions and various powerful lobbies, rather than being conducted within the official institutional channels. The infiltration and intimidation of such a system was particularly easy for an organisation such as the Camorra.

The danger signal of widespread 'a-legality' or illegality within public administration was already becoming clear by the mid-1970s. Southern regions only make up 36 per cent of the population, yet, according to official statistics, southern politicians are rather overrepresented among those Italian officials charged with 'neglect of public duty' (see Table 4). It should always be remembered that such statistics only indicate a general trend during that period; yet this trend has since been confirmed by the explosion of charges and convictions since 1992.

Table 4: Southern politicians charged with 'neglect of public duty' (as a percentage of charges nationwide)[18]

Year	%
1976	56
1977	48
1979	51
1980	52
1982	63
1983	61
1984	60

During the period of surreptitious Camorra growth, i.e. during the 1970s, the local political system was itself passing through a transitional phase. This relative weakness of the political structure, coupled with the at best semi-democratic traditions of the structure itself, allowed the Camorra to begin to condition local politicians and to effectively penetrate the 'first level' of politics.

By this period the Camorra was making huge drug profits,

which it urgently needed to recycle and protect, and the old-style politicians, who were unable or unwilling to accept this new state of affairs, began to suffer from both Camorra threats and pressure applied by their younger colleagues. Furthermore, the tension between these rapidly growing criminal organisations and a new and semi-corrupt political elite also led to 'the breakup of another monopoly, namely political control over public spending in the South, through the emergence of a fearful competitor in this area, namely a Camorra elite'.[19]

The beginning of a series of political murders carried out by Camorra gangs is clear evidence of organised crime's growing power and its relative autonomy from the political structure, in comparison with the preceding period when it had been subordinate. Although there were many woundings and attempted murders during the late 1970s, the first significant political murder was that of Socialist Party councillor Pasquale Cappuccio, killed in Cutolo's stronghold of Ottaviano in September 1978. Another councillor, a Communist called Domenico Beneventano, was killed in the month of the earthquake, November 1980. The following month the Mayor of Pagani, Marcello Torre (an independent Christian Democrat), was gunned down.[20]

So even before the earthquake struck, the Camorra had begun to act independently of its political protectors, in some cases killing local politicians who either did not keep their promises or would not give in to their demands. This tendency was to worsen tragically following the 1980 earthquake.

THE CONSEQUENCES OF THE EARTHQUAKE

The most disturbing aspect of the reconstruction scandal in the aftermath of the earthquake is that so much of the money siphoned off was diverted quite legally; allegations of shady deals are widespread but proof of straightforward illegality is only beginning to emerge now. Nevertheless the billions that have disappeared remain, at the time of writing, Europe's largest financial scandal. A good part of this amount disappeared without direct Camorra involvement, revealing a corrupt ethos that has since become an undisputed fact with the emergence of the *Tangentopoli* scandal in early 1992.

One of the first moves made by the authorities was to

Table 5: Councils classified as damaged before and after May 1981[21]

Province	No. of local councils	No. of councils classified as damaged	
		before May 1981	in May 1981
Avellino	119	104	119
Naples	91	67	86
Potenza	98	46	98
Salerno	157	66	157
Benevento	78	0	78
Caserta	104	0	102
Matera	31	0	31
Foggia	64	0	14

overstate the extent of the damage. Table 5 illustrates a sudden increase in the number of councils defined as damaged six months after the earthquake.

As the months passed, it became clear that reconstruction was proceeding at a very slow pace. Consequently, in October 1982, two decrees extended the right of private individuals to obtain advances from bank accounts set up by local councils for reconstruction,

> as long as they showed a document stamped by the Mayor and the Secretary of the Council, in which the following phrase had to be written: 'Following verification of entitlement and the correct nature of the documentation presented, pay Mr X the sum of Y lire.'[22]

Never before had local mayors wielded such powers or controlled such large amounts of money. Banks were now flooded with deposits set aside for reconstruction.

Months of delay turned into years, and these delays also gave time to inflate the size of projects, and consequently their total cost. For example, the cost of repairs to the ring road around Lago di Patria was estimated at $102 million in February 1985, rising to $136 million in October 1985, $272 million in 1986, and $370 million in 1988. Similarly, the estimated cost of rebuilding the Conte Sarno Canal rose from $37 million to $82 million in 1987 and to $400 million in 1988.[23]

One of the myths surrounding the earthquake is that it was a strictly southern affair. In reality 28 of the 50 companies that won the largest contracts were based in central or northern Italy.[24] These big consortia quickly realised that they could make huge profits from delaying the start of building work, as they were given an advance of between 20 and 37 per cent of the project's total cost once it had been officially approved. With the actual work often delayed by months or even years, companies could use these large sums of money to finance other operations in the meantime.[25]

These consortia then often subcontracted the work to local building companies, normally at prices 40–70 per cent below those agreed between the consortia and public authorities, thus creating another huge source of profit. Indeed, a mere 11 per cent of the companies that actually engaged in reconstruction were part of the original consortia that had won the contracts. And many of the local subcontractors were controlled by the Camorra, as we shall see below.

The important point to remember is that this system benefited both the Camorra and major construction consortia. The mechanics of the system are outlined in the following hypothesis published by the major opposition party, the Partito Communista Italiano (PCI):

How to earn $80 million without setting foot on a building site
Let's imagine a contract worth $80 million, with a building firm receiving an advance of $28 million, an amount that is only detracted once the contractor has spent $40 million. Let's suppose that it takes three years to complete half the project (18 months to actually start work, and another 18 months to complete half the work). In three years the contractor has earned interest worth over 40 per cent, taking into account the interest rates of the early 1980s.

What can therefore happen is that from an initial projected cost of $80 million a firm receives $28 million immediately (twenty days after signing the contract), $11 million in interest from the bank, another $32 million due to rising prices, and if the project is then subcontracted at half price, another $40 million. In net terms, a firm can therefore make over $80 million without ever having set foot on a building site.[26]

While the national government was promoting a 'carpetbagger' mentality, the local political structure lacked a tradition of openness and decision-making based on an applicant's merit. This had not escaped the notice of the local police, and on 10 October 1982 the prefect of Avellino, the main town within the area most affected by the earthquake and reconstruction,

> convened the representatives of the 119 councils of the province in order to agree upon common action to be taken against the Camorra and organised crime. During the meeting it was established that there had to be a full council meeting once a month, that greater space should be given to smaller opposition parties, and that the council must become a 'glass-house' in terms of its general administrative management.[27]

Speaking to the assembled politicians, the prefect's warnings were prophetic:

> The mobilisation of councils cannot and must not end up a ritual, similar to a religious litany, because it is in the badly lit areas of certain administrations that the Camorra makes headway. In many councils the opposition is well and truly ghettoised, council meetings are only held in exceptional cases, often everything is decided without ordinary people being aware of anything.[28]

Two years later the Neapolitan sociologist Amato Lamberti, who had researched twenty of these councils in detail, assessed the outcome of the meeting:

> The most important decisions, those on the contracts to be awarded, are only made in meetings of the ruling group. It has become a fixed rule that there is no monitoring of the subcontracting firm at all, while there are large gaps in checking up on the firms which have actually won contracts.[29]

This sequence of events illustrates two facts: contracts were being awarded to companies without any checks being made on them: decisions made behind closed doors were far more likely to be influenced by the Camorra and to lack the accountability which would have characterised full and public council meetings. What it also illustrates, crucially, is the unwillingness of local politicians to make themselves accountable.

Fourteen Inspection Committees were set up to monitor the

progress of construction work, although they had very little technical expertise:

> operations of a purely technical nature, such as an inspection of the progress of building work, or projects of primary or secondary urbanisation, motorway link roads, the rerouting of rivers and streams, the restructuring of railway lines, etc., were all entrusted to committees that lacked any technical support. On the contrary, they were led by and made up of magistrates, state attorneys, prefects, bureaucrats of the re-gional council, academics, magistrates of the regional court and the state finance commission, MPs, ex-regional council-lors, mayors, etc. What is impossible to understand is how such committees were able to ascertain and verify anything from a technical point of view, given their composition.[30]

Indeed, of the original 143 members of these committees, 30 were ordinary magistrates.[31]

Yet it would be wrong to think that the judiciary was the only high-level institution involved. Most sectors of the legal and state bureaucracy also played a role:

> when the names of the other inspectors are scrutinised one finds even more surprises: three prefects, including those of Naples and Salerno (the Prefect of Naples resigned in 1987, while his counterpart in Salerno never did, even though he was also employed at the Special Office for Reconstruction in the 'earthquake crater'), seven deputy prefects, the president of the Campania regional court along with other members of both the Latium regional court and the Campania regional court, four magistrates from the state finance commission, including the president of the Campania section, Silvino Covelli. He was also an inspector at Monteruscello, and apart from being an inspector, managed to see to it that his daughter was employed within the commission's bureaucracy as well. The chief registrar of the Naples law court was also an inspector, as was the head of personnel.
>
> Furthermore, members and officials of the control com-mission of the Campania Region were inspectors, as were ordinary employees of the same commission who effectively carried out regulatory checks. This is not to forget ex-regional

councillors, office staff employed by particular Ministers, officials of the regional council, and a local director of education, and so on.[32]

Inspectors were paid 1 per cent of the value of the projects they inspected.

Senior public servants were therefore legitimising the whole reconstruction, but many of them would also be called upon to adjudicate if any legal controversies or accusations arose concerning the legitimacy and legality of such a huge programme of works.

And conflicts of interest did arise. For example, Neapolitan magistrates began an investigation into Camorra involvement in the building of thousands of houses at Monteruscello, and the fact that the new flats were already showing serious signs of decay. Yet the people who had previously inspected the flats were their colleagues at the Naples law courts.[33] A similar conflict of interest arose concerning water infiltration in new houses built in Casoria and Casalnuovo.

Apart from these conflicts of interest, there is another very good reason why magistrates should not be involved in work such as this – it takes them away from their work within the legal system. The Campania region has one of Italy's highest crime rates, yet its magistrates are also at the top of the table as regards extra-judicial activities.

Perhaps the most telling detail of this scandal is that many local politicians became millionaires as a result of the earthquake. In addition to being elected mayors and councillors, they were, as private individuals, also allowed to win contracts as practising architects, construction engineers or consultants. Of the eighteen mayors in the Province of Avellino in the 1982–90 period, fifteen won a total of 1,334 reconstruction contracts, an average of 89 contracts per mayor. These figures need to be roughly quadrupled to include all the councillors who also won reconstruction contracts.[34]

It has been estimated that between 20 and 30 per cent of a project's entire cost was taken up by the fees of architects, engineers and those generally involved in planning, and that an individual contract was worth an average of $80,000.[35]

Yet there was a perfectly viable alternative:

Instead of building useless roads one could have created tens of thousands of jobs by activating productive sectors. But elevated sections were as useless as they were expensive, and therefore extremely profitable for builders and the politicians associated with them. But directing these huge amounts of public expenditure towards productive investments would have given rise to a real process of development; which would have meant the collapse of that unhealthy link between power politics and the parasitical economic interests of the public, private and criminal sectors.[36]

The inescapable conclusion from the fiasco of earthquake reconstruction is that the greatest beneficiaries have been local politicians, senior members of the judiciary and the state bureaucracy, and the Camorra. Another important point to bear in mind is that *all* the major political parties were involved. The political affiliations of those Avellino councillors who had won reconstruction contracts closely mirrored their political strength within local councils: 44 Christian Democrat councillors had won contracts, 24 Socialists and 12 Communists.[37]

Although vast amounts of money were earned legally by individual politicians, the huge *Tangentopoli* scandal of 1992–3 has led to the discovery of an illegal system of financing political parties. Over the years a widespread system of kickbacks developed in which politicians demanded that a fixed percentage of contracts be diverted into party coffers. One of the reasons why this particular system came to light in 1992 was that demands had become too high, as one local businessman explained: 'In recent years kickbacks increased from 3 to 7 per cent. Extortion had become even worse, businesses were being strangled.'[38]

If one steps back a moment from the activities of leading politicians and business people, one is faced with the plain fact that the earthquake has been a traumatic experience for many ordinary people. For example, in early 1994, more than thirteen years after the earthquake, at least 700 families – 4,000 people – were still living in steel containers of 12 m². It is also fitting, in terms of his political traditions, that over a hundred of these families live in Castellammare di Stabia, Antonio Gava's home town.[39]

Despite the billions that have been spent, unemployment levels in Campania are higher than fifteen years ago; similarly, the standard of living in relative terms is still amongst the lowest in the country. In many areas the only real innovation has been the growth of organised crime.

Chapter 4

The 'business Camorra' of the Nuvoletta gang

The Jolly Roger is the banner of competitive business.

— Sean O'Casey

THE NUVOLETTA GANG AND THE EARTHQUAKE

When Lorenzo Nuvoletta was finally arrested in December 1990 it was widely believed that he was the leader of the Camorra's second most powerful gang, second only to the one led by Carmine Alfieri. The rapid rise of Nuvoletta's gang was largely owing to its intervention in earthquake reconstruction, which involved relaundering money and winning contracts. The well-documented rise of this gang, based around four brothers – Angelo, Ciro, Gaetano and Lorenzo – is an excellent case study in the transformation of an insignificant family from the provinces into multimillionaires.[1]

In the early 1960s one of the Camorra gangs operating to the north of Naples and dealing mainly in contraband cigarettes was led by Antonio Maisto. When he had to go into hiding in 1971–2 the reins were taken over by his sons, Luigi and Enrico.

Ciro and Lorenzo Nuvoletta initially joined this gang as minor members. Stefano Bontade was another member during this period, son of the old Mafioso Francesco Paolo Bontade, a member of Michele Greco's Mafia gang. In a disastrous government policy Bontade, along with many other Mafiosi suspected but not convicted of serious crimes, was obliged to live in 'external exile' in the Naples area, where he naturally continued his criminal activities. This quickly brought the Nuvolettas into contact with the Sicilian Mafia, a link which was to prove vital in their rise to power. During the early 1970s Bontade, along with Salvatore Riina and Gaetano Badalamenti, began to set up a new Mafia committee, or *cupola*.[2]

The Nuvolettas are from Marano, a town of 46,000 just north of Naples. After their early exploits in the Maisto gang, they made their first independent move which came to characterise them: in the mid-1960s they diversified and became significant landowners; using state funds designed to set up small agricultural landholdings, they bought up a total of some 100 ha of land from various smallholders. A company called 'Viticola Nova', founded in July 1966 and run by Giuseppe Iacolare, had the function of paying their farm labourers. The first loan to the Nuvolettas, in this case Angelo, was received in 1969 from the Bank of Naples: $40,000 repayable over forty years.[3] This was the start of a fifteen-year relationship between the Nuvoletta gang and the South's major bank.

They were soon supplying many military and civilian establishments with various foodstuffs, and were not surprisingly implicated in swindles against the Italian government and the EEC, 'for the non-delivery of fruit and vegetables'.[4]

During this period the Nuvolettas made large amounts of money by intimidating insurance officials investigating a variety of claims made, and much of their power within local agriculture derived from the intimidation of local farmers. Two *carabinieri* reports from 1976 detail the threats made against two local farmers by the Nuvoletta gang; in one case they demanded to become co-owners and in the other to become suppliers.[5] But it was not only brute force that allowed them to wield such influence – many farmers took out loans from finance companies managed by the Nuvolettas.

And it was not long before they moved into an even more lucrative sector, that of hard drugs. It was here that they made most of their illegal money from then on.[6] Aniello and Antonio Nuvoletta, both sons of Gaetano, are believed to have been involved in a large cocaine trade with another major Camorra leader, Umberto Ammaturo; indeed Antonio was convicted of cocaine trafficking in March 1977.

In the same period arrest warrants were issued for the Nuvolettas accusing them of importing a consignment of cocaine worth $208,000. The charges also mentioned phone calls to Germany made by Aniello Nuvoletta about the purchase of Leopard and

Centurion tanks costing between $800,000 and $1,600,000, although the German police found no evidence of this.[7]

So by the mid-1970s the Nuvoletta brothers were well known to the police, having been arrested on a variety of charges. What is particularly significant is that according to the Mafia super-grasses Tommaso Buscetta, Antonino Calderone and Salvatore Contorno, the Nuvolettas had very close links with Sicily, normally arranged through Ciro Nuvoletta.

Before he was murdered, the Mafioso Giuseppe Di Cristina confirmed the Nuvolettas' links with Luciano Liggio's Sicilian gang, specifying that somewhere between Naples and Caserta there was a large fruit production factory that provided a cover for a drugs depot and possibly a heroin refinery, owned by Liggio himself. The Nuvolettas managed the whole enterprise on his behalf.[8] According to police reports the Nuvolettas were allowing Mafia men on the run to stay in their houses as early as 1971, one of the most important Mafia bosses being Liggio himself. When Liggio was finally arrested police found a cheque stub detailing a payment made to the Nuvolettas' bank account.[9]

It was these links with top Mafiosi which led to the Nuvolet-tas' rapid rise. Apparently the first meetings between the Nuvolet-tas and the Greco family from Palermo were held in Marano in 1974. The timing is particularly significant as many believe that Michele Greco was at that time the leader of the Sicilian Mafia's *cupola*, the Mafia's supreme decision-making body. Furthermore, other Mafia supergrasses have detailed two top Mafia–Camorra summits held in Marano in 1978 and 1979, involving the Nuvo-letta and Zaza brothers from Naples, Salvatore Riina and other top Mafiosi.[10]

This is how Mafia supergrass Antonino Calderone recalls the links:

> In 1974, during one of my visits to Naples, an old man of honour originally from Palermo, who lived in a building in the Santa Lucia area, told me of the family (i.e. the Mafia) which went back to the 1930s. The most important members of the family in Naples were the Mazzarella, Nuvoletta and Zaza brothers. Then there were other people such as Nunzio Barbarossa, the Sciorio brothers, and others. The entire Naples family was controlled by Michele Greco, but within it the Nuvoletta gang had about ten members with an even closer

and more direct relationship with Michele Greco, who could direct them without the mediation of the family itself.[11]

A major Camorra supergrass, Pasquale Galasso, has revealed details of further meetings held at one of the Nuvolettas' villas in 1981. What was remarkable about these meetings is that they often involved representatives of all the major Camorra families, and so there were often a hundred people present, many of them on the run, as well as dozens of cars. But as he explains:

> Our worries arose from the possibility that the police might arrive during our meetings and cause a bloodbath, yet Nuvoletta always managed to calm us down. Sometimes, when Carmine Alfieri and I looked out at his farmhouse on leaving Vallesana, we would see a few police cars parked outside Nuvoletta's house. That proved to us he was well protected . . . in the course of these meetings we had to sort out once and for all the tensions Cutolo had created. I can recall that Riina, Provenzano and Bagarella were in Nuvoletta's farmhouse at the same time.[12]

It is generally thought that the influence of the Mafia gave the Nuvolettas a key advantage over their rivals, making them particularly efficient and business-orientated, although they could also engage in cold-blooded acts of violence when necessary. Having Mafia support also meant they enjoyed both increased political protection and a comparative lack of aggression from other gangs.

With their economic growth through heroin and cocaine activity the Nuvolettas felt they had to rapidly diversify their wealth and set about laundering their 'dirty' money by investing it in legal projects. Like many other *camorristi* they chose the construction industry and in particular cement factories. The reason for this choice has very little to do with the ease of disposing of victims, the main advantage being the low level of technological knowhow required. Also, concrete can only be transported for approximately 10 miles, so major building projects are virtually obliged to use local suppliers of concrete.

The Nuvolettas founded their first cement company, SOGEME, in April 1979. It had assets of $16,000 and a sole director, Luigi Romano, a fruit and vegetable trader. (It is possible that Romano initially acted as a *prestanome*, literally a 'name-lender', as the Nuvolettas' criminal record prevented them from exercising official control of the company – although the fact that Romano was more than he seemed is shown by his purchase of a luxury hotel in 1978 for $2,400,000.) Just two years later, in April 1981, SOGEME's capital had increased to $80,000, an increase of 500 per cent over two years.[13] A year later, in March 1982, capital had reached $1,720,000. Growth rates were clearly phenomenal, and in the first three years of trading alone the company's capital increased more than hundredfold.

The crucial factor in these developments was the November 1980 earthquake. The Nuvolettas had moved fast, renaming the company Bitum Beton the month after the earthquake, restructuring their factory and buying new vehicles. Cement is perhaps the most vital raw material in building work and is normally estimated to make up 30 per cent of the cost in building a house.[14] Bitum Beton's turnover mushroomed alarmingly, from $3.2 million in 1981, to $8.8 million in 1982, $13.4 million in 1983 and $18.4 million in 1984.[15]

According to Judge Mancuso, these huge increases are a classic sign of money laundering. As regards the 1981–4 period, 'Not one piece of evidence has been provided for the legal origin of the approximately $2 million difference between the finances available and actual investments.'[16] It appears that sometimes the Nuvolettas made up this difference through an ingenious if rather crude method: with shareholders providing 'loans' to the company.

Control of the company moved back and forth between Luigi Romano and his cousin, Vincenzo Agizza, who in turn was the major shareholder of a cleaning company which held the contracts for Naples University, Naples Central Station and other major public buildings. Neither Romano nor Agizza had anything to do with the building trade by profession. Their staggering success, as Mancuso laconically comments, 'was achieved by a company led by a fruit and vegetable trader and the owner of cleaning firm, without any real experience in this area'.[17]

Judge Mancuso has named Vincenzo Simonelli, unknown to the authorities until December 1983, as the *eminence grise* of the Nuvolettas, their effective intermediary with the local and national business world.[18] According to his tax declaration he was virtually destitute, having declared an income of $2,560 in 1980 and $1,360 in 1981; his desperation was such that he was twice convicted in 1983 of writing uncreditworthy cheques. Yet in December 1982 he bought a piece of land for $72,000 upon which a factory would be built and spent another $290,000 on another piece of real estate.[19] And even earlier, in March 1981, he had written a valid cheque for $41,000.[20] Simonelli is believed to have been the Nuvolettas' main *prestanome*, and when they realised that much of their property was about to be seized, they gave him dozens of pedigree racehorses, so many, in fact, that by the summer of 1985 Simonelli was the proud owner of some sixty horses, although he never convincingly explained how he had come into possession of them.[21]

Not only do the business inexperience of these individuals and their inexplicable financial operations cause suspicion, their associates and connections give rise to further concern. In 1983 Romano had asked Giovanni Napolitano, a convicted heroin trafficker who had already received a nine-year sentence, to become a shareholder. Indeed, Mancuso possesses documentary evidence to suggest that Romano exchanged many cheques with the Napolitano brothers, visiting their house in Canada at least once a year. They in turn are suspected of involvement in illegal gold trading and drug trafficking, and were also said to be on close terms with Sebastiano Aloi, reputedly the head of the Italo-American Mafia in Miami, who is connected with the Columbo and Gambino families of New York. This particular connection was apparently useful in setting up facilities for heroin refining in Canada.

Vincenzo Agizza's role appears to have been that of providing financial services. He was the head of a huge cleaning company, which in 1984 provided services worth over $16 million to a variety of institutions: state railways, the Alfa Romeo/Nissan factory just outside Naples, the state electricity company and Venice council. What is particularly disturbing in this context, given the Camorra's widespread use of minors who cannot be brought to trial, is the contract to clean Naples' two main borstals, Filangieri and Nisida. Not to mention the contract to clean the flat of the Prefect of Naples, the major representative of the government in the city.[22] Furthermore, Agizza's cousin owned a company which had the cleaning contract for one of the major law courts in Campania, at Santa Maria Capua Vetere.[23]

In this particular case it is clear that the company concerned was very successful, but it is important to understand in detail how that success was achieved, chiefly because it gives an indication of how difficult it is to defeat the Camorra.

Compared with their competitors, Camorra companies have an advantage for the following three reasons: intimidation of workers, potential clients and politicians; varying degrees of political collusion and protection; and financial advantages obtained as a result of their economic success.

Intimidation

There is no direct evidence of the intimidation of workers in the Bitum Beton case. Yet intimidating workers is a vital component in keeping down labour costs, and not surprisingly there have been many Camorra attacks throughout the 1980s on local trade union leaders and workplace activists. Given the unifying nature of large workplaces, it is not surprising that one of the first demonstrations against the 'modern Camorra' in Campania occurred in the shipbuilding town of Castellammare in the summer of 1980. Workers at the shipyards felt that the entrance of the Camorra, with its demands for protection money, would significantly raise costs in comparison with competing northern and central Italian shipyards. In 1983, for example, Castellammare workers claimed that a ship built by them, identical to one built in Genoa, cost $800,000 more due to the infiltration of the Camorra.[24]

This is not to say that workers are not affected by fear or by their own historical and cultural traditions, which could often lead them to believe that the Camorra only bothers those with power and money. Nevertheless, as one trade union leader from Caserta has stated:

> in this area [the Camorra] has only one antagonist, trade unionists: we are the only social group to fight for control over the economy and the openness of political institutions, and we are the only ones able to organise popular mobilisations.[25]

Apart from direct intimidation, the Camorra has also practised a more insidious strategy: that of long-term infiltration of trade unions, and in Naples, the infiltration of the organised unemployed movement.

The Bitum Beton case provides greater detail of intimidation in the world of business. In 1982 a building cooperative called CMC won a contract to build 1,000 houses and due to their long-term connections considered Calcestruzzi Ltd as their natural suppliers of concrete.

Yet, as the CMC supplies manager recounts, things went rather differently:

> As early as 1982 I sent one of my technicians to the Naples area to ascertain who were the biggest and most reliable cement companies . . . Bitum Beton offered us a price which was about 80 cents lower per cubic metre than the others. At that point, the common practice is to contact all the other companies and try to obtain further reductions, but in this case we received information from our orders manager, Marco Abbondanza, who stated that it was best to leave things with Bitum Beton both in technical terms and for reasons concerning the 'social peace' which this kind of supplier could guarantee us.[26]

Indeed he later states that CMC were extremely happy with Bitum Beton's performance, particularly their guarantee of providing 'social peace' in a very turbulent area. And in terms of competitive business, CMC's choice also appears to have been the most rational.

A Mr Rambaldi, a witness from the firm which lost the contract, Calcestruzzi Ltd (part of the giant Gardini group), has made a fascinating deposition. Writing before the company's involvement in *Tangentopoli*, Mancuso describes Rambaldi as being a 'witness above suspicion, the Naples representative of one of the largest European business groups':

> following the setting up of Bitum Beton's factory I soon noticed that, against all my expectations – i.e. that the firm concerned, given the owners' total lack of experience, would have had just as much trouble as we had had, or as any other company had had, to launch themselves on the market. Yet reality completely overturned this expectation: the reality was that Bitum Beton acquired important market sectors in a rapid and completely unexpected fashion.[27]

The final consequence of Bitum Beton's rapid rise was the formation of a cement consortium in 1983, the Consorzio Campania Costruzioni. For Bitum Beton's competitors, it was a case of 'if you can't beat 'em, join 'em'; stability was finally achieved by a general agreement on market share. Given the dynamic growth of Bitum Beton, it might seem strange that they called a halt to a competition they had been winning, but the creation of a consortium meant that Bitum Beton gained credibility, legitimacy and also expertise. Mancuso is extremely perceptive on Bitum Beton's motivation: 'one should repeat that the objective is civil society, and not simply profit, and this has now been reached.'[28]

The final area of intimidation concerns politicians, although discussion of this point here will be brief as this argument will be dealt with in greater depth in a later chapter. For now I will again concentrate on the Nuvolettas' activities in a very specific field – their battle for building contracts in Quarto, a town next to their stronghold of Marano.

This occurred in 1982–3 and revolved around the Nuvolettas' desire to obtain building contracts before the passing of a new town development plan. Given the reputation of the Nuvolettas and their empire, there was resistance within the council to awarding them the contract. At one point the council even prevented the building committee from meeting in order to block the awarding of the contract. The Nuvolettas allegedly responded by blowing up the cars of the mayor, Carendente Giarusso Castrese, and of Russo, another senior council official.

These bombs had the desired effect: the council resigned and the new administration installed in January 1983 agreed to the Nuvolettas' demands. Police had tapped their phones, and it appears that Lorenzo Nuvoletta and others were even in close contact with Quarto councillors just before the approval of the Quarto town development plan. Other council officials, the government's Extraordinary Commissioner for Quarto and individuals who were selling land were also involved. Mancuso laments the fact that the documentation concerning these contracts has disappeared from council files.

In any event, just a few months later council planners discovered that three quarters of the projected 10,000 rooms had already been built, virtually without permission or contract.

Political collusion and protection

A 1988 *carabinieri* report states that, as regards their wider political contacts, the gang 'is definitely in a position to control and deliver a huge amount of votes in favour of a given local political candidate'.

The Nuvolettas were certainly well connected: Vincenzo Agizza, who is reputed to have committed serious crimes as a member of the Nuvoletta gang, was a Christian Democrat councillor from 1980 to 1983 in the inner city area of Poggioreale. A 1990 report from the Naples police headquarters reveals that all members of the ruling group on the 1984 Marano council have been committed for trial on charges of forgery and promoting private business interests.[29] Furthermore, according to a June 1990 *carabinieri* report, two Christian Democrat councillors elected in May 1990 are close relations of leading members of the Nuvoletta gang; and another DC councillor in Marano has been arrested by revenue officers for illegally exporting currency.[30] Not surprisingly, the council was disbanded by government decree in the same year and a special commissioner appointed to run local administration.

It appears that famous Camorra names are often a guarantee of a high number of votes. One of the candidates elected for the first time in the May 1990 council elections was Carmine Romano, nephew of Luigi Romano, who was elected as a Socialist Party candidate at the nearby town of Brusciano with 1,164 preferential votes.[31]

The percentage swings in the May 1990 local elections also give rise to suspicion. In a country where until 1992 even a 2 or 3 per cent swing was seen as very important, the swing in Marano compared with previous elections was 6.3 per cent in the elections for the regional parliament and a massive 18.5 per cent in the council elections.[32] The concern expressed in the 1988 *carabinieri* report appears to be fully justified: it is very unlikely that the percentage swing was caused by mass attraction towards the political programmes of the respective parties or some local political issue. The most likely explanation is that the Camorra, in this case the Nuvoletta gang, had delivered the vote to its own candidates, or to candidates it had come to an agreement with. Indeed in towns such as Marano political parties no longer match the normal stereotype, according to the current Special Commissioner: 'one does not identify with the national party. Here there are councillors who change party every year.'[33]

Political 'networking' is engaged in to a vast extent. Antonio Saracino was a Republican Party councillor in Marano during the 1980s, and from 1983 until 1985 he was personal secretary to Giuseppe Galasso during his period as Under-Secretary for the Ministry of Culture; Galasso's importance is that he is probably the major living historian of the city of Naples and perhaps the leading intellectual based in the city. In December 1984 Saracino phoned the director of the Naples National Library to enquire about a cleaning contract for Agizza Ltd, and openly used his political influence: 'The Under-Secretary is asking for news, haven't you got any for him, I don't get it?'[34]

Then there are also classic examples of 'friendship', such as Nicola Di Muro's participation in the 1987 wedding of Luigi Romano's daughter, Leonilde; Di Muro was Christian Democrat deputy mayor in the town of Santa Maria Capua Vetere.[35]

Furthermore, when he was arrested for membership of the Nuvoletta gang, Luigi Romano's address book contained many private phone numbers or direct office numbers of important government ministers. He had a particularly close relationship with Christian Democrat politician Vincenzo Scotti during his period as Minister of the Interior – Scotti also came to the opening of the Castelsandra Hotel. Romano admitted at his trial that he had met another important Christian Democrat minister, Paolo Cirino Pomicino: 'I met him twice in the company of Scotti, and then never again.' But Romano was obviously being economical with the truth as it also emerged that he had four different numbers for Cirino Pomicino, Budget Minister during this period.

He also had the phone number of Casertan Christian Democrat MP Gaetano Vairo, who after his re-election in April 1991 became president of the parliamentary committee responsible for removing MPs' parliamentary immunity from prosecution.[36] Yet there was perhaps nothing surprising in this: until 1987, over a period of many years, Vairo had been Romano's lawyer.

Once Luigi Romano and Vincenzo Agizza had been convicted of several crimes (although not of belonging to a criminal organisation) their power and credibility were seriously undermined. Hence the later revelation of their apparent links with Vairo – they allegedly supplied free cement for Vairo's villa in Maddaloni and funded his 1987 election campaign with $100,000 – has been interpreted as a personal vendetta by Romano and Agizza.[37] Yet one wonders what the reaction would have been if they had not yet been convicted and had simply made the same accusations without having a criminal record.

Although none of these details is irrefutable proof of close links between organised crime and major politicians, it is inevitable that major businessmen such as Romano and Agizza regularly meet and discuss a whole series of issues with politicians, whether they be broad discussions of policy or illegal arrangements.

Financial advantages

It is important to deal with finance too because it illustrates very well how the dividing line between legality and illegality can become blurred, making criminal activity almost unstoppable.

According to Amato Lamberti, Director of the *Osservatorio sulla Camorra*,

> When the Camorra invests in residential development or tourism, or in other words in 'clean' business activities, it must have its own experts on tax, finance, commercial law, indeed its own legal office; there has to be a 'brains' to advise on what kind of investments to make. Today, the professionals of the Camorra are still anonymous figures.[38]

However, it is not only academic observers who are of this opinion; Judge Mancuso, for instance, also recognises that the Camorra enjoys

> comprehensive relationships with the world of finance, and with the most knowledgeable experts of financial and commercial companies, where the dividing line between legality and illegality seems to dissolve, making the ascertainment of individual responsibilities extremely difficult.[39]

Indeed it has been in the world of finance that the Nuvolettas have been particularly innovatory, as outlined in the March 1988 conviction of Marano businessman Domenico Di Maro, found guilty of criminal association:

the infiltration of capital from illegal activities into the business world permitted, on the one hand, extremely advantageous re-investment (thanks to financial liquidity and the ease in obtaining clients through the use of intimidation), and on the other hand it allowed entrance into the less risky area of civil society (the world of finance, politics, public administration). These are the typical methods adopted by the Sicilian Mafia, and they strongly influenced the innovatory decisions made by the Nuvolettas, who then introduced these ideas within the Camorra as a whole.[40]

Di Maro had been involved in suspect financial dealings for many years, providing, for example, easy loans from his property company to a Sicilian Mafioso as far back as April 1979,[41] as well as writing cheques payable to various members of the Nuvoletta family from as early as 1976.[42]

The huge liquidity enjoyed by Camorra companies allows them to engage in massive investment, thus quickly outstripping their rivals. For example, Agizza Ltd increased its capital from $1,200,000 in 1981 to $3,500,000 in 1982, but this occurred without an increase in the firm's turnover, i.e. in the volume of its activities.[43] 'Legal' Camorra companies can quickly create large operating profits and are able to outbid rival established companies for public contracts. Once credit institutions hear of their performance the rules of the market dictate the creation of a close relationship:

> All the offers made by Camorra firms are 20–25 per cent below the real costs. In order to compete for a contract, a healthy firm knows it has to estimate costs and the amount of advances it receives from banks. Yet the Camorra enjoys such a financial liquidity that it always wins the tender, and in many cases the banks are making a profit from this situation.[44]

The result is a vicious circle. Camorra firms become excellent investments in rational free market terms: as far as banks are concerned only the most successful companies will be offered the most enticing repayment schemes on loans, which gives Camorra companies a further advantage over their fully legal rivals. For example, in 1981–2 Bitum Beton received 'easy-term financing' of more than $800,000 from ISVEIMER, the Institute for the Economic Development of the South.[45] And during their 1990 trial the prosecuting judge declared that the Nuvolettas' gang 'enjoyed very firm and important alliances within the Bank of Naples'. Contacts can extend down to a very low level; one piece of evidence presented to the trial detailed a telephone conversation between the clerk of a local bank, who empathised with Vincenzo Agizza about the manager of the local bank in question, and thanked Agizza for the Christmas present his wife had received.[46]

Once these major companies develop close relationships with large banks, many strange details are likely to be ignored; Judge Mancuso cites the revealing example of a Monte dei Paschi di Siena bank report dated 10 March 1983, which expressed concern about 'the inexplicable concentration of enormous liquidity in a brief period, for no reason and without any apparent cause'.[47]

The most prominent case of the 'legitimate' business world's involvement with the Nuvolettas concerns the South's largest credit institution, the Bank of Naples. The general manager of the bank from 1980 to 1983, Raffaele Di Somma, has been convicted of providing illegal credit to a series of companies owned by an associate of the Nuvoletta gang, Domenico Di Maro. That Di Maro was even allowed any credit in this period is surprising, as the *carabinieri* had been making investigations within the bank during 1982, making it clear he was suspected of involvement with the Camorra.[48] Nevertheless Di Maro was allowed credit for $7.2 million.

Given his background, it is not surprising to discover that Di Maro took advantage of his special relationship with the bank, illegally obtaining a further $3.2 million in credit and causing severe financial problems for the bank.[49] Di Somma, however, gained an immediate benefit from all this, in the shape of two silver plates worth $800 given to him by Di Maro every Easter and Christmas.[50]

But this was not simply a case of a hardened criminal corrupting a mild-mannered banker. Independently of any Camorra involvement, Di Somma was also convicted of forcing ninety-one companies indebted to the Bank of Naples to take out loan insurance policies with his son's insurance company.[51] Indeed the power of intimidation of such a major financial institution is likely to be very extensive indeed; businesses on the verge of bankruptcy are clearly likely to remain silent even if they believe that the bank is involved in sharp or illegal practice, as they would risk having vital credit immediately denied.

Even more alarming is that a crossover may now be occurring in an unexpected direction. The classic business figure has always been that of the *mafioso imprenditore*, i.e. the gangster who moves into legitimate business. Today, given the power of the Camorra in some areas, one can see the emergence of an *imprenditore mafioso* – an individual who previously worked within the law by and large, acting as a banker or consultant to a firm known to have Camorra connections, advising on areas of investment, profit distribution and a whole host of legitimate financial problems. Once this *imprenditore mafioso* learns the tricks of the criminal trade, he or she is in an excellent position to strike out independently, as appears to be the case with Di Somma.

THE STRENGTHS AND WEAKNESSES OF THE NUVOLETTA GANG

During the 1980s the Nuvoletta gang transformed itself into a huge international holding company investing in agriculture, cleaning contracts, construction, drugs, fraud and stud farming. And like any major conglomerate, it also diversified into the leisure industry, with Luigi Romano buying a huge luxury hotel on the coast south of Salerno, worth approximately $8 million before its seizure. The Castelsandra Hotel has 124 rooms, 8 suites, 30 villas, tennis courts and even a small zoo, during the construction of which a hill containing rare wildlife was destroyed.[52]

The value of the real estate seized when the judiciary acted against the Nuvolettas' empire in 1988 gives some idea of their wealth, although this is very probably just the tip of the iceberg. Luigi Romano and the Agizza brothers had the following properties seized: two flats in Brusciano worth $320,000, a villa near Paestum worth $240,000, a block of flats in Naples worth $1,050,000 as well as other minor properties. Land, buildings, flats, villas, machinery and vehicles worth $16 million were seized from the Bitum Beton company, while Agizza Ltd had $20 million of property seized.[53] The finance police have calculated that the Nuvolettas' 'legal' investments were worth $280 million at that point.[54] The final order to seize that gang's possessions in October 1992 involved holdings valued at $240 million.[55]

But despite this huge growth the Nuvolettas were unable to immerse themselves completely in 'civil society'; although they had created a huge 'legal' empire their illegal activities were still central to their operations. The fact that a war broke out between the Nuvolettas and the Bardellinos at the end of 1983, both previously part of the New Family alliance against Cutolo, is proof that as yet the Camorra seems to have failed to create a lasting peace within its own ranks.

A long series of events had led to mistrust and finally open war between the Bardellino and Nuvoletta gangs. Towards the end of 1982 Antonio Bardellino, probably thanks to a warning from the local police, just managed to escape capture in his Rio de Janeiro hideout. Despite this setback, a meeting was soon arranged between Bardellino and the Nuvolettas in Zurich, but Aniello Nuvoletta was arrested at the rendezvous. Many other leading members of the Nuvoletta gang would also have been arrested had they not suffered a chance accident in northern Italy, near the Swiss border.[56] Soon after this, however, the wheel turned full circle with Bardellino's arrest in Spain; but he was inexplicably released on bail and predictably disappeared soon afterwards.

Given this sequence of events, it is not surprising that the two groups came to mistrust each other and subsequently started a gang war. A turning point in the battle was reached when Lorenzo Nuvoletta's younger brother Ciro was killed in his Marano 'bunker' in June 1984. Two months later events culminated with an attack at Torre Annunziata, which saw eight people killed and twenty-four wounded, Italy's worst ever gangland massacre.

The feud rumbled on for several years, with the Nuvolettas emerging as victors due to their immense financial strength and the fact that their leaders were all locally based, whereas Bardellino spent most of his time in South America.

The rise of the Nuvoletta gang is a good illustration of the combination of 'old' and 'new' elements of criminality that characterises the Camorra – the continuing importance of the use of violence combined with sophisticated financial manoeuvres. Yet the Nuvolettas were ultimately unable to resolve a central contradiction as outlined by a senior investigator: 'If they become respectable people there is the free market law of competition, which could see them end up as losers.'[57]

The story of the Nuvolettas also illustrates the common interest of *camorristi* and the most influential levels of 'legal' society. As a Bank of Naples clerk once told police investigators with extreme frankness and admirable accuracy: 'It certainly isn't the Bank of Naples which must take the fight to the Camorra; it must simply look after its own interests.'[58]

Although the Nuvolettas' operations were distinctive for their entrepreneurial specialisation, they could never have been successful without strong political connections. And the best overall example in the modern era of the links between politics and the Camorra is undoubtedly the kidnapping and release of Christian Democrat politician Ciro Cirillo in 1981.

Chapter 5

The Cirillo affair

> Whether 'tis nobler in the mind to suffer
> The slings and arrows of outrageous fortune.
> Or to take arms against a sea of troubles,
> And by opposing end them.
>
> — Shakespeare

On the evening of 27 April 1981 the Red Brigades kidnapped a senior Christian Democrat named Ciro Cirillo in a town just outside Naples; in order to abduct him they killed two body-guards and wounded his secretary. Almost three months later, on 25 July, Cirillo was released unharmed.

The kidnapping and eventual release of Cirillo saw the involvement of three major players: the Brigate Rosse (BR), the Christian Democrat party machine and the various secret service groups linked to it, and the Camorra – principally Raffaele Cutolo's NCO, then at the height of its powers. The Cirillo affair undoubtedly reveals the DC's duplicity and lack of morals, but it also clearly illustrates the power that the Camorra had now come to wield in Neapolitan society and politics.

Not only were the highest levels of the state machinery mobilised on behalf of the Christian Democrats – fully accepting negotiations and payments to both the Camorra and the Red Brigades during the kidnapping – the subsequent seven-year judicial investigation was frequently obstructed and vilified. When the verdict was finally announced in 1988, Christian Democrat Prime Minister Ciriaco De Mita described the investigating magistrate, Carlo Alemi, in the following terms: 'a Judge who acts outside procedures, and who abuses procedures as a vehicle for his own suspicion, places himself outside the institutional network',[1] and called for disciplinary measures to be taken against him. These were subsequently set in motion although no disciplinary steps were ever taken. Vincenzo Scotti, one of the Christian Democrat ministers mentioned in the final verdict, also attempted to sue Judge Alemi for libel but without success.

The main Naples newspaper, *Il Mattino*, faithfully echoed its Christian Democrat owners, with the editor Pasquale Nonno writing that Alemi was only looking for

> a negotiation between the Christian Democrats and the Red Brigades through the Camorra ... everything objectively takes on the aspect of support for communist propaganda, which has an entirely political proposition: the Christian Democrats' negotiation ... Public opinion is convinced that judges believe they are above the law.[2]

The general climate of institutional hostility surrounding the whole affair also emerged in an unusual fashion in 1986, when the first film directed by Giuseppe Tornatore (who later won an Oscar for his *Cinema Paradiso*), was withdrawn after just two months following threats by Cirillo to take out a lawsuit.[3]

WHY WAS CIRILLO KIDNAPPED?

The minor player in this affair is dealt with relatively easily. If the NCO was at the height of its powers in 1981, the Red Brigades' star was starting to wane. They had achieved their greatest success in 1978, with the kidnapping and subsequent murder of senior Christian Democrat politician Aldo Moro.

One of the weaknesses of the BR was that they were a largely northern grouping. Broadly speaking, they were an offshoot of the student movement which had erupted in Italy in 1968, followed by a wave of militant workers' struggles in the 'Hot Autumn' of 1969.

The founding leadership of the BR was made up of revolutionary students who had become frustrated with the meagre gains won by such a mass radical movement of students and workers. They sought to speed up events by 'carrying the attack to the heart of the state' through selective assassinations and kidnappings of leading politicians, trade unionists, journalists and company managers. This would in turn force a repressive reaction from the state which would, in theory, provoke a revolutionary counter-reaction by the masses.

Through such a strategy the Red Brigades effectively sought to substitute themselves for a mass revolutionary working class. But during the 1970s elements within the government's secret services began to view the BR as a useful tool. In recent years it has emerged that the BR were penetrated during the 1970s by secret service agents, who would sometimes 'pilot' the BR into certain actions that would be convenient for a given faction with the Christian Democrat party. It does not appear that the Cirillo kidnapping was a 'piloted' operation, although the secret services did play a significant role in the negotiations.

For the 'genuine' BR, the Cirillo kidnapping represented an opportunity to recruit members in the South's capital. Hundreds of thousands of people had been made homeless or were living in accommodation rendered unsafe by the earthquake. Many families had been placed in huge hotels along the coast, which were closed down for the winter, and were effectively isolated from their original place of work, as they were far away from the main lines of public transport.

Many of those living in the city were housed in either old or dangerous accommodation, and in the months following the earthquake there were almost daily demonstrations of people demanding to be rehoused. The 12,000 homeless before the earthquake had now risen to 150,000. Roads were often blocked by demonstrators, and sometimes buses were seized and burnt in order to make temporary barricades; indeed in one afternoon alone fifteen buses were seized and destroyed.

At the same time, however, there were thousands of empty flats within the city and its immediate outskirts, which were the 'second' or 'third' homes of the wealthy. In such an emergency, it clearly would have made sense to house homeless families temporarily in these flats. Many schools had been immediately occupied by 'earthquaked' families as they were often modern and low-level buildings. But this obviously created chaos as the number of available schools was drastically reduced, often requiring a three-shift system in the primary sector.

For the BR the existence of a Communist Party council in Naples was a highly significant factor. The council's refusal to requisition these second homes was concrete proof of the Communists' conservatism and accommodation with bourgeois society, one of the key arguments in the Red Brigades' political analysis.

The kidnapping of Cirillo, combined with the demand to requisition second homes, enabled the BR to present themselves as the defenders of the city's poor, in the hope of creating a stable base in one of Italy's major cities. But the choice of Cirillo was far from random, as the BR explained in the first communiqué they released after his capture:

> It is easy to explain who Ciro Cirillo is: this murderer represents the continuity of power of the Christian Democrat party regime in the Campania area. If yesterday, together with his friend and godfather [Antonio] Gava, he was the man of unbridled property speculation, he is today in the front line of imperialist restructuring in the urban area of Naples.
>
> His strong and numerous links with all the economic and political forces of regional government have given him the role of both guide and strategist of restructuring and reconstruction on a regional level.[4]

For many years Cirillo had been nominated by the Gavas' faction at Christian Democrat congresses as president of the electoral commission; he was effectively the party's main power broker in Naples and therefore the custodian of many secrets. Having been president of the regional council in the past, in 1981 he was president of the regional council committee for urban planning. His most important role in this period was that of vice-president of the regional committee for reconstruction, a position which in practice meant control of the committee. In other words, Cirillo was the politician who made the most important day-to-day decisions concerning the massive earthquake reconstruction programme.

It is also likely that Cirillo, like all powerful Neapolitan politicians, had had links with the Camorra before his kidnapping. For example, in one trial against the NCO, the prosecution produced a letter from Michele Gaglione to Andrea Quintosegno, both members of the New Family alliance, written almost a year before the kidnapping, in May 1980. Gaglione urged Quintosegno to become active in Cirillo's re-election campaign, 'because if he is re-elected there is a good chance that he will help me to get out on parole'.[5]

One of the dangers was that if Cirillo were to talk to the BR it would not only be the DC that would suffer. The general political destabilisation, and the possible revelation of DC links with the Camorra, would also have harmed both wings of the Camorra currently engaged in a massive gang war.

THE NEGOTIATIONS

It would appear that the BR's strategy during the Cirillo affair differed markedly from that of Aldo Moro's kidnapping three years earlier. In 1978 the primary BR objective had been to gain open political recognition through negotiations for the release of Moro, which would have involved the release of some jailed BR members. On this occasion it appears that their main objective was to gain a following in Naples by demanding urgent government measures to help the homeless and to stop widespread profiteering from the reconstruction.

The different nature of their demands compared with the Moro kidnapping eventually led the BR to decide to release Cirillo; however, perhaps more important than this was the DC's immediate willingness to negotiate for Cirillo's release. The existence of this channel of communication did not emerge publicly during the kidnapping itself, as it coincided with three other, more newsworthy, events: the attempted murder of the Pope, the publication of the membership list of the secret P2 Freemason lodge and the subsequent resignation of the government.

Negotiations only took place because the secret services requested them: they moved with astonishing rapidity – asking the National Prisons Office for permission to visit Cutolo the day after Cirillo's capture, and actually seeing Cutolo within just sixteen hours of the abduction.[6] The early meetings were attended by a delegation of two secret service agents, two senior NCO members and Giuliano Granata, Christian Democrat mayor of Giugliano. The action of the secret service was in no way opposed by government ministers; in fact, on the very same day that the secret services first met Cutolo, the Minister of the Interior Virginio Rognoni declared: 'the Camorra could have an interest in helping to free councillor Cirillo. Sometimes organised crime and terrorism are intertwined, other times they are separate. All possible channels must therefore be opened.'[7]

One of the main reasons the Camorra was willing to intervene in the kidnapping was that the massive police presence in urban areas – principally in the form of road blocks and searches of houses and buildings – got in the way of many of their activities, such as smuggling, extortion and the distribution of drugs. The drop in the number of murders gives a chilling indication of the Camorra's reduced room for manoeuvre during this period: both before and after Cirillo's kidnapping the number of gang-land deaths reached almost one a day – yet during his three months in captivity the number fell to just over one a month.

This is how one leading NCO member, Giovanni Pandico, recalled the period and Cutolo's response:

> This situation had practically paralysed all our activities: from murders to bank robberies, from theft to picking up money due from protection rackets; it also prevented the unloading of contraband cigarettes and drugs as the coast was under surveillance.
>
> Cutolo was immediately informed of the situation and decided to intervene, getting the word outside that he was prepared to get involved in the problem.[8]

The initial messenger between Cutolo and the BR was Luigi Bosso, an ordinary inmate who had declared himself a left-wing 'political' prisoner while serving a sentence for a series of common crimes. In another trial Bosso stated: 'Cutolo asked me to contact the Red Brigades members in Palmi prison and give them the following message: "The Christian Democrats are willing to negotiate at any level, using Cutolo as a middleman."'[9]

Giovanni Pandico, a leading NCO member held in the same jail as Cutolo, has stated that on 5 May he and Cutolo met Silvio Gava, secret service agents and NCO members Vincenzo Casillo and Corrado Iacolare. (Casillo was a notorious *camorrista*, widely considered to be the number two in the NCO chain of command, and although he was not on the run at that time, Iacolare was). At the end of the meeting it was agreed that Cutolo would use his influence within jails to persuade the BR to release Cirillo.[10] It is important to remember that in all these meetings there is no evidence whatsoever of any desire of the secret service or the DC to discover Cirillo's whereabouts. From the first day negotiations were based on Cutolo's NCO acting as go-between with a view to obtaining the safe release of Cirillo. Subtle details such as this show clearly the DC's toleration of illegality.

Several other meetings followed between the negotiators, some of them held at the high-security Ascoli Piceno jail where Cutolo was imprisoned – an incredible venue considering that notorious criminals who were wanted for serious crimes also took part in the meetings and were apparently given *carabinieri* uniforms and identity cards.[11] Not only was Silvio Gava probably a frequent visitor to Cutolo's jail, along with DC Senator Francesco Patriarca; according to many other witnesses interviewed during the investigation, DC ministers Antonio Gava and Vincenzo Scotti also attended meetings in the jail. Indeed, Cutolo recently claimed that Scotti arranged for the NCO to receive a consignment of machine guns as evidence of his willingness to negotiate.[12]

Although he has given different versions on different occasions, Francesco Pazienza, one of the key secret service agents involved in these meetings, has also stated that he met Vincenzo Casillo and that he negotiated directly on behalf of DC national secretary Flaminio Piccoli.[13]

In the short term, Cutolo wanted an end to the intense police activity; in the medium term he hoped to be transferred to a more relaxed prison environment; and in the long term he hoped to gain large numbers of important reconstruction contracts and perhaps one day be released on parole earlier than he might have expected prior to the kidnapping.

Meetings continued at a frenetic pace both inside and outside the jail. The deputy director of the secret services has admitted that one of his men had frequent meetings with Vincenzo Casillo during the kidnapping,[14] and added: 'The presence of Casillo was also essential, inasmuch as without an introduction which vouched for the visitors, Cutolo would have never accepted to give out information.'[15] He also specified that three official meetings, authorised by the Ministry of Justice, took place between Cutolo and the secret services in Ascoli Piceno jail.

Eventually an agreement was reached amongst the three parties: it was absolutely clear that a large sum of money would be paid to the BR, and there were many other details which to this day have never been clarified.

None of the BR's political demands were met (an end to the 'deportation' of the homeless from the city, the requisitioning of empty flats and the closure of a huge 'caravan city' rapidly erected to house hundreds of families), but in the end they accepted that a ransom was enough for them to release Cirillo. It appears that the BR kidnappers managing the operation were less 'principled' than those who had kidnapped Moro, in the sense that they were quite willing to use the Camorra as mediators, thus deflecting the crucial impact which any direct BR–DC communication would have had. Indeed the failure of the BR to achieve any of their political demands, and Cirillo's subsequent release, might suggest either a successful intervention by the secret services within the BR or sheer political ineptitude. However, a far more likely explanation is the potential for NCO gangsters to attack BR members inside jails, one of the factors that probably induced the secret service to contact Cutolo in the first place.

In any case, once an agreement was reached, a collection was held amongst the managers of large building companies who supported the Christian Democrats. A ransom of at least $1,200,000 was then paid to the BR, and the NCO also received a minimum of $720,000.[16] It is also likely that the same building companies subcontracted a large number of reconstruction projects to NCO-controlled companies.

Indeed, while the major building companies may have eventually subcontracted work to the NCO, these businessmen probably won many contracts from the DC as they had paid the ransom to get the DC's man out of the hands of the BR. One example of this was the $70 million contract for building 1,000 prefabricated houses in the Avellino area.[17] In a pattern typical of earthquake reconstruction contracts, the company which received the initial contract, Volani, based near Venice, then subcontracted it to another central Italian company based in Bologna, with the final subcontract involving a company linked to Cutolo's son Roberto.

In its fantasy world the BR apparently saw no contradiction in claiming to be a party of the working class while financing itself through donations from the highest levels of capitalism. In their last communiqué before Cirillo's release they wrote: 'the Red Brigades have expropriated from Cirillo the murderer, from his family of speculators, his party of bloodsuckers and his social class of exploiters the sum of $1,200,000.' And they continued, 'the Cirillo campaign, through the dialectic of revolutionary initiative and the struggles of the marginalised proletariat, has built and reinforced the linkage between the party and the masses.' The release of Cirillo had suddenly become irrelevant, 'purely a problem for the regime'.[18]

This last assessment was absolutely correct – the Cirillo kidnapping has continued to haunt the DC for more than a decade. The problems started as soon as he was released. Cirillo was freed after nearly three months of imprisonment, early on the morning of 24 July, and found by a traffic police patrol car. The traffic police telephoned their superiors who told them to take him to police headquarters for the customary debriefing. Two hundred yards down the road, however, their car was surrounded and stopped by four state police cars and Cirillo was 'kidnapped' a second time. This second group of officers was led by Biagio Ciliberti, a face Cirillo recognised as '[he was] the son of Bettino, an old party comrade'.[19]

He was bundled out of the patrol car and taken to his home, where his doctors refused access to investigating magistrates for three days, saying he was 'unable to make any statement' because of the 'trauma' he had suffered. The primary motive of investigators at this point was not to unearth the truth surrounding the negotiations, but to locate the terrorists while the trail was still hot.

Despite Cirillo's alleged nervous exhaustion he immediately received visits from leading Christian Democrat politicians, such as Antonio Gava and the party's national secretary Flaminio Piccoli. During subsequent questioning Piccoli has admitted that the day after Cirillo's release 'we were left on our own to chat and Cirillo outlined his beliefs on the current situation of terrorism in Italy, which he had deduced from the ideas he heard Senzani and others outline during the period of his imprisonment.'[20] In other words, Cirillo was lucid enough to talk to leading Christian Democrats for two days, during which it is presumed they established a common version of events, before he agreed to be questioned by investigating magistrates.

THE COVER-UP

During the kidnapping, and immediately afterwards, there were rumours about negotiations. It has to be said that the rumours were caused by an obvious puzzle – the Red Brigades would have never released Cirillo without having obtained something in return, and for this to have happened some form of negotiation must have taken place. Less than three weeks after Cirillo's release even magazines sympathetic to the DC were writing: 'It was the Camorra that saved Cirillo – Don Raffaele Cutolo, boss of the Neapolitan underworld, was the intermediary with the terrorists, who received $2.4 million.'[21]

A cover-up would clearly be necessary, and the first 'deviation' from the truth concerned a leaked document published in the PCI daily *L'Unità* the following year, which named the leading Christian Democrats who had gone to see Cutolo in jail. A few days later it emerged that the document was a forgery organised by Cutolo; it was apparently designed to remind the politicians who had negotiated that they ran the risk of exposure if they did not keep their part of the bargain.

More important than this isolated example is a long series of facts, events and statements that, taken as a whole, can only lead to the conclusion that there has been a cover-up. For example, many of the pages covering the time of the Cirillo kidnapping have been ripped out of the visitors' book at the high-security prison where Cutolo was held; on others the names of visitors have been cancelled out. Tape recordings of Cutolo's telephone calls during this period were inexplicably erased on order of the appropriate ministry; similarly, Cutolo's normally copious correspondence appears to have trickled down to virtually nothing during these three months. Furthermore, the recordings of telephone conversations between the Red Brigades and the person due to bring them the ransom were tampered with in an attempt to present a completely different version of events, and the tapes of Cirillo's revelations to the BR while imprisoned have never been found.

Even more disturbing is the number of 'illustrious corpses' linked to the kidnapping – the two main victims being Antonio Ammaturo in 1982 and Vincenzo Casillo in 1983.

Ammaturo, the head of the Naples Flying Squad, was murdered on 15 July 1982. Although the official version of events places sole responsibility on the BR, the car used in the attack was provided by two *camorristi* with whom the BR were in contact.[22] Furthermore, one of the terrorists wounded in the attack was hidden and nursed back to health in the house of a known *camorrista*.[23]

Ammaturo's position obviously made him an enemy of both the Red Brigades and the NCO, but the fact that he appears to have been investigating the Cirillo kidnapping inevitably leads one to suspect that the same 'unholy trinity' of terrorists, *camorristi* and politicians conspired to silence him. His brother Grazio recalls that just a few days before his death Antonio told him, 'I've finished, it's really big – all of Naples will tremble; I've sent everything to the Ministry',[24] but no trace has ever been found of his report. His sister has testified that the last time she saw him, two weeks before his murder, he told her that he had been working on the Cirillo case: 'If they don't rub me out first, many important heads will roll.'[25] Ten days before his death, he told one of his police team that he was finishing a report on the Cirillo affair.[26]

The murder of Vincenzo Casillo, Cutolo's main negotiator during the kidnapping, is even more important, as it represents a turning point in the relationship between the Camorra and local politicians. Although there are some rumours that Cutolo had Casillo killed because he had stolen Cutolo's part of the Cirillo ransom, Cutolo has stated that he was worried by the untrustworthiness of politicians, and he claims to have warned Casillo after the kidnapping:

> It was me who told Casillo to keep documentary evidence of the meetings he had with these people, whom I didn't trust because all they do is *sell hope by the ton to poor people*, and then, when things don't work out as they expected or when they've got what they wanted, *they cast you adrift*.[27]

The whole question of the murder is further complicated by the fact that a secret service card that could be used by Casillo was found in his burnt-out car.

But Ammaturo's and Casillo's are far from being the only deaths linked to the Cirillo kidnapping. Casillo's partner disappeared a few weeks after his death, and her body was eventually found in a ditch under a motorway in December 1983, while Ammaturo's brother Grazio died in an unusual hunting accident in the same year. Another clearly related murder was that of criminologist Aldo Semerari, often employed to give psychological profiles of Cutolo and other Camorra leaders, who was decapitated in 1982.

Nicola Nuzzo, a key NCO member involved in the

negotiations, was battered to death in the ward of a Roman hospital in 1986, soon after a meeting with investigating magistrate Carlo Alemi. Salvatore Imperatrice, Casillo's bodyguard and also a member of the NCO negotiating team, died mysteriously in jail in March 1989. Mario Cuomo, who lost his legs in the explosion that killed Casillo, was eventually murdered in October 1990. A secret service agent, Adalberto Titta, who had several meetings with Cutolo in prison, died of a sudden heart attack, as did Luigi Bosso at the age of 42. Not only was such a series of deaths highly suspicious, it was clearly harming Cutolo's NCO, and the involvement of a rival gang seemed likely.

A possible link between some of these deaths was explained to Judge Alemi in 1987 by Enrico Madonna, who was Cutolo's preferred lawyer during the Cirillo kidnapping and probably took part in several meetings: 'amongst the bearers of [the politicians'] promises there were Casillo, Iacolare, Giuliano Granata, Nicola Nuzzo, Semerari'.[28] Madonna was himself murdered in October 1993, three days after telling a journalist he was willing to tell a parliamentary commission all he knew about the Cirillo affair.

Indeed, the ramifications of the affair may reach as far as London. Vincenzo Casillo once told Madonna that he had murdered the bankrupt financier, Roberto Calvi, who was found hanged under Blackfriars Bridge in 1982.[29] It appears that in an attempt to avoid imprisonment and further criminal charges Calvi had intervened in the kidnapping to help the DC, contacting the Camorra and paying some of the ransom money. However, as his legal situation did not improve afterwards, he was apparently threatening to reveal the political connections behind his corrupt financial operations, and the order was therefore given to eliminate him.

In view of all these events it is not at all surprising that a judicial investigation was set up to establish what really happened during the kidnapping, and it is hard not to agree with its conclusion:

> in judgement it seems clear that the evidence unequivocally points to an attitude on the part of leading Christian Democrats that was markedly different from the party's 'official line', namely to react with firmness to all Red Brigades blackmail and to reject all hypotheses of a negotiation or a

compromise. In reality there were members of the party who did not follow this official line but were active in various ways to obtain Cirillo's release, turning above all to the mediation of Raffaele Cutolo and accepting negotiations with the Red Brigades.[30]

In other words, the truth established in law was that a group of leading Christian Democrats negotiated with the Red Brigades through Raffaele Cutolo. Although no individual politician was named, it was clear who Judge Alemi was referring to.

But instead of being 'grounded' by the party hierarchy, the politicians involved in freeing Cirillo were subsequently promoted. Antonio Gava became a minister for the first time in 1983, which was followed by the even more incredible decision to make him Minister of the Interior in 1988. Vincenzo Scotti also went on to hold a succession of important ministries throughout the 1980s, and was Minister of the Interior between 1990 and 1992. Biagio Ciliberti, the man who led Cirillo's 'second kidnapping', was promoted to a senior role within the Ministry of the Interior soon after Gava's appointment and became Italy's youngest ever police chief when he was put in charge of the city of Trieste.

The whole issue came up once again in July 1993 when the Court of Appeal turned down the demand for a reopening of the investigation, regardless of the fact that important protagonists in the kidnapping had decided to give new testimony and had been legally judged to be credible witnesses. While investigating magistrates in the North had brought down virtually all major politicians in the *Tangentopoli* investigations of 1992–3, it seems that the wind of change had not yet made such a strong impact in Naples. Judge Carlo Alemi, leader of the investigation during the 1980s, resigned himself to the court's decision: 'It doesn't surprise me, I didn't expect anything else, I had predicted it for a whole series of reasons. Maybe it called for too much courage.'[31]

The case has recently been reopened, however, and the new Federal Prosecutor of Naples, Agostino Cordova, is optimistic about the possibilities, while at the same time revealing his own view of the affair:

We will soon discover the whole truth about the Cirillo

affair. We will reassemble tile by tile the mosaic of negotiations between Christian Democrats, the Camorra and the
secret service. We will also be able to find out who ordered
the political murders connected to that affair and why.[32]

Cordova's optimism is probably based on the revelations of
Camorra supergrass Pasquale Galasso, which have shed light on the
reticence of the legal system to get to the bottom of the affair.[33] The
Christian Democrat Senator and lawyer Alfredo Bargi, who
defended both Cirillo and his party in various trials linked to the
affair, apparently became a senator thanks to a $32,000 contribution
by Galasso's gang to his April 1992 election campaign.[34] Galasso
also bought him a new office, obviously with the intention of
gaining preferential treatment within the legal system. One lowly
lawyer, however, would obviously not be enough to guarantee
preferential treatment, and Galasso has stated that he bought an
office for Judge Armando Cono Lancuba, too, and that he let them
both have free holidays in a hotel he owned.[35] The involvement of
Judge Cono Lancuba is of particular interest here: he was the public
prosecutor in the preliminary proceedings of the main Cirillo trial.
With hindsight it is easy to understand why press accounts of the
trial described his attitude towards those who denied or diminished
their role in negotiations as that of a goalkeeper rather than a centre
forward – in other words, he did not attack them at all.

Whatever we may think of their methods, it is difficult not to
share the analysis of a member of the Red Brigades involved in
the kidnapping:

All these elements led us to the historical and political conclusion that all high levels of organised crime and the *Nuova
Camorra Organizzata* were nothing but the other side of the
coin of the state, in other words the worst and most reaction-
ary elements within the state.[36]

THE LONG-TERM CONSEQUENCES OF THE NEGOTIATIONS

The Cirillo affair reveals the symbiosis that had developed
between the Christian Democrat party machine and the top
level of organised crime.[37]

The precise nature and consequences of this joint venture

began to emerge in greater detail in 1993 as a result of Pasquale Galasso's revelations. Galasso claims that he killed Casillo to free Gava and other Christian Democrats 'from Cutolo's threats'. In a meeting held nine months after the kidnapping, in April 1982, Vincenzo Casillo reportedly told Giuliano Granata, the DC mayor who had taken part with him in the negotiations: 'you did what you wanted and then washed your hands'.[38] This is Galasso's view of the post-kidnapping tension between the two parties involved in the negotiations:

> the Gavas were feeling the pressure of Raffaele Cutolo's demands, as he expected the agreement to be kept . . . and he threatened to unleash a scandal that would have involved the institutional apparatus that had conspired with him for the liberation of Cirillo. So, as the Gavas were feeling threatened by Cutolo, they turned to, and formed an alliance with, the only person who at that moment could fight Cutolo. That person was Carmine Alfieri.[39]

It appears that the advantages Cutolo hoped to gain from his involvement in freeing Cirillo did not materialise. But if that was the case, Cutolo was unlikely to meekly accept the politicians' lack of faith, and he continually threatened to release information showing the direct involvement of DC politicians in negotiations.

If this interpretation of events is correct, the defeat of a powerful organisation such as Cutolo's NCO necessitated the successful coordination of an intricate strategy. To obtain Cutolo's defeat it seems that the DC machine simply turned and provided support and protection to another gang, that led by Carmine Alfieri in Nola.

It was also in Alfieri's interest to destroy Cutolo. It was widely believed that Cutolo had negotiated with leading politicians, and if he had received the advantages he hoped for, then he would not have hesitated to annihilate any rival gang. As Galasso has stated:

> When Cirillo was freed we were well aware that his release was due to Cutolo's intervention, and we were afraid that he had reinforced his association with Gava and Scotti . . . The murder of Salvatore Alfieri was a signal that Cutolo would never look back, as he felt that he had his back covered by the

politicians and the secret service that had been involved in the Cirillo affair.[40]

It was decided to kill Casillo, Cutolo's right-hand man, with a car bomb, one of the first times that the Camorra had used this kind of technique – in logistic terms this is a method that requires far more resources and planning than one man with a pistol. According to Galasso, the reasons for this decision were

> first of all, to make it clear to Cutolo that he was finished, and that once and for all he had to stop blackmailing the politicians and the institutions he had dealt with during the Cirillo affair. It is also beyond doubt that through that action Alfieri wanted to demonstrate to the politicians – mainly the Dorotea faction and perhaps to Antonio Gava in particular – that he had to be reckoned with ... The car bomb was therefore intended to demonstrate Alfieri's real importance.[41]

All the available evidence points unequivocally to negotiations taking place between Cutolo and Christian Democrat politicians during the Cirillo kidnapping. A year or two after the kidnapping, however, Cutolo's empire had collapsed: he was transferred from the mainland to a high-security prison off the coast of Sardinia in April 1982, and many of his leading men were either murdered in the gang war of the early 1980s or arrested in the series of 'maxi-blitzes' of 1983–4.

The Cirillo kidnapping and its consequences therefore mark a turning point in the relationship between powerful criminals and corrupt politicians – they were now coming together as a single group that often pursued a common purpose. Just as the DC felt that the best way to respond to the crisis unleashed by Cirillo's kidnapping was to turn to Cutolo for help and thereby legitimise him, it later felt unable to deal with Cutolo's threats without turning to the Alfieri–Galasso gang.

As the Anti-Mafia Commission has written:

> from that moment [Casillo's death in January 1983] until today Alfieri and his men were to stain Campania with blood and obtain large slices of the reconstruction cake; for a long time they would also constitute an uncontested effective government in large areas of the region.[42]

Alfieri and Galasso were also aware that a turning point had been reached with the murder of Casillo; as Galasso states: 'As far as I can recall that was the only time we talked about a crime in euphoric terms. Alfieri embraced [here a name has been censored in the original document] and congratulated him for the courage he had shown; I know that he later gave him a Rolex.'[43]

Not only Cutolo, but many other Camorra gangs understood the shift in the balance of power that Casillo's death represented; they subsequently abandoned Cutolo and aligned themselves with Alfieri.

What the Cirillo affair demonstrates is that for leading Christian Democrats in Campania the problem was never one of trying to eradicate organised crime but deciding what arrangements to make with it. In turn, major Camorra gangs have been part of the local political and economic elite, not something outside it.

Chapter 6

How the Camorra works

With adequate profit, capital is very bold. A certain 10 per cent will ensure its employment anywhere; 20 per cent will produce eagerness; 50 per cent positive audacity; 100 per cent will make it ready to trample on all human laws; 300 per cent, and there is not a crime at which it will scruple.

— Karl Marx

Although most of the activities detailed in this chapter are clearly illegal, two factors should be borne in mind: the line between legality and illegality is often very nebulous, and there are many other activities involving the Camorra that are generally run along legal lines.

TERRITORIAL CONTROL

Direct physical control over a given area, as exerted by the Mafia, is of vital importance for the growth of Camorra gangs. Once this control is won, criminal gangs can not only extend their protection rackets, illegal gambling, usury, cigarette and drug trading; they can begin to become power brokers, mediating between ordinary people and ruling politicians. Acting as brokers not only increases their general social legitimacy, it also makes them more important in the eyes of corrupt politicians worried about getting elected.

Just as the Mafia evolved over time from guarding rural estates through managing tenant farms to property speculation and public sector contracts in the postwar period, so the Camorra's role and its use of violence, too, have changed. During the last century Camorra violence involved direct acts of intimidation and robbery, without the Camorra playing any sophisticated economic role.

But with the growth of the contraband trade in the post-war period, the role of the Camorra began to change. While many *guappi* had traditionally controlled fairly large and significant sectors, such as fruit, vegetable and meat markets, the growth of the contraband industry required not only a more dynamic attitude and greater financial investment, but also defence against increased police activity. The addition of drugs to contraband cigarettes obviously involved even greater financial investment, higher risks in terms of prison sentences and more competition from rival gangs. Territorial control has thus become increasingly important to the Camorra in the postwar decades.

It is important to understand the *dynamism* of this process. The growth of the contraband industry meant that the Camorra was no longer simply reacting to what was around it, it was making large investments that needed to be defended. Camorra gangs were therefore beginning to consciously transform the conditions surrounding them rather than simply reacting to them. Easier communication, improvements in transportation as well as the competition between rival gangs all led to greater territorial control. The massive increase in profits brought about first by contraband cigarettes and then by the drug trade explains the higher level of violence: just as nation states militarily defend their wealth and privilege against both external and internal threats, so Camorra gangs defend their activities through increased militarisation.

The greater frequency of violence between rival Camorra gangs in comparison with the Mafia is explained by the relative lack of mediation between gangs, at least at the lower and medium level of Camorra activity: the Camorra has never had the equivalent of the Mafia's hierarchical *cupola* or 'commission'.

It is not only the level of violence that indicates Camorra control over a given territory; the selling of contraband cigarettes, for example, requires the regular, visible presence of considerable numbers of people. In this respect certain aspects of the Camorra have always been different from the Mafia – the difference in environment between rural Sicily and urban Campania, and the different activities taken on, have always made the Camorra far more visible than its Sicilian counterpart.

However, one important similarity is that organised crime in both regions has come to take the shape of an alternative form of power, described by many as an 'anti-state'. The Camorra is actually much more of a 'parallel state' than an organisation committed to destroying or taking over governmental power. But once systematic criminal influence within the political structure, with its consequent protection from legal sanctions and harassment, becomes generally accepted, territorial control can take on a literal meaning: Camorra control becomes a widely known fact, conditioning both the local population and the political structure. When this position of power is reached, all manner of criminal activities can flourish, privately sanctioned by local political leaders.

No less a figure than the Federal Prosecutor of Naples, Agostino Cordova, has recently outlined the fundamental importance of territorial control:

> Recent investigations have allowed us to ascertain that it is through complete control over an area, and in particular control of elections and financial activities, that the leaders of the Camorra – Carmine Alfieri in the Province of Naples, Gennaro Licciardi in the city and Francesco Schiavone in the area of Caserta – have been able to dominate the politicians and businessmen with whom they had dealings.[1]

Even though physical control of an area through intimidation may be more important than the possibility of total political control, it would be a mistake to view the Camorra as a purely criminal organisation. The Camorra's governing drive remains economic and not political or social: physical control over a given territory and domination of local politicians, i.e. the exercise of power, are means towards the end of capital accumulation and enrichment.

In recent years some Camorra gangs seem to have undergone a further mutation: from total physical control of a given territory there appears to be a tendency towards concentration on particular activities such as cocaine distribution, illegal gambling, the selling of cigarettes, and so on. Another development is the growing number of organisations dealing primarily with public sector contracts, in contrast to other gangs whose primary activities remain clearly within the 'illegal' economy.[2]

DEFINING CAMORRA MEMBERSHIP

It may be more accurate to describe activities such as racketeering, illegal gambling and the street selling of drugs and cigarettes as *Camorra-controlled* rather than as activities directly engaged in by leading members of major gangs. Drug dealing, for example, is sometimes carried out by addicts themselves, who because of their erratic lifestyle are not considered reliable enough to join a gang, or more often by juveniles who are too young to be prosecuted.

However, once young people's delinquency brings them into direct contact with a gang, as with selling drugs, we are normally dealing with activities that involve the threat or use of violence.

For most ordinary people, the fear of violence is far more threatening than any specific criminal activity, and politicians tend to devote much of their time and ultimately public and police resources to this low-level crime, thus leaving higher Camorra levels untouched. Indeed it is arguably the 'foot-soldiers' who are the 'fall guys' for the real *camorristi*.

The thousands of young people who sell contraband cigarettes and small amounts of drugs, extort money through protection rackets and organise illegal gambling rings are individuals with no direct influence on a gang's policy; they simply have to accept their boss's word and decisions as law. These people are likely to die very young or spend long periods in jail, as they lack the money to either hire good lawyers or make friends within the judiciary, which would enable them to secure acquittals or suspended sentences. They are also useful cannon fodder for politicians who need to silence any criticisms that they are 'soft on crime'.

Some youngsters do make the leap into a criminal gang, and at this point their personal situation can change at an astonishing speed. As one observer has written of the Mafia:

> there is a kind of 'criminal career' which often begins with theft or hold-ups carried out individually or by small gangs, which then leads boys of 16 or 17 into contact with the Mafia and eventual membership. These are extremely upwardly mobile careers which sometimes end in death as a result of the frequent shootings that punctuate life in our country.[3]

Young men under the age of 18 are particularly encouraged by Camorra gangs to take part in armed robberies or murders as they cannot be tried as adults. In the 1984–5 period alone the Naples Juvenile Court dealt with fifty cases of alleged murder.[4] The number of under-age boys and girls charged with crimes doubled during the 1980s and increased by 28 per cent between 1990 and 1992 alone, with the largest increase, 93 per cent, relating to under-14-year-olds, who cannot even appear in court. Although Campania only contains 10 per cent of the national population, the number of under-age Campanians held in detention centres and awaiting trial in 1992 (see Table 6) clearly illustrates the Camorra's ability to recruit young people and so to reproduce itself extremely effectively.

Table 6: Number of inmates in Campania's youth detention centres as a percentage of detention centre inmates nationwide[5]

Charge	Percentage of national total
Murder	8.0
Attempted murder	22.6
Attempted robbery	10.6
Robbery	8.9
Violent robbery	36.5
Extortion	21.3
Drug-related crimes	23.8

Whereas thirty years ago a 'criminal career' leading to the top of a major gang might have taken decades to complete, with the huge financial profits nowadays available mainly through drug trafficking, a young man can be a major gang leader and billionaire before he is thirty.[6]

This tendency towards rapid growth, as well as its lack of a clear hierarchy and division of interests, distinguishes the Camorra from the Mafia, as it has never managed to create a stable federal structure. This makes the Camorra more difficult to eradicate through crude repression: while the Mafia is like an octopus (a single head with powerful tentacles), the Camorra is more akin to the Hydra, the monster of Greek legend which sprouted two heads for every one that was cut off. Indeed, a rapid rise to immense wealth in just a few short years is an irresistible temptation for young people who otherwise face a lifetime of unemployment or at best underemployment. This prospect guarantees the social reproduction of criminal gangs regardless of new laws or investigative techniques.

It is important to stress again the distinction between working under Camorra control and membership of an organised gang, as it has been repeatedly shown that repression of criminal-controlled activities such as the sale of contraband cigarettes does nothing to stop the socio-economic conditions that force so many people to work illegally. The only effective strategy is to target the criminal bosses at the top, but even this would be pointless unless it is combined with a total change in the conditions that enable powerful criminals to provide employment and to gain some form of respect and social acceptance.

A young man generally becomes a member of a Camorra gang without any kind of ceremony; Cutolo's NCO appears to be an exception – an unrepresentative throwback to the rituals of the last century. However, one common feature of all Camorra groups is the fact that family links, while important, are not always essential. This is a fundamental difference from the family-based Mafia structure.

The people who eventually become gang leaders tend to be members of a family notorious for its criminal behaviour and/or those who are clearly willing to engage in acts of violence. As Pasquale Galasso has explained:

> Every Camorra group has a leader, around whom there are a number of trusted members who have distinguished themselves during gang wars and in difficult times either through their ferocity, their managerial skills or their ability to communicate with the non-criminal world and other social classes. These figures emerge and surround the leader, who is at the centre of this leadership group. This group then decides everything.[7]

And in Alfieri's gang at least, these decisions also included murders, as Galasso again explains:

> The choice is made over whom to kill and you wait for the right moment, in the sense that the victims might be in jail, not live locally or be well protected; when all the signs are good the boss and the leadership group decide how to carry it out and the killers are chosen and organised.[8]

In Alfieri's gang the killers were normally part of the leadership

group itself, whereas in many other gangs this is not the case –
although it is common practice to use drug addicts as assassins,
who are themselves killed afterwards.

INTIMIDATION AND EXTORTION

This is the oldest form of Camorra activity which is still
important today. Often the first rung on the ladder of a criminal
career, it is also one of the most 'invisible' activities since it is
one of the least reported crimes.

Compared with other activities such as usury, drug dealing
and public sector contracts, it is labour intensive, risky and
brings in relatively meagre profits. Intimidation and extortion
are generally *Camorra-controlled* activities, in that a gang's control
of a given territory gives it the right to expect a cut from any
protection racket taking place.

In 1992 the shopowners' association ASCOM estimated that
46 per cent of shops pay protection money in Naples, compared
with a national average of 12 per cent.[9] The arrangements
between shopowners and criminals may not always involve cash
payments – shopowners may be required to assist with money
laundering by cashing cheques or, as is often the case with usury,
they may find their businesses slowly bought up. Alternatively,
their premises may become a drug distribution centre like an
electrical goods shop in Secondigliano, for example, where a
day's supply of heroin for the area, 120 doses, was stored in, and
collected from, a microwave oven on display.[10]

The relationship may not be solely based on the threat of
violence. The establishment of public links with shopowners, a
generally respected group in society, is also a means of gaining
public recognition. Further legitimacy can then be obtained by
demanding largely symbolic contributions for family members
in jail, or even the placing of special street lights during traditional festivals. One example of this was the series of identical
stars placed above dozens of shop fronts in the main street of
Secondigliano before Christmas 1991. Each one cost the owner
between $100 and $150, but perhaps the main importance was
the demonstration of being under the control of Gennaro
Licciardi's gang.[11]

There is another, equally important reason for developing a
relationship with shopowners – they are economic agents who

regularly order a whole range of goods and services. Not only can gangs then think about providing these goods and services in exchange for reducing the protection payment, they can also make offers to buy into the business.

The money extracted is in the region of several billions of dollars a year, and several thousand people are involved. Perhaps the chief importance of this activity is the legitimacy that gangs gain from what can often be small payments: the very fact that prominent members of the community feel obliged to pay extortion money is a clear sign that organised crime has come to dominate a particular area.

ILLEGAL GAMBLING

Illegal gambling, like extortion, is another activity that has been carried out in an organised form in Naples since at least the start of the last century. It takes two forms: placing bets in an illegal system and illegal gaming houses.

The latter have always existed in many urban areas of Campania, and in Naples small printing shops were particularly favoured as premises for many years, although now all manner of places are used.

An illegal betting system, in contrast, requires quite a high level of organisation, and the extent of this activity should not be underestimated. For example, in Naples in October 1982 police discovered an illegal bookmaker's office containing 500,000 receipts, and in 1986 another office was found with receipts worth $8 million.[12] In 1989 it was estimated that the annual turnover throughout Italy for illegal betting reached the incredible figure of $4.4 billion, with clear profits of around $16 million.[13] In 1991 the finance police estimated the annual turnover to be $3.2–$4 billion, or over $80 million a week.[14] (These national figures include systems run under Camorra control in Florence, Milan, Rome and Sicily.)

In Naples itself it is estimated that more people bet illegally than in the state-run lotteries, as payouts are almost immediate and winnings are not taxed. Like the trade in contraband cigarettes, it is commonly seen as harmless and as providing both jobs – up to 5,000 people are employed, mainly women – and winnings. For the Camorra it generates not only profits, it is also a means of laundering drug money when payouts are made.

Furthermore, the prompt and full payment of large prizes massively increases a local gang's popularity and prestige. In Naples, the main area of illegal gambling in Campania, it is currently estimated that the turnover per week reaches several million dollars.[15]

One example that illustrates the potential scope of this activity allegedly took place in the late 1980s. In 1987 the Naples football team led by Diego Maradona, arguably the world's best player at that time, won the Italian league title for the first time in the club's history. The celebrations went on for days, yet many Neapolitans also had something else to celebrate – their winnings on the illegal betting racket run by the Camorra, in which they had bet on Naples winning the championship.

The following season, Naples played just as well until, with only a few games to go to the end of the season, their form suffered an inexplicable collapse. The rumour that circulated then, and which has recently resurfaced in specific allegations concerning Maradona and other players, was that players accepted bribes from the Camorra to lose matches: paying large sums of money to players would have cost the Camorra less than paying out winnings to half the city.[16]

USURY

The widespread practice of usury (specifically, private money-lending) is closely linked to the historical development of employment in Naples and the major towns of Campania. Because so many people have no permanent full-time job, they normally have no access to credit, so in cases of emergency they have turned to private moneylenders.

Usury increased widely in Italy during the economic recession of the early 1990s. Compared with other European countries, Italy had been relatively untouched by the recession of the early 1980s, and so the impact of the new economic world order caught many people unprepared. Small businesses desperate for a loan because banks are unwilling to grant credit are the main users of this system, although it also provides finance for many individuals who find themselves unemployed for the first time.

Shopowners need to pay for supplies, rent or taxes, while the unemployed face all manner of direct needs. The Association of Italian Bank and Finance Customers (ADUSBEF) estimates that usury has a national turnover of $10 billion.[17] And the main shopkeepers' association, CONFESERCENTI, estimates that one in five shops, bars and restaurants is caught in a private debt trap.

Because of their dire economic position, many individuals and small businesses may not be able to keep up repayments, often fixed at around 10 per cent per month; their debt quickly escalates as interest rates spiral to 30 or 40 per cent per month, and debt collection then falls into the hands of organised crime, if it was not already under their control. If repayment is impossible, the Camorra has various 'solutions' available: it may take control of the enterprise concerned, demand that the debtor carry out some illegal action such as transporting drugs or simply force the debtor to provide employment to certain individuals.

It is particularly difficult to prove the existence of this crime, and if so-called 'financial consultants' fail to provide tax inspectors with documentary evidence of the source of their earnings, the fines for not abiding by the regulations are very minor.

The whole system provides an excellent opportunity for money laundering as well as for investment in legal enterprises.

PUBLIC SECTOR CONTRACTS

As the scandal of earthquake reconstruction shows, public sector contracts are of vital importance to the Camorra. In fact, one can say without fear of contradiction that the Camorra has only achieved its present position of strength thanks to the help it has received from politicians in gaining contracts.

The relationship can be so close that criminals and politicians appear indistinguishable, as was the case with Carmine Alfieri's economic empire:

> In many cases business relations with public administration appear to have taken on the character of an authentic symbiosis. Indeed, this was demonstrated by the fact that the continual awarding of contracts, subcontracts and authorisations to the business segments of the criminal organisation had its accompanying counterpoint in violent and intimidatory actions aimed at eliminating even marginal competition.[18]

And, as a leading member of the Alfieri gang, Pasquale Galasso, has outlined:

the relationship between politicians and bureaucrats, business-men and then *camorristi* is ultimately realised and achieves total fusion in the mechanism of public sector contracts. On the basis of all that I have noticed personally in my legitimate business activities and my work with Carmine Alfieri and other *camorristi* and businessmen, it has been clear to me that the politician who manages the financing of a contract, and therefore the awarding of a contract, is a mediator between the Camorra and a large company, which is nearly always from northern or central Italy. Such mediation takes the form of demanding a bribe from the company for himself or his representatives, and the awarding of subcontracts to companies directly controlled by Camorra groups.[19]

Yet the relationship between a 'clean' firm and the Camorra does not remain a distant one for long:

even if it did not exist at the start, what happens is that all the firms holding contracts slowly become subject to Camorra influence and end up being entirely at the disposal of the leadership of a criminal gang. This occurs in various ways: from outright intimidation to joint financial and econ-omic operations. At the end of this process of a Camorra group's total control over a single firm, you will notice that the individual businessman is always available for the Camorra; this obviously includes [the Camorra's] general business capacity and its whole public relations structure.[20]

And there are simply so many contracts to be awarded. One fairly representative example, which illustrates the amount of money involved and the environment in which contracts are awarded, dates from September 1990, when rubbish collection contracts for Naples city estimated at $280 million were awarded to five private companies. When the new companies took over, their workers were repeatedly intimidated through warning shots and physical attacks. They eventually went out with a police escort of over a hundred – many rubbish bins had also been deliberately destroyed. It was presumed that rival gangs whose tenders had failed were demanding a 'piece of the action'.[21] Just over a year later further threats made by armed men wearing balaclavas necessitated further police escorts –

Naples must be the only city in the world where rubbish has a police escort.[22]

Although the awarding of public sector contracts has been a national scandal for many years, 55 per cent of public sector contracts in the 1985–90 period were still awarded on the basis of private tendering and bidding, 25 per cent even as a result of private negotiations; a mere 15 per cent were awarded as a result of competitive public tendering.[23] Not surprisingly, an investigation of local authorities by the National Audit Office in 1990 found that in 67 per cent of cases the rules governing contract tendering had been violated, affecting contracts worth $3.2 billion.[24]

Although new laws have since been introduced, they can be by-passed in various ways: costs can be inflated over the term of the contract due to the 'discovery of unforeseen problems'; after a contract has been awarded, many tasks may be subcontracted for 'technical reasons' to other companies purported to be the only ones competent in those particular fields.

Another technique is the creation of a cartel of interested companies (often linked to the same Camorra group) in order to inflate the average price of tenders. A good example of this was revealed by investigations carried out by the finance police in late 1991 into contracts for rubbish removal and disposal awarded by 104 councils in the Province of Caserta. In depressingly familiar tones the Anti-Mafia Commission commented:

> In the councils disbanded for Mafia infiltration in line with the anti-Mafia laws, it has been noted that the presence of Camorra companies was a general phenomenon. Firms with all kinds of names submitted tenders, but in effect it was always the same Camorra group through its local networks and company managers. Tenders were submitted at levels two or three times higher than the market average, and there was no space for competitors.[25]

THE TRADE IN CIGARETTES AND DRUGS

Contraband cigarettes normally cost 40 per cent less than the official government price in the state monopoly sector. In Naples legal sales of cigarettes have fallen every year since 1985, with a 27 per cent drop recorded in 1993 alone – although this may have been partly due to a state tobacconists' strike early in the year.[26]

The contraband market was restructured in the mid-1980s, when prices were lowered primarily with the aim of creating more jobs, although the chain of distribution was also modified. Instead of fast motorboats racing through the Bay of Naples, articulated lorries now picked up deliveries along the coast of Puglia and drove overland in convoy.

Profits are probably in the region of several billion dollars a year, although the market's importance for the Camorra lies not solely in the profits generated but in the number of people who directly earn their living through this trade, estimated to be at least 30,000. Of all the activities described in this chapter, the sale of contraband cigarettes creates the greatest popular support for Camorra organisations, even though the actual street selling is again a Camorra-controlled activity rather than something in which gang members take a direct part.

As the major Camorra cigarette smuggler of the 1970s and 1980s, Michele Zaza once said (in terms that go some way towards explaining his nickname of 'Mad Mike'):

> At least 700,000 people live off contraband, which is for Naples what Fiat is to Turin. They have called me the Agnelli of Naples ... Yes – it could all be eliminated in thirty minutes. And then those who work would be finished. They'd all become thieves, robbers, muggers. Naples would become the worst city in the world. Instead, this city should thank the twenty, thirty men who arrange for ships laden with cigarettes to be discharged and thus stop crime![27]

Indeed, Zaza has consistently denied that trading in contraband cigarettes is a criminal activity, once declaring 'I'm not a Mafioso, I'm not a *camorrista*, I'm a simple cigarette trader.'[28] His wider criticisms are not without foundation:

> Isn't it a crime to demand 20 per cent of public sector contracts too? Who punishes politicians for that? And the mysteries of Italy – the Lockheed affair, the petrol scandal – who remembers them any more? A cigarette smuggler doesn't hurt anyone, he pays for the cigarettes and creates work for loads of people.[29]

What is remarkable about this attitude is not the fact that it is taken by a particular Camorra leader, but that it is probably shared by tens if not hundreds of thousands of people in Campania. As one cigarette smuggler said, echoing Zaza's sentiments entirely: 'It's tax evasion; don't industrialists avoid paying taxes? Only we do it risking our lives.'[30] The deaths of four cigarette smugglers in the Puglian town of Brindisi in 1991–2 alone are evidence of the accuracy of this statement.

For gang leaders the profit margin is enormous. Despite the fact that they are just one element in a three-link chain consisting of the Camorra boss who organises imports from overseas factories, the local gang leader who controls distribution, and the street vendor, the profit overall in terms of street value compared with factory prices has been calculated at 342 per cent.[31]

Given the scale of contraband sales, it is not surprising to learn that, according to Italian police, US tobacco multinationals such as Philip Morris and Reynolds (manufacturers of Marlboro, Camel and Winston) run a parallel system – 'export 2' – for selling their products to smugglers. A police report from the mid-1980s identified concessionary agents in Switzerland 'which directly supply Italian smugglers, who identify themselves as the representatives of specific criminal groups'.[32] Supergrass Salvatore Migliorino has made the same accusation: 'We went and bought cigarettes in Switzerland and paid the multinationals . . . We negotiated with people who represented Philip Morris, with whom we signed contracts for a thousand, two thousand or ten thousand crates of cigarettes.'[33]

Government exasperation turned to action in late 1991 when the Finance Minister rushed through a decree temporarily banning the sale in state-controlled tobacconists of Marlboro, Merit and Muratti, directly accusing Philip Morris of dealing with cigarette smugglers.[34]

Profits in the drug trade are even larger. The Financial Action Task Force, a group set up at the Paris G7 summit in 1989, currently values the world turnover of drug trafficking at $320 billion a year, yielding profits of $90 billion.[35]

In Italy itself, the government's statistical office estimated in 1992 that the total turnover of the Italian drug market amounted to $6.4–$9.6 billion per year.[36]

In Campania, according to Neapolitan sociologist Amato Lamberti, the local drug market was worth $3.2 billion a year in

1990 and employed a total workforce of 25,000.[37] More recent studies have estimated that there are 30,000 regular heroin users in Naples, who must spend at least $80 a day on their habit, producing a daily turnover of $2.4 million, a monthly turnover of $72 million and an annual turnover of $860 million.[38] Cocaine is thought to be even bigger business than heroin; and one should also add on large amounts for marijuana, amphetamines and synthetic drugs. In recent years a crack-based chocolate, *totaretto*, has also become popular.

The current structure of Camorra drug trafficking appears to point towards a European base of operations somewhere in Spain, probably in Camorra-owned restaurants in Granada and Armilla, with local distribution centres in Naples, Aversa, Portici, Salerno, Torre del Greco and Torre Annunziata employing about a thousand people directly. It is likely that there are other distribution centres in Florence, Milan and Rome.

Although serious Camorra involvement in drugs only began in the mid-1970s under the control of the Mafia, trade so mushroomed that by the early 1980s the Neapolitans' gang warfare had spread even as far as Peru, where they would fight over the control of exports and where a large laboratory for refining coca leaves was also discovered.

It seems that during the mid-1980s Michele Zaza had a contract for cocaine from Peru and Bolivia worth $800 million a year, making it the third largest commercial operation in Campania – after the Alfa Romeo car factory in Pomigliano d'Arco and the steelworks at Bagnoli on the western edge of Naples. Around 70 kg a month were imported, almost a tonne a year, and the operation was run jointly by South Americans and Neapolitans, until a series of arrest warrants was issued in 1987. The drug was sent from Bogotá by air couriers passing through Frankfurt and Madrid, and was then distributed throughout Italy.[39] Zaza was also involved in the 'Pizza Connection' case of the early 1980s, and his name came up in connection with a September 1982 Paris meeting with other Mafiosi in which a 600 kg package of cocaine held in Brazil was discussed.[40]

The drug trade is international by definition, and its international nature was again confirmed quite recently in the 'Green Ice' operation, revealed in September 1992 by Italian and US authorities. This saw the arrest of 34 people in Italy, 167 in the US and 2 in Costa Rica. A total of 682 kg of cocaine was seized, along with goods and currency worth $58 million, including a 22m³ storeroom in London stuffed full of dollars waiting to be laundered. Carmine Alfieri's gang were the Camorra representatives in this huge operation, relaundering money through the current account of an 80-year-old former primary-school teacher. The Italian laundering quota was $400,000 per week.[41]

One of the Camorra's specific methods of dealing in drugs, as opposed to all other major criminal gangs, who predominantly use addicts, is to use whole families in their distribution network. Adults normally negotiate the price and receive the money while their under-age children deliver the drugs. In such a system it is almost impossible to obtain convictions, as the adults are, for obvious reasons, extremely unwilling to confess.

The massive profits to be made in the drug trade may well be leading to changes in the Camorra's organisational structure. The fact that profits are so vast could lead to a decision to concentrate on the drug trade alone rather than run the risk of further harassment by branching out into the other illegal activities outlined in this chapter. And the level of profits can also produce 'career changes': 'The very availability of large amounts of money which arrive continuously favours the faster and faster conversion of a *camorrista* into a businessman.'[42] It would therefore be in the interest of these 'Camorra businessmen' to withdraw completely from low-level criminality such as theft, extortion and illegal gambling, and to let these areas be managed by violent raw youngsters.

MONEY LAUNDERING AND GOING 'LEGIT'

The term 'dirty' money is a misnomer, as the only major cases in which it is necessary to launder specific banknotes are kidnap ransoms and bank robberies, both fairly rare activities for organised crime in general and for the Camorra in particular. The problem for most criminals is not so much 'dirty' money as 'funny' money – the possession of large amounts of money that cannot be accounted for. For major criminals the problem is finding the means to render legitimate, anonymous or untraceable huge amounts of money that have been earned illegally, and not the fact that possession of individual banknotes might somehow constitute proof of illegal activities.

In general, laundering involves three stages: the first is the *placement stage* – the depositing of cash. This has traditionally been done by opening a variety of accounts using the names of people without criminal records, both at one individual bank and at several different banks. However, due to recent Italian legislation, which requires personal details to be kept for anyone depositing over $16,000, much of this now takes place in other countries. The second stage, *layering*, involves the movement of money, and even its reconversion back into cash, in order to lose all trace of its origin. Only then is the *integration stage* reached – the full absorption of previously 'dirty' money into the 'legal' system.[43]

A friendly relationship with a bank or credit institution, or even outright ownership, is the simplest way of recycling 'hot' money. In recent years banking activity and deposits have grown rapidly in the Naples area: in the 1989–92 period the number of banking outlets in Campania grew by 21 per cent, almost double the national average of 11 per cent, while deposits increased by 19 per cent as against a national average of 13.6 per cent. The province of Caserta, where more local councils have been disbanded due to the infiltration of organised crime than anywhere else in Italy, enjoyed an increase of 29 per cent in banking outlets and 24 per cent in new deposits.[44]

Investigators also face obstacles placed in their path by the banks themselves. A bank manager may well be aware that behind the *testa di legno* (the straw man opening an account, who does not have a criminal record) there is in reality a wealthy *camorrista*; any refusal to open an account and to grant credit will mean the loss of an account often involving millions. However, if police later begin making enquiries, the bank is unlikely to divulge all it knows about the real account holder, as it would then be implicated and possibly prosecuted for facilitating money laundering.

The use of offshore financial operations is also widespread. Although the actual financial operation may take place in the country of origin, in legal and accounting terms the transaction takes place in the Bahamas, Bermuda, the Cayman or Channel Islands, Gibraltar, Hong Kong, Liechtenstein, Switzerland, and so on. One of the reasons why the lax controls are never significantly tightened up is that many 'legal' businesses and financiers – such as Robert Maxwell – make use of the same facilities, often for the same reason – the need to lose all trace of origin.

Large commercial operations also provide a common method of laundering: the value of goods delivered or ordered is simply exaggerated, or non-existent goods are apparently sent or received. Alternatively, once the Camorra gains control of a smaller commercial enterprise, its financial inflows and outflows can be used to launder 'funny money'. Property speculation is a classic example of this particular method: buying land and building on it involves large sums of money in rapid circulation – a good example of this is the land bought by the Alfieri gang just outside Nola.[45]

The ownership and use of gambling casinos is a traditional means of money laundering for any large organisation dealing in drugs. This is why, from the early 1980s, New Family gangs began to invest heavily in casinos near the borders between France, Italy and Switzerland, as well as on the Franco-Spanish border.

Apart from this rather exotic kind of investment, one of the most common and economically important targets of money laundering and legal investment is the service sector, where illegal earnings can be recycled in a range of retailing, tourist and cleaning services. For example, in late 1991 the Camorra boss Ciro Mariano almost gained control of the city's major theatre, the Politeama.[46]

This may also be why there are still so many retail outlets in southern Italy: rapid inflows and outflows of cash are completely normal and are difficult to trace. The resources needed to even begin monitoring these activities are clearly massive, and the offences committed often fairly minor. A restaurant owner, for example, faced with the charge that his huge operating profit is in fact due to laundering drug money, could easily reply that he understated his real turnover in order to avoid tax payments. The owner might still have to pay a fine for tax evasion, but would nevertheless be able to carry on his operations and take further precautions in the future.

It would appear that the modern Camorra (beginning with the growth of Cutolo's NCO) initially recycled much of its money through Pippo Calò, the Mafia's 'cashier' and 'ambassador' in Rome from the early 1970s until his arrest in March 1985.

Other Camorra gangs have also made use of their links with the Mafia. For example, one of the Nuvolettas' key money laundries was the Stella d'Oriente (Star of the East) company, founded in February 1974 in the Sicilian fishing town of Marzara del Vallo. The firm was initially controlled by Luciano Liggio and Salvatore Riina, but after a few years members of the Nuvoletta clan also became shareholders. It specialised in importing and exporting frozen fish and was widely held to be a means for money laundering.[47]

It is important to remember that laundering 'dirty money' is not always essential for the Camorra if, as in the case of Carmine Alfieri's gang, the bulk of profits comes from public sector contracts. In historical terms, however, money laundering is an important development: in the space of three decades many Camorra leaders have moved from crude protection rackets and control over agricultural markets to become sophisticated financial operators.

The ultimate investment move is into government bonds, particularly US Treasury securities, and speculation on the stock exchange. And unfortunately, countries such as Italy, with its chronic public sector debt, are frequently obliged to hurriedly issue government bonds as a means of obtaining finance.

THE CAMORRA'S INTERNATIONAL LINKS

The extent of the Camorra's international links is severely restricted by its need to maintain power and influence through territorial control. With a few exceptions, such as Michele Zaza and possibly Umberto Ammaturo, moving overseas, whether it is motivated by entrepreneurial motives or by sheer self-preservation, is a step backwards in a *camorrista*'s criminal career.

Once they move abroad major criminals do not wield the same influence they enjoyed at home; in particular, they lack the political protection which often enables them to avoid arrest. Their anonymity overseas also makes it difficult for them to become involved in criminal activities at a level similar to that at which they operated at home; and in major industrialised countries Italians are normally just one amongst a number of competing ethnic groups outside the majority population. Then there is often a fundamental language barrier which can be an even greater obstacle to the creation of a criminal reputation.[48]

A long stay abroad inevitably means that their power base at home starts to crumble. Not only will a strong rival be more likely to launch some kind of attack; rising stars within the gang can be tempted to make a bid for power, a move that can easily start with giving police overseas a tip-off to the address where their leader is living.

All these reasons make it very unlikely that top criminals will go and live permanently in other countries, although there is little doubt that they regularly visit a whole range of nations. This is why reports that top Mafia leaders now reside in London[49] are probably wildly inaccurate. It is far more likely that Italian criminal gangs are investing in a range of activities throughout Europe, and apart from drug deals these will usually be activities that either are 'legitimate' or do not involve the use or threat of violence. The main attraction of a country such as the UK for Italian organised crime appears to be twofold: the opportunity to launder money within the City of London, and the ease with which fugitives can merge into the population and, even if questioned, avoid returning to Italy as charges of conspiracy and Mafia association are not grounds for extradition.

The semi-racist debate in the UK about organised crime and the relaxation of passport and customs checks in January 1993 missed two very simple points concerning criminal infiltration: leading criminals had already created their own 'internal market' within Europe at least a decade before '1992'; and anyone with a serious criminal record will simply obtain forgeries enabling them to pass through a normal passport check. A senior British detective, specialising in Italian organised crime, played down the effect of a relaxation in frontier checks on Italian criminal groups:

> they've been moving drugs and illicit articles, in huge amounts, over a very long period of time. And to be honest, I don't see that the dropping of frontier barriers, so far as goods or people are concerned, is going to make any difference. They've moved enough in anyway – and they've not had a problem in the past.[50]

The only reported case of a presumed *camorrista*'s presence in the UK, that of Antonio La Torre and his ownership of a restaurant in Aberdeen, can at the moment only be seen as an exception to the rule. Although he appears to have been in contact with known criminals both in Italy and in Venezuela, La Torre has never been arrested or questioned in Britain.[51]

Yet in recent years the La Torre gang, from its home town base in Mondragone, has extended its control into the province of Caserta and into southern Lazio, specialising in heroin, cocaine and arms deals[52] – so much so that in July 1992 police impounded villas, import–export companies, supermarkets and luxury cars worth a grand total of $400 million, all linked to the clan.[53]

The fact that street prices for hard drugs in Britain are the highest in Europe makes the UK a prime target for international criminal infiltration as profits are likely to be higher than elsewhere.[54] But, apart from a small number of major gang leaders, the street level and intermediate levels of the Camorra do not have the connections to visit foreign countries except on holiday or as couriers. The presence of top gang leaders normally indicates that they want to make major business deals, rather than an attempt to set up or gain control of organised crime.

Nevertheless, the growth of the drug trade, money laundering and the rapid general increase in the Camorra's strength in recent years has led to a greater presence overseas. Just as the world's economic and political systems have become far more integrated over the last two decades, so have the operations of top criminals. Given the complex international nature of drug trafficking and money laundering, a high-level criminal who operates in one country alone is likely to be superseded by criminals who try to harness resources and opportunities on a global scale.

A brief survey of Camorra activities outside Italy is therefore not only a legitimate concern for non-Italians, it also provides another viewpoint from which to gauge the power of the Camorra within Italy itself.

The career of Michele Zaza, who made his first fortune in the contraband cigarette trade during the 1970s, is probably the best illustration of a *camorrista*'s international development.

Born in 1945, Zaza had his first brush with the law in 1961 when he was arrested for being involved in a street fight. He was later sentenced for carrying a knife, then on another occasion a pistol, and then again for fighting. But by 1974 there was evidence that he had made a qualitative leap when he was arrested with some top Mafiosi closely linked to Luciano Liggio, one of the Mafia's top three leaders during that period.[55]

His widely recognised cunning helped him to slowly emerge from the shadow of his Mafia protectors. The 1974 Marano agreement between Sicilians and Neapolitans concerning the contraband cigarette trade was wound up at a second Marano meeting in 1979, partly because Zaza had become uncontrollable. As Tommaso Buscetta has said: 'According to what Stefano Bontade told me, laughing, Michele Zaza used every trick in the book to unload his own cigarettes rather than those of the Palermo families.'[56]

Zaza became known as 'the King of the blondes', as cigarettes are called in slang, and ran a fully multinational operation. Having by now moved into drug trafficking as well, he was immensely wealthy. For example, when he was arrested in Rome in June 1981 police found cheques worth $950,000 in his pockets.

He is rumoured to have set up a heroin refinery in the French city of Rouen in 1982, buying premises worth $2 million. Zaza hoped to make between $20,000 and $32,000 a day profit until the plan was interrupted by his arrest.[57]

But he soon escaped from custody in Italy, and by 1989 the US Treasury Department estimated that his assets in the US alone were worth $3.2 million. At the same time the FBI also estimated that he had $15 million deposited in Swiss banks.[58] For many years his daughter has been the official owner of a ten-bedroom villa in Beverley Hills, not to mention his Paris flat, a villa just outside Nice and several properties in Naples.

In recent years, in an attempt to avoid harassment from Italian authorities (particularly new laws which allow the seizure of assets whose origin cannot be accounted for), he moved his base of operations to the South of France.

Until his arrest in Nice in March 1989 (following the discovery of a lorry carrying 500,000 packets of contraband cigarettes), he appears to have engaged in top-level criminal activity, apparently hosting a European drugs summit at the Elysée Palace hotel in Nice on St Valentine's Day 1989, when the Camorra was given control of supplies from South America.[59] And in 1990 Zaza's associates almost managed to buy the casino at Mentone, on the French side of the Franco–Italian border.[60]

Another *camorrista* operating on a global scale was Umberto Ammaturo, who specialised in cocaine trafficking from South America. Born in 1941 and first arrested in 1962, he first came to warrant serious police attention when he was arrested with the Camorra's leader in Milan, Nunzio Guida, in 1972.

Until his arrest in Peru in May 1993 and his extradition back to Italy, Ammaturo had been on the run for many years, spending most of his time in South America. He was arrested in São Paulo in Brazil in August 1990 and spent three months in jail in Brasilia, before he managed to escape, having paid $105,000 in bribes. According to a Drug Enforcement Administration report, Ammaturo has been one of the financiers of the Shining Path guerrilla movement in Peru, and like Michele Zaza he has diversified his interests on a global scale. For example, he once bought a tourist centre in Senegal through a large bank account at the Unione Banche Svizzere.[61]

One of his most recent operations came to light with the arrest in Naples of nine of his associates in March 1992, following the discovery of 10kg of cocaine which had arrived from Colombia. The cocaine was 'soaked' into clothes that were then smeared with solvents to distract sniffer dogs; the clothes would then be chemically treated in Castellammare and the cocaine reconstituted.[62] An even larger operation was discovered in July of the same year, involving the importation of 300kg of cocaine a month from Colombia via Peru.[63] The particular success of Ammaturo during the 1980s was often the result of his creation of a triangular system of cocaine smuggling, involving the use of several African countries as staging posts, rather than solely using the traditional South American–European axis.

In recent years Eastern Europe has become an important area for Camorra expansion. It seems that many Camorra operators, short of predicting the fall of the Berlin Wall, nevertheless understood that the whole Eastern bloc was desperate for hard currency. They also realised that many people were curious to try drugs for the first time and so often offered them at very low 'promotional' prices.

The breakup of the old Soviet Union, with the beginning of widespread privatisation and financial reform, has allowed organised crime to make investments from abroad. Arms dealing and drug trafficking have mushroomed, as has trade in antiques, at such a rate that in the first half of 1993 it was estimated that 531 criminal gangs were operating within the Commonwealth of Independent States, and by the second half of the year this climbed to 3,000 gangs with a membership of 15,000. Apart from selling drugs, arms and stolen cars, many criminal gangs are able to recycle their money through buying into privatised companies and illegal trading of the rouble, as well as setting up prostitution rings, protection rackets and robbing banks.

Production of opium has already reached significant levels in Uzbekistan and Tadzhikistan, although for the moment this is aimed mainly at the CIS market. The overland heroin route from Afghanistan, Iran, Pakistan and South-East Asia now often passes through the CIS; alternatively heroin is brought into Italy by Central African couriers who work as illegal labourers around Caserta.[64]

The war in former Yugoslavia has made Germany strategically more important, and the Camorra has been buying up restaurants all over the country. For example, Lorenzo Nuvoletta was once almost arrested in a restaurant in Baden-Baden but managed to escape. Gennaro Licciardi, boss of Secondigliano and one of Campania's top five gang leaders, established his base of operations in Rostock, in eastern Germany, where his brother opened a whole range of shops. Edoardo Contini's clan is reported to have sent ten men to Leipzig, where they have opened restaurants as well as clothes and food shops.[65] Furthermore, two Camorra money laundries were discovered in Munich in early 1992.

The south of France has been important for its casinos, many of which – in Nice, Cannes, Menton and Boulier-sur-Mer – have suffered Camorra infiltration and have been closed down by authorities for long periods. One of the first indications of Camorra infiltration was the arrest of long-term Camorra leaders Nunzio Barbarossa and Nunzio Guida in Nice in February 1989. Another important area of investment in France for money laundering is private clinics, which account for 37 per cent of French hospital beds. In these institutions money can be recycled quite simply, as a fake kidney transplant can easily 'cost' $160,000.[66] The murder of the deputy mayor of Marseilles in January 1990 was viewed by police as linked to this laundering system, and their suspicion was heightened by the fact that he was also a private doctor.

Frauds concerning the European Union could virtually fill a separate book given their sheer scale – in recent years it has been estimated that fraud amounts to at least 10 per cent of the EU's Common Agricultural Policy expenditure. Yet these frauds are more the result of the general climate of illegality rather than operations run under the control of Camorra gangs.

Nevertheless, EU fraud can involve: false receipts for activities never carried out, non-existent companies making orders, false declarations concerning the quality of a particular product, or the addition of water to goods to increase their weight.

One example in the 1991–3 period concerned false receipts amounting to $37 million in the Puglia–Campania area, which led to the release of $4 million of EU subsidies for the apparent sale of olive oil. Companies issued receipts for non-existent activities, while bottling plants declared they had produced non-existent goods, hence the EU easily fell into the trap.[67]

In conclusion, the Camorra's economic and social power means it creates huge profits, recycling massive amounts of money into the legal economy and directly or indirectly providing work and subsistence for up to half a million people. Indeed, the broad picture provided here has not even discussed other highly relevant Camorra activities, such as prostitution, arms trafficking and the production of counterfeit goods. As one of Naples' leading policemen has noted:

> the Camorra has probably become more dangerous than the Mafia because the presence of organised crime in Campania is so widespread that it is definitely more difficult to eradicate. Given that it is not a monolithic group [i.e. it does not have the same structure as the Mafia, in which the following scenario could develop] – you get the boss and his deputy, you decapitate the strongest gang and the others get disorientated – on the contrary here [in Campania] you decapitate one and the others remain as they were.[68]

If the activities detailed in this chapter comprised the full extent of Camorra power then their defeat would be extremely difficult. The creation of such power, however, could never have been achieved without the support and connivance of local politicians, the very people entrusted with any solution to the problem of organised crime.

Chapter 7

Criminal politics

The old mayor, a Christian Democrat, was a thief – but he helped everyone. He stole but he gave us welfare cheques, cheese as well – he never made us pay for water or electricity. Now there's a new communist mayor and he has reported us to the police because we don't pay our bills.

— Unemployed Castellammare man

> There must be sincerity and justice in the activities of the council and of the state, and it is necessary that citizens have faith in them. In Naples, on the contrary, citizens have lost all faith in their rights and in the justice handed down by the council and the state.
>
> This is not due to ancient traditions which should have disappeared by now, but to new forms of private despotism, clientelism and Camorra, which are different forms of private organisation which tend to administer justice in their own fashion, outside the law and the state and, where necessary, against the law and the state. Citizens only have faith in favours.[1]

The reality of recent political life in Campania makes the above report, written almost one hundred years ago, extremely relevant today. The underlying theme of this chapter is that if the problem of links between politicians and professional criminals recurs so frequently, then perhaps another solution needs to be found, rather than simply repeating variations of solutions which have been found wanting over more than a century.

The most worrying aspect of the links between politicians and professional criminals is that the relationship has not only become closer and more intertwined over the last two decades; the balance of power moved in the criminals' favour throughout the 1980s. It could easily be argued that at the moment of their 'fall' in 1993, Antonio Gava and his Christian Democrat machine in Campania needed the Camorra for their political survival far more than individual Camorra bosses needed leading politicians to survive.

The decade between the decline of Cutolo in the early 1980s and the arrest and subsequent collaboration of first Pasquale Galasso and then Carmine Alfieri in the early 1990s is the crucial period in this evolution. Cutolo's 'mass Camorra' remained largely outside the political structure: it simply and consistently delivered votes and received in return contracts and protection from politicians. In some senses the NCO was a more modern and violent version of the Camorra racketeering dominant in the first two or three decades of the postwar period. It was the rise of the Nuvoletta and other New Family gangs that represented the development of a more sophisticated Camorra, both economically and politically.

In economic terms Camorra gangs became far wealthier – and their turnover and subsequent reinvestment in legal activities became a vital element in the survival of the precarious Campanian economy. The mechanics of money laundering and diversification into legal areas necessitated working relationships with the local political ruling class, who became increasingly aware of the Camorra's enormous financial wealth. These relationships often started thanks to politicians' encouragement – although if this was not forthcoming, connections would be nurtured by the Camorra through intimidation, violence and alternative candidates.

Strong economic and political relationships had been formed from the late 1970s onwards, and by the end of the 1980s these links appear to have become essential for senior politicians and their parties. By that time Carmine Alfieri's 'political Camorra' had arguably won the upper hand in its relationship with the local political structure.

THE ASSAULT AGAINST LOCAL COUNCILS: THE FIRST LEVEL OF POLITICAL CRIMINALITY

During the early 1980s the relationship between the Camorra and local politicians was still rather unstable, but over the next few years it became clear that many local politicians were at least under the influence of the Camorra and very often conniving with it.

The late 1970s and early 1980s saw a large number of political murders. In April 1981, the Christian Democrat regional councillor and ex-mayor of Marigliano, Alfredo Mundo, was murdered; a Social Democrat councillor, Giuliano Pennacchio, was killed in Giugliano in July 1982; the following month, a DC councillor, Giuseppe Caso, was killed in Poggiomarino; and in October the PSI mayor of San Gennaro Vesuviano was gunned down. In December 1984 they killed Crescenzo Casillo – an especially important target as he was the mayor of a major town, Casoria.[2]

If one looks beyond murders to the underlying level of intimidation, the picture becomes even clearer: between April 1982 and March 1983 there were 17 bomb attacks against local administrators, 5 attacks against trade union offices, 16 assaults on trade unionists, 5 murders of council committee chairpersons and 14 attacks on councillors.[3] This sudden rise in systematic violence was the result of two factors: the internal growth of Camorra gangs in the second half of the 1970s and the massive increase in council budgets following the earthquake.

By the mid-1980s the Camorra was engaged in a campaign for direct political involvement. Its economic strength had increased massively thanks to reconstruction, and in social terms association with the Camorra also provided both an economic and a political niche for a class of young architects and engineers. A new professional middle class was emerging during reconstruction, unwilling to be dominated by the old Christian Democrat method of clientelism.

A new type of politician had also emerged, different from the old-style political liberals of the 1950s and 1960s who had used Camorra *guappi* for clientelistic mediation. These new men, often from relatively poor backgrounds and with a limited education, were ambitious and not afraid to take risks. In many cases they represented 'a new low-quality political grouping, who have totally committed their professional future to politics, and whose relationship with the Camorra is not so much based on personal enrichment as on the means to begin and maintain their political career.'[4] The Camorra was thus being fully integrated into the political system. ~~very stupid~~

These 'rampant' elements were often either members or close associates of the Socialist Party. For example, Ernesto Bardellino was the Socialist Party mayor of San Cipriano d'Aversa in 1982–4, and it was widely known he was the brother of one of the Camorra's most notorious gang leaders, Antonio.

For those politicians who opposed the Camorra, or who were perhaps associated with a gang that was losing a war, the price continued to be high. In what can only be seen as a deliberate strategy, twelve councillors were assassinated in Campania between 1984 and 1985. Yet assassinations are generally the exception – kneecappings, beatings, threats against the individual politician or their family normally suffice.

Intimidation is therefore widespread, and the lack of activity of politicians threatened by *camorristi* can allow openly corrupt politicians to do the Camorra's bidding. Throughout July 1992, for example, the drivers of a company that had suddenly lost its contract with Acerra council over suspicion of Camorra links demonstrated in front of the town hall, so the Mayor simply decided not to go to work for the entire month.[5] Although the number of local councillors elected directly from the ranks of criminal gangs may well be very low, the number of politicians who knowingly accept votes from the Camorra and grant them favours is probably very high. In addition, there are also 'honest' councillors who simply turn a blind eye.

The physical attacks, the threats and the whole process of conditioning and direct criminal infiltration all helped to do serious damage to basic democracy. However, it should always be remembered that many politicians had a traditional disposition to high levels of illegality. In 1985 the PCI sent out a questionnaire to thirty Campanian councils and found that on average they held full council meetings only once every two months, although even this was within the legal requirement of two per year.[6] The absurd situation could easily be reached when there were literally hundreds of items for approval or debate – indeed in one meeting the Naples provincial council had 1,300 items on the agenda! On one occasion in Nocera Superiore, the mayor demanded that 323 items be voted on as one block.[7] The point to be borne in mind is that most of these items concerned ratification of contracts awarded. Furthermore, many of these contracts had been awarded solely as a result of private negotiation rather than public tendering, as was the case of Campania's third largest town council, that of Torre del Greco, which awarded contracts almost exclusively as a result of private negotiations in the 1984–5 period.[8]

By the end of the 1980s the Camorra had established itself within many local councils – indeed, rather than *camorristi* facing charges of intimidating politicians, many politicians were now facing charges of involvement with the Camorra. A *carabinieri* report detailed that in the 1988–9 period police investigated 192 local administrators and brought official charges against 126, of which 21 were accused of membership of a Camorra gang; 5 of these people were then arrested.[9]

The May 1990 council elections are a useful barometer of the Camorra's direct move into municipal politics. In a declaration that gives a clear indication of its severe impotence, the Naples police headquarters stated prior to the elections that fifty-two of the candidates were suspected of having close links with the Camorra. Despite this warning, or perhaps in some cases because of it, 31 of these candidates were elected: 17 Christian Democrats, 8 Socialists and 4 Social Democrats.

Not surprisingly, during the election campaign senior magistrates were sounding the alarm:

> nowadays Camorra clans are able to determine majorities and to guarantee the electoral success of a candidate – above all in the Province of Naples . . . the Camorra boss contacts the politician directly, he speaks to him personally, and it all ends with a joint decision on building projects or anything else.[10]

The mutual nature of the relationship had been understood, too: 'It is an exchange of favours amongst equals: the godfather guarantees votes, public order, in other words total support. On the other hand the politician commits himself to dividing up the cake.'[11] Yet warnings like these fell on deaf ears, as the politicians responsible for fighting organised crime had often become partners in a whole range of illegal activities.

Vittorio Sbordone, Naples' Chief Federal Prosecutor, commented six months later on the effect the publication of 'suspicious' candidates had had: 'it is an ethical question. These lists have had no effect, nobody has been removed from office.'[12] Sbordone continued: 'All I want to do is to outline a culture of implicit tolerance of illegality; and it is in this institutional environment that organised crime prospers.'[13]

It should therefore come as no surprise that a judicial inquiry into the May elections published in December 1990 revealed voting irregularities in seven constituencies: Casoria, Naples (2), Pozzuoli, San Giuseppe Vesuviano, Saviano and Torre del Greco. In some cases the number of votes cast was higher than the number of people on the electoral register.[14]

The problem of illegality and links with organised crime is dramatically brought into focus in Naples, the capital of both Campania and the whole South. Events within the council, the city's largest employer, are particularly illuminating. During the late 1980s, the warning signs had been numerous. For example, during his period as the Socialist Party's mayor of Naples from 1987 to 1990, Pietro Lezzi had to testify or make statements before judicial inquiries on ten separate occasions.[15] And in December 1991 Socialist councillor Silvano Masciari, who had been groomed to succeed his party colleague Lezzi, was sentenced to fourteen months in jail for having provided council jobs to two known members of the Mariano gang.[16]

In September 1990 it emerged that out of the 80 city councillors, 38 were under police investigation for association with the Camorra. One of them was a communist, but the rest belonged to the five ruling parties, with only 19 councillors from the governing coalition not under investigation.[17]

It was hoped that things would improve as a result of the June 1992 Naples council elections, yet even before voting took place it was clear that any potential clean-up had little chance: of the 923 candidates, 189 already had criminal records.[18] And over the following year 18 councillors out of 80 ended up facing charges for various crimes: 7 Socialists, 5 Christian Democrats, 2 Republicans, 1 neo-fascist of the MSI and 1 member of the PDS. The various parties only addressed the symptom rather than the cause when they replaced fourteen of these councillors – some of these 'substitutes' were soon arrested and accused of other crimes![19]

By early 1993 the collapse had become total. A new ruling group was cobbled together, but politics had by now taken on a surreal tinge, as many of the difficulties in creating a new administration were due to councillors being under arrest, on the run, or continually helping police with their enquiries. During the spring several meetings were inquorate due to the fact that many councillors were either under arrest or undergoing questioning in the police barracks next door.[20]

In May the ruling group on the city council passed a motion declaring its bankruptcy, with debts amounting to approximately $800 million. Three months later, as councillors were again bickering over forming a new ruling alliance, black gunge instead of water started coming out of many taps in the city, a problem that, though not new, had supposedly been resolved. Fearing a repeat of the rioting which had ensued in Ponticelli in May 1990, and had led to the resignation of Mayor Lezzi, the President of the Republic signed a decree on 12 August disbanding the council and providing emergency funding. The most important reason given was that of maintaining public order.

Apart from this generalised illegality and inefficiency, it is difficult to monitor who may have links with the Camorra. The Mayor of Naples Francesco Tagliamonte admitted in mid-1993: 'In this great confusion of things that need to be done concerning 17,000 council employees, identifying who has connections with *camorristi* is a totally impossible task.'[21] His position appears to be perfectly rational, however. Official statistics show that in the period from 1984 to 1993, in the Province of Naples, 902 council administrators were the subject of legal proceedings, 60 of them for Camorra membership.[22]

If large numbers of politicians behave in this fashion, then it is only to be expected that bureaucrats will do so as well. The main cases of bureaucratic corruption in Naples' council during 1992 were the following: in June two librarians were arrested and charged with usury, forgery of legal documents, embezzlement and membership of a criminal organisation; in July a maintenance worker at the council court was sacked when it emerged that his sons were members of a Camorra gang; in October the chief technical officer of the food supplies division was arrested for extortion; in February 1993 the head of the council police and another employee were arrested and charged with extorting money from a businessman who had applied for a trading licence. A water board official was also arrested and charged with defrauding the board.[23] This brief outline of bureaucratic corruption and criminality is enough to show that any 'clean' administration that is elected will find itself being serviced by a bureaucracy with these kinds of ingrained habits.

The long history of political corruption in Campania has rendered its existence normal at all levels of society, including the bureaucracy; and its working relationship with the Camorra is just one part of a much larger picture of corruption and illegality. However, although Naples' city council may carry a particular weight due to its size and general influence, it is nevertheless a paragon of virtue compared with many other local councils.

'ABANDON HOPE ALL YE WHO ENTER': POLITICAL CRIMINALITY IN SANT'ANTONIO ABATE

The symbiosis of politics and crime in Sant'Antonio Abate, to the south-east of Naples and Vesuvius, is probably no worse than in dozens of other towns in Campania. The choice of presenting this particular town as an example of the intermeshing of criminal and political activities is dictated to a large extent by the details that have come to light in a number of recent trials; although the town also has its specific interest as one of the power bases of Antonio Gava, who was arguably the most important politician in Campania over a 25-year-period that began in 1968 and ended in 1993, when he was charged with membership of a criminal organisation.

The town has a population of 17,000 and an electorate of 9,000, and for many years has been the fiefdom of Giuseppe D'Antuono, described by supergrass Pasquale Galasso as 'simultaneously, a man of Antonio Gava and of Carmine Alfieri'.[24] D'Antuono was first elected mayor in 1973, and held the position for almost fifteen years until September 1988, although there was an interruption between December 1981 and March 1983 when he was in jail accused of membership of Cutolo's NCO.[25] Although the charge was dismissed in court due to lack of evidence, it probably furthered his political career rather than handicapping it.

In the early years of D'Antuono's rule, Sant'Antonio Abate seemed a normal small town politically dominated by the Christian Democrats. In typically clientilist fashion he illegally took on twenty-eight people as council employees in 1978,[26] and the overall council workforce rose from 42 in 1973 to 292 in 1988, even though regulations stated that no more than 206 could be employed.[27] Administrative decisions such as these contributed to the $8 million debt the council had accumulated by the time it was finally disbanded in 1993.

As we have seen in earlier chapters, it was during the early 1980s that a huge gang war broke out across Campania over the contraband and drugs trade as well as earthquake reconstruction contracts. Sant'Antonio Abate was by no means immune to these pressures, and D'Antuono's release from jail in March 1983, in time for the council elections, brought some of these tensions out into the open.

Five electoral lists were presented during the 1983 elections, the two moderate ones being the Christian Democrats (DC) and another Catholic-inspired list named 'Renewal and Democracy', which used the olive branch as its symbol. The DC list won 5,913 votes out of a total of 8,886, gaining 21 seats, while 'Renewal and Democracy' gained 1,909 votes and 6 seats, with three other seats going to minor parties.[28]

D'Antuono, a member of Antonio Gava's DC faction, was due to become mayor again, but then internal dissent broke out. The alternative list had been led by Mario Savarese and Giuseppe Abagnale – at that time the latter was a member of Carmine Alfieri's gang. After the election seven DC councillors led a breakaway group which intended to stop D'Antuono from becoming mayor. Negotiations were held between these seven and the Savarese/Abagnale grouping, and in the meantime many of these councillors abandoned council meetings to make them inquorate and therefore unworkable.

However, negotiations soon stopped once a series of violent attacks began: DC councillor Orlando Cinque was shot at, while three others received phone threats.[29] Not surprisingly, a few days later they stopped their factional activities, rejoined the DC group, and D'Antuono became mayor once again.

Behind the scenes an agreement appears to have been reached which allowed Abagnale to cross over from his original grouping to become in effect a DC councillor. His nominal political affiliation, however, meant little when compared with his membership of Alfieri's gang: in the past Abagnale had been convicted of murder, attempted murder and membership of a Camorra gang.[30]

Despite the fact that he was a wholesale butcher by trade Abagnale became chairman of the public works committee, and soon after his appointment a decision was made to build a slaughterhouse worth $330,000. But as happened so often with earthquake reconstruction contracts, once the project was approved the price quickly rose to $490,000 and later to $1,920,000.[31] It would appear that this was mainly a manoeuvre to gain access to money, as the actual building work was delayed for many years, probably to allow Abagnale to keep his monopoly position in meat production. As outlined previously, the Christian Democrats have always been riven by internal faction fights over resources: it is the internal pecking order that dictates the amount of resources and privileges a political faction controls. Although feuding within the party seemed to be fairly subdued in 1983, it slowly began to increase over the subsequent period.

Abagnale's behaviour is a good example of the intermeshing of 'criminal' and 'political' interests. Ten years after these events, the disgraced Christian Democrat MP Alfredo Vito recalled that after the 1983 elections 'Antonio D'Auria forced D'Antuono to bring the alternative list into the council, and in particular Abagnale, who in later years became a friend of D'Antuono, so much so that he followed him into the DC list in 1988'.[32] The political importance of this lies in the fact that Antonio D'Auria has been Antonio Gava's personal secretary since 1972; so it can only be presumed that his intervention was made on Gava's behalf.

However, in the mid-1980s the millions which began to filter through for earthquake reconstruction caused increasing tension between competing political and criminal factions. As regards his criminal affiliation, Abagnale left the Alfieri gang in the mid-1980s and joined the locally based Rosanova clan. One of the Rosanova brothers later recounted that during this period 'Abagnale and we had enormous economic and business resources thanks to the contracts we obtained from Fantini'.[33] Antonio Fantini, a Christian Democrat politician currently facing six separate charges linked to earthquake reconstruction, was president of the Campanian regional council from March 1983 to November 1988, a position that automatically made him one of two Special Commissioners appointed by the government to supervise reconstruction. He was therefore a linchpin in the distribution of major contracts and favours, such as a $200 million contract for a water recycling plant, and he seemed to be linked to the Rosanova gang.

On a national level Fantini was part of Giulio Andreotti's faction within the Christian Democrats, in opposition to that of Antonio Gava, as Alfonso Ferrara Rosanova explains:

> After Giuseppe Abagnale moved towards Fantini, a politician of Andreotti's faction, and obtained the contracts I've already mentioned, D'Antuono automatically moved towards Andreotti's faction . . . It was clear that Gava was losing power at S. Antonio Abate; and after the contract for the water recycling plant had been awarded, Fantini, along with Giuseppe Abagnale, had created a very strong electoral base.[34]

In the typically indirect fashion in which these factional battles are normally fought out, a Christian Democrat study centre named 'The South in Europe' was founded in the town in January 1986. Its charter 'supported civic progress and the country's democratic growth, through its encouragement of social and educational activities, its promotion of increased associational initiatives and a free exchange of ideas, experience and knowledge'.[35] The brutal reality behind these supposedly lofty ideals can be glimpsed from the fact that the organiser of this manoeuvre, Gava's secretary Antonio D'Auria, is currently facing charges of Camorra membership.

The May 1988 council elections, in which D'Antuono and Abagnale's Christian Democrat list gained 4,987 votes and 15 seats, became a focal point for the growing tension. As Abagnale had now passed over into their 'sphere of influence', the Rosanova gang supported the DC list.[36]

The 'opposition' to the Christian Democrats was once more led by a 'civic list', although it had given itself a new and not particularly original name for this election – Catholic Christian Democrats (CCD) – and was led by Antonio D'Auria. The CCD gained 4,070 votes and 12 seats, while the socialists gained 1 seat, and the real opposition of the MSI and the PCI also gained 1 seat each.[37]

The former Christian Democrat MP Alfredo Vito has testified that

> it was absolutely obvious that the list that was officially closest to Gava was the civic one and not D'Antuono's: and you could notice this from hundreds of signals that could not go unobserved – the Ministerial machine put itself at the civic list's disposal.[38]

Gava's own personal actions also illustrate his factional position; his refusal to come and speak in the town, given that he would have been duty-bound to support the official DC candidate, went against his own long-standing traditions during election campaigns. Superficially there did not seem to be any real political differences between the two lists, apart from some rather vague references to local issues in the 'civic list'; what was really at stake, of course, was control over the Christian Democrat spoils system.

Yet the election did not resolve the issue, as the DC list failed to achieve an absolute majority. One of the reasons for their failure was the fact that a few days before the election a Dr Calabrese suddenly withdrew his candidature, thus depriving them of a majority – apparently his withdrawal was due to pressure from four *camorristi*: Ciro D'Auria, Catello De Riso, Gaetano Mercurio and Bernardo Santonicola.[39]

Most of these men had been released from prison in the mid-1980s and appeared to earn their living mainly by extorting money from canning factories in the area. Mercurio had been acquitted of the 1984 Torre Annunziata massacre for lack of evidence, Santonicola had been convicted of murder, and De Riso had been acquitted of attempted murder, although, when he was arrested for threatening Dr Calabrese, a brush and a spray for cleaning pistols were found hidden in his car.[40]

The intimidation of a Christian Democrat candidate, who was supported in turn by Fantini at regional level, Andreotti at national level, and by the Rosanovas at a criminal level obviously suggests that it was the politician Antonio Gava and the gang leader Carmine Alfieri who were applying pressure. The involvement of Mercurio, suspected of the Alfieri-inspired Torre Annunziata massacre, lends weight to this hypothesis.

A clear division emerged five weeks after the election, when Pasquale Galasso ordered the killing of two Rosanova brothers,

Aniello and Luigi, as well as of Diodato D'Auria, a DC council-lor who was also coincidentally a distant relative of Antonio D'Auria. The murders had the desired effect: three DC council-lors immediately moved over to support the other list, thus giving the Catholic Christian Democrats the majority. Giuseppe Abagnale, the ex-Alfieri gang member who had crossed over to the Rosanovas and become a DC councillor, went into hiding in fear of his life.[41]

The balance of power in the town was now clearly established: the losers were the official Christian Democrat list and its councillors, and therefore Antonio Fantini at regional level, Giulio Andreotti at the national level and the Rosanovas at the criminal level. Given the circumstances, it is not surprising that one of the Rosanova brothers has stated: 'I believe Antonio D'Auria and Antonio Gava to be morally responsible for my brothers' murder.'[42]

The motive behind these murders and acts of intimidation was clearly political power and the financial resources that came with it. One other point to bear in mind is that during this period (1988–90) Antonio Gava was Minister of the Interior and ultimately responsible for police activities.

The new council, agreed upon in December 1988, excluded both D'Antuono and Abagnale and elected Bonaventura Rispoli as mayor. It quickly revealed the illegality of D'Antuono's administration and its $8 million debt. They released damaging details, such as the fact that in eight council meetings held between May and September 1988 an average of forty resolutions per meeting was approved. These resolutions included: author-isations for payments, approval of contracts to be tendered, approval of contracts recently awarded and approval of the ext-ension of contracts already in progress for a total value of $9.6 million.[43]

The change in political power was also confirmed at the level of crime. Once Abagnale was stripped of his position as council-lor he clearly lost a degree of protection, and both Giuseppe Abagnale and his brother Carmine were murdered by the Alfieri clan in June 1990.

Yet D'Antuono was far from resigned to his fate and made accusations against the four men involved in anti-Christian Democrat intimidation during the 1988 election campaign – who were subsequently convicted of extortion but not Camorra membership at their first trial. However, Pasquale Galasso has spoken of a meeting held in late 1990 or early 1991, involving himself, the four men in question and Luigi Riccio, Mayor of San Paolo Belsito and member of Antonio Gava's faction:

> The opening speech was made by Riccio who, with his typically arrogant attitude and in his limited and crude diction said, all the while keeping a cigar in his mouth, that 'my boss' (everybody knew that with this expression he was referring to his political godfather Antonio Gava; it was an expression he continued to use during our discussion, and it was absolutely clear to me and to the others who he was referring to) was tired of having to put up with the fact that D'Antuono had been forced to go 'on the run', as he put it − for fear of a revenge attack by those four. Riccio explained that Gava had already helped them by influencing the appropriate magistrates and by convincing D'Antuono to withdraw at the main trial the accusations he had made during preliminary proceedings.[44]

It would appear that things progressed in this direction, as D'Antuono felt able to resurface and eventually resume his political career.

By this point we have reached the early 1990s, a period in which the Christian Democrats were promising 'renewal' and 'transparency' in government and an end to their links with organised crime. At the same time, D'Antuono was facing two separate trials concerning his past administrations, as well as the possibility of being placed under preventative house arrest for five years and having property confiscated as a result of demands by the State Prosecutor's office in Naples.[45]

Despite all this, D'Antuono made a successful political comeback in 1993 and was elected Christian Democrat mayor once again in June. He won his election under a new electoral system, which had been strongly supported by Christian Democrat reformers such as Mario Segni and the ex-communist PDS, as they believed that the elimination of preference voting and the institution of a second ballot for the position of mayor would somehow magically end the links between criminal politicians and political criminals.

Soon after D'Antuono's election, the authorities began to receive complaints of threats he apparently made to rival candidates, and he was subsequently charged with membership of a criminal organisation and ballot rigging and suspended from his post in August 1993. There is evidence that D'Antuono openly favoured intimidation such as occurred during a council meeting called on 5 July to discuss whether the candidates presented were appropriate to become mayor and presidents of council commissions. During this meeting

> there were unjustified and excessive interruptions made from the public gallery which harshly criticised any speech attempted by members of the opposition to such an extent that the right to democratic debate was denied; in all this the mayor and the senior councillor, also the chair of the meeting, did not ask the police present in the chamber to intervene.[46]

In a forlorn attempt to salvage some shred of credibility, the authorities decided to disband the council the following month and appoint an unelected government commissioner for eighteen months. The motivation behind this presidential decree was 'the restoration of democratic principles and collective freedom'.[47] In any event, government commissioners are subject to the same pressures as elected representatives as regards Camorra intimidation and influence. Despite this latest move the problems in Sant'Antonio Abate, as in dozens of other towns, remain the same: socioeconomic conditions which perpetuate the reproduction of criminal gangs and a political tradition that tolerates and often encourages illegality.

THE SECOND LEVEL OF POLITICAL CRIMINALITY: REGIONAL COUNCILS AND THE HEALTH SERVICE

Barely twenty years after their foundation in 1970, Italy's twenty regional authorities now account for nearly 10 per cent of the country's gross domestic product. They are generally responsible for agriculture, economic development, housing, hospitals and health services, public works and urban affairs.

Yet despite their demands for more power to raise taxes independently, in 1989 they were financially tied to national government for 98.2 per cent of their expenditure.[48] Perhaps even more important than this is the fact that regional government has no real history in modern Italy – to a large extent these authorities are hollow shells, devoid of any political tradition, colonised by national parties and politicians, who have also brought in their traditional practices. Furthermore, election as a regional councillor is very often a stage in an upwardly mobile trajectory: while over the 1970–90 period 19.2 per cent of Campanian regional councillors were elected from the ranks of the Naples city council alone,[49] at a national level at least 20 per cent of all regional councillors left for seats in the national parliament.[50]

Apart from this general picture, in relative terms it is not surprising to learn that major research conducted over this period has shown Campania to come nineteenth out of Italy's twenty regions in terms of general administrative performance, and last as regards public satisfaction and bureaucratic responsiveness.[51] In other words, the local political culture of inefficiency and illegality has simply been reproduced on a grander scale.

There is, however, one very obvious difference compared with municipal administration: the lack of political murders. It is highly likely that regional politicians have been conditioned by the Camorra's move into local politics during the 1980s and, given their own political traditions, were quite willing to come to an arrangement with it. Indeed, we are often dealing with the same politicians who have previously been elected as municipal councillors.

The major area of regional government expenditure is the financing and management of local health authorities, the *unità sanitarie locali* or USLs. Although Campania comes only seventh nationally in terms of its total number of public hospital beds, in line with a familiar pattern it is second in terms of its public health budget, which in 1992 amounted to $6 billion.[52]

In recent years the most scandalous example of wastage and Camorra infiltration concerns USL 35 in Castellammare di Stabia, Antonio Gava's home town. The first example of corruption was a contract signed in 1982 for in-patient catering, which cost $10 per meal, an improbably high figure for the period. Not surprisingly, an investigation was begun in 1986 when a new contract was signed that reduced costs by more than half. In the long term, however, this was not a solution – in late 1991 patients refused to eat meals in protest at the poor-quality food they were being served.

The construction of a new hospital wing took more than ten years to complete, while costs increased from $1.6 to $8 million;

it also appears that up to 20 per cent of the total cost may have been spent on bribes.

In 1988 the son of the local hospital's main cardiologist and the son of the Socialist vice-president of the USL were both promoted to jobs they were not qualified to perform. In October 1989 an investigation began into the legitimacy of the decision to let a flat for $650 per month to an employee of the USL, Dr Adriana Ingenito, who also happened to be the wife of DC Senator Francesco Patriarca.[53]

The level of nepotism became even more bloated in the spring of 1991 when dozens of sons, daughters, grandchildren and other relations of the USL 35 management committee and local councillors were all given jobs.

These are only a few specific examples to help explain why by 1992 USL 35 had an operating deficit of over $80 million and over a thousand workers on its payroll. This scandal involved not only politicians, but also trade union officials within the local hospitals, who are also facing charges of membership of a criminal organisation and extortion.

It seems that the Camorra's murder, in March 1992, of Sebastiano Corrado, a PDS councillor and member of the USL 35 management committee, was linked to his involvement in a bribe regarding the refurbishing of a nursing school – in this case 15 per cent of a $200,000 contract.[54] Most of the companies concerned with building work or cleaning services were controlled by *camorristi*, and it seems that Corrado, who worked in the authority's finance office, had done something to anger a particular gang.

Once again, it is the patients who suffer the most: orders for new equipment mysteriously disappear, wards and kitchens are infested with cockroaches due to lack of cleaning, and so on. As a doctor based in a cardiology department stated: 'We are operating without being able to offer guarantees to a patient who comes to us asking to be cured.'[55]

THE THIRD LEVEL OF POLITICAL CRIMINALITY: NATIONAL GOVERNMENT

Until mid-1993 there was little evidence of direct Camorra involvement at the national political level, although some circumstantial evidence had previously pointed in that direction.

For example, during a police raid on Lorenzo Nuvoletta's

house in the 1980s, a letter from a lawyer named Palumbo was found in which he urged the Nuvolettas to 'direct their votes towards Antonio Gava'.[56] During another *carabinieri* raid, Antonio Gava's visiting card was found in the pocket of Domenico Di Maro, a builder later convicted of a series of crimes, including membership of the Nuvoletta gang.

A raid on Carmine Alfieri's house as far back as March 1976 revealed that he had six different telephone numbers for the DC Senator Francesco Patriarca, known in Camorra circles as 'Frankie the Promise' for the favours he would often try to do.[57] Futher evidence of Patriarca's contacts emerged in 1983: between 1974 and 1976 he had written three letters to Ciro Iavarone, an NCO member in jail, in which he thanked him, among other things, 'for your help during the election campaign, which led to my election'. Even more disturbing is the fact that Patriarca was a member of the Parliamentary Justice Commission and later the Anti-Mafia Commission.[58]

Although these examples (and many others one could give), do not constitute definite proof of illegality, the undisputed power of the Camorra makes it very likely that close links with politicians do exist. The sheer size of the Camorra's economic empire makes it highly improbable that the most entrepreneurial and powerful gang leaders are not consulted regularly by politicians.

The examples cited here are therefore in many senses the tip of the iceberg – they are just a few of the cases which have come to light so far. However, in both the economic and the political spheres, the Camorra naturally has to use personnel without criminal records, so its influence and actual penetration within political institutions is impossible to quantify.

Evidence has recently started to accumulate concerning Camorra infiltration of national politics. But its relationship with national politicians is less organic and direct than with local councillors; the main role of the national politician is one of delaying or deflecting government policies that might damage their criminal friends, while approving laws that facilitate criminal penetration of the public sector.

A brief examination of the activities of a few MPs brings into focus a disturbing picture, as in the case of Socialist MP Raffaele Mastrantuono, former vice-president of the Parliamentary Justice Commission, which has the role of monitoring and amending laws relating to organised crime. The delicacy of this position is not, one would think, entirely in keeping with the fact that the town council of Villaricca, of which he was mayor from 1975 to 1984 and again in 1990–3, has been dissolved due to Camorra infiltration.[59]

Mastrantuono became the right-hand man of the Socialist Party's Deputy National Secretary Giulio Di Donato and has often had a strange relationship with the judiciary. As part of the Justice Commission he once repeatedly interrupted a trial and insisted on telling two judges details about a local Camorra gang operating in his home town. Not only was this completely inappropriate behaviour, it also created suspicion that Mastrantuono wanted to damage a rival gang.[60]

The vice-president of the Justice Commission between 1992 and 1994 was the Liberal MP Alfonso Martucci, elected at Casal di Principe near Caserta. Before becoming an MP he had been a lawyer, specialising first in defending NCO members and later members of the Bardellino and Mariano gangs. When he decided to stand as a Liberal candidate, the party's vote in the town leapt from 1.2 per cent to 26.7 per cent, giving rise to strong suspicions of Camorra support.[61]

In more general terms, however, the accusations made by Pasquale Galasso in 1992–3 have thrown a different light on the traditional view of the relationship between politics and organised crime. It is no longer simply a question of the Camorra manoeuvring votes towards 'friendly' politicians in exchange for favours and protection. The accusations currently facing Antonio Gava and other senior Neapolitan politicians are not 'corruption' or 'breaking the law on the public financing of political parties', which are the major accusations in the northern *Tangentopoli* scandals. These politicians are not accused of merely making arrangements with the Camorra, but of being part of the Camorra themselves.

The issue is no longer one of 'bad government' or clientelism but in some cases total commitment to a violent and illegal organisation. Once again, these accusations also point to the fact that the Camorra is far more than an organisation that relies primarily on acts of violence and its control of the drugs trade – in fact, public sector contracts could even be its largest source of profits.

The most powerful politician in this scenario is undoubtedly

Antonio Gava, who could easily be called the godfather of Campania. This ex-Minister of the Interior and other leading Christian Democrats in Campania are currently held in jail, facing a trial in which they are accused of

> having been part of a Mafia-type criminal organisation initiated, organised and led by Carmine Alfieri and other leaders of the Campanian Camorra, contributing in a regular fashion to the attaining of this organisation's goals: in particular, control over economic activities, the granting of licences and authorisations, the awarding of public sector contracts and the obtaining of illicit profit and advantage for themselves and others. And furthermore, of having impeded and hampered free voting, and of having acquired votes during electoral campaigns.[62]

Although the precise nature of the links may never be proved satisfactorily, it is certain that close links exist, and the weight of evidence appears convincing. Alfieri recently recalled for magistrates a meeting held at Lorenzo Nuvoletta's house in late 1980 or 1981: 'Antonio Gava was at that meeting. You can appreciate, your Honour, that with this kind of protection *you sort out* trials, you can do business, the police leave you alone.'[63] A more graphic example of this protection was given several years later, when Gava was Minister of the Interior: in a major report on organised crime presented to Parliament on 5 December 1989, Gava omitted to even mention the existence of Alfieri's gang, despite the fact that it had been common knowledge for several years that Alfieri had superseded Cutolo as the Camorra's strongest leader in 1981–2. This is how Alfieri describes his response:

> A few days after this piece of news came out in the newspapers, at one of the meetings at my farmhouse to which I summoned Senator Vincenzo Meo, I asked him to thank Antonio Gava for the 'interest' he had shown in not mentioning my name. Meo assured me that he would have communicated my gratitude to Gava.[64]

Once again, though, it is Pasquale Galasso who gives the best overall outline of Gava's system of power, telling magistrates in December 1992:

Such relationships exist and there are many political figures involved in them. Amongst these Senator Antonio Gava is undoubtedly the most important; he has a number of faithful allies throughout Campania who manage his political interests in a variety of social situations. Amongst these, I can recall Vincenzo Meo in the Nola area, Ciccio Catapano and his son Pasquale in S. Giuseppe Vesuviano, Dr Liguori in Poggio-marino . . . the Riccio brothers of S. Paolo Belsito, Giuseppe D'Antonio in Palma Campania, Giuseppe D'Antuono in S. Antonio Abate, and so on.

Furthermore, nearly all of these people were in close contact with Carmine Alfieri, who guaranteed them both a powerful electoral base and also a very solid and efficient interface for managing that system of contracts and subcontracts.[65]

So far we have focused on how criminals seek to exploit their relationship with politicians, but for criminals to gain these advantages, politicians must receive something in return. And as far as local, regional and national politicians are concerned, the vital link with Camorra gangs is their ability to deliver votes, the very lifeblood of professional politicians.

GETTING THE VOTE OUT

Given the political history of Naples and Campania over the last century and a half, it is not surprising that politics has almost lost any pretence to honesty or genuine democratic debate. The following scenario, sketched out by a senior investigator, paints an accurate but at times almost incomprehensible picture of political criminality, beginning with a *camorrista*'s approach to a voter:

> They know who is going to vote in that individual ballot box, so the *camorrista* says to himself: from family X (who has been contacted) there have to be so many votes . . .
>
> Apart from voting for this candidate because I tell you to, if you vote for Fred Smith you get something in return: there are council jobs to be given out, contracts to be awarded, certification of disabilities in order to get a pension, and so on . . .

They check up on and control the voting, but above all they control the successful candidate. The candidate then has to act so that the promises made beforehand are actually kept afterwards.

If a politician says: 'Dear voter, if you vote for me, and after my election I'm sure you voted for me, I'll get your daughter a job in this particular office' – then the person in question who has been promised this by the politician, and who knows that if he is elected he will probably keep his promise, will go out and vote for him.

At the very least he signs a blank cheque, but what choice does he have? There is this politician who has promised a job for his daughter, and another who has promised nothing.

But the politician hasn't promised these things to individual voters but to a Camorra leader . . .

The *camorrista* never worries about whether somebody is going to keep their promises because he can solve the problem. If a businessman or politician gets elected he has to keep the agreement he made previously with the *camorrista*, when he told him, 'Don't worry, you get me elected and then I'll always act in your favour.' If he then becomes mayor or chairman of a committee and doesn't keep to this agreement, the *camorrista* doesn't have many options, he's not going to wait for five years . . . as a matter of course they kill him. And there have been several local politicians eliminated in this fashion – and the background is always the same – the agreement had been broken and at a certain point they have been eliminated . . .

It is not unusual to see politicians who belong to different party factions, or even to different parties, being elected with votes controlled by one individual Camorra gang.[66]

In other words, one might argue that a politician elected with Camorra votes is more 'honest' than one elected without help from the criminals, in the sense that promises are generally kept, and expectations accurately reflect what is then achieved by the politician elected. This scenario also partly explains why right-wing and centre parties such as the neofascist MSI and the Christian Democrats have generally performed better than the left, which is far less likely to make deals with organised crime;

the left is therefore deprived of a reservoir of votes that goes to those candidates who make deals with *camorristi*.

The crucial element here is the *camorrista*'s influence within a given community. Not only does he enjoy obedience as a result of his violent reputation, he also enjoys a certain level of support as it is known that many semi-legal jobs, such as selling contraband cigarettes, have been created thanks to his illegal activities. The most important factor, however, is the common knowledge that he is the mediator with the political system in terms of public sector jobs, contracts, pensions, various services, and so on. As Galasso puts it, a relationship previously based on fear, respect, or semi-friendship is transformed

> when a person comes to ask us for favours, such as a low-class job, and it is given to them – at that moment this person swears allegiance towards whoever has done him the favour. There are other favours as well: whoever has problems with VAT, a builder's licence, the tax office, the bureaucracy, permits, and so many other problems that are part of our society.[67]

Long-term unemployment and poverty are the vital elements in explaining the strength of this system: there are simply so many people desperate for a job or some kind of financial help that they are prepared to accept arrangements of this kind.

Camorra leaders often recognise that providing electoral support is a vital component in their own self-preservation, as a *camorrista* once explained:

> This [electoral] support may not even cost a candidate anything. If he is a capable politician and the organisation sees that they can exploit his election in the future they won't ask him for a penny; on the contrary they will spend money on posters, leaflets, meetings . . . It is an investment, because once he is elected the candidate will make himself available.
>
> But if he just wants a bit of help, then he has to pay. A thousand guaranteed first-preference votes from a given area in Naples council elections cost $240,000–$320,000. The person who wants this help normally has a strong electoral base of around 10,000 votes, and those extra preference votes are intended to gain him chairmanship of a council committee . . .

The Camorra isn't interested in parties but in people. A local Camorra leader needs just a single afternoon to get a thousand votes: seven youths on mopeds who give people written or verbal 'messages'.[68]

When votes are counted many observers stand near the tellers, some of them members of Camorra gangs. Using a prearranged system, voters sometimes write their own name near that of the candidate they have voted for, or write a number somewhere which will not invalidate the ballot paper but identify the voter. Ballot papers completed in this fashion are evidence that the request made beforehand to vote for a particular candidate has been acted upon. Alternatively, pre-prepared ballot papers can be smuggled into the voting booths, scrutineers at polling stations can be intimidated, and so on.[69]

Nowadays there are many factors that link politicians to the Camorra, the major one obviously being the need for election, preferably with more votes than rival candidates within the same party. Yet there is also the persuasive power of intimidation, or blackmail as a result of previous links with *camorristi*, the need to finance party organisations or factions, or simply personal greed. Given the nature of the Camorra, it is impossible to quantify its general political influence and the extent to which it can dictate voting patterns, but it seems beyond doubt that its influence is highly significant, in that Camorra votes probably make the difference between electoral defeat and victory, either in absolute or factional terms.[70]

According to Galasso, by the early 1990s Carmine Alfieri's gang virtually held the upper hand in its relationship with politicians:

In the six-month period preceding elections there is a coming and going of all those politicians who have had links with our Camorra group, who push themselves forward in order to get votes – they therefore demonstrate their continuing availability – and at that point things turn into a market place.

At the end Alfieri and the rest of us measure up what a politician can offer us in exchange: if he is useful as a politician or if we can use him for his friendships within institutions, particularly the judiciary. In the end politician X is 'weighed' to see whether he really has that power.

It's a bit like in our own Camorra group: what Pasquale Galasso says has a certain power, but if someone else says the same thing it's hot air. Basically it's the same thing.[71]

Carmine Alfieri's cousin Francesco has made a similar appraisal during questioning by magistrates, although in a more boastful fashion: 'in admitting his own frequent meetings with politicians, often with national MPs, as he repeatedly claimed, he arrogantly declared that it was they who needed him for electoral reasons, and not he who needed them.'[72]

Galasso tells a revealing story concerning his first meeting in September 1991 with Alfredo Vito, who was then preparing his campaign for election as an MP in the April 1992 elections, in which he was elected with the highest personal vote of all Campanian candidates. Galasso was on the run at the time from a 10-year sentence for Camorra membership and extortion:

> What made me almost laugh was to hear the ideas put forward by this future MP; I heard Vito talking about fighting the Camorra, and even though I was on the run I was due to meet him in a few minutes . . . He told me that he knew all about my situation and promised to take an interest in it particularly as regards my trial at the Court of Appeal in Naples, as he had lots of friends within the judiciary . . .
>
> After the March 1992 sentence, in which all my family was acquitted of the charge of constituting a Camorra gang . . . I respected our agreement, which [here a name has been censored in the original document] reminded me of; I think that Vito drew heavily on the Camorra's vote.[73]

Vito later confirmed that he met Galasso at a DC election meeting, telling magistrates: 'It's true, I have met Pasquale Galasso. But it was a trap, your Honour, believe me – I was naively caught in a snare without being guilty of anything.'[74]

If this is the situation of politicians belonging to the traditional parties of government, for the ordinary voter it has become clear in recent years that the once reformist Socialist Party (which entered national government in the early 1960s) has also been transformed into a fully corrupt party and that the ex-communist PDS has suffered a similar, if not identical fate. In other words, the left has adapted to the right's political outlook, absorbed many of its values and methods of operation and has discarded any possibility of a different system. The *inevitability* of corruption – the predominance of political favours over rights – has become pervasive.

This lack of hope for the future, and the common knowledge of cross-party corruption, creates great difficulties in terms of effecting real changes:

> In the South elections no longer represent consensus or dissent towards whoever is administering the political system, as it does in other democracies. In the South votes represent economic hardship and are directed towards whoever controls resources; it is not consensus but necessity; you vote for them but you hate them.[75]

And it is to this area – the social, political and judicial forces outside the Christian Democrat and Socialist regime, which are normally seen as an alternative to the criminal politics of these two parties – to which we now turn.

Chapter 8

Who will stop the Camorra?

Why don't all those people do something?
Don't they get angry about anything?
Aren't they angry about the police on every street corner?
Aren't they angry about the homeless without even a cigarette?
Aren't they angry about the pissed-off unemployed hanging around?

If you're not really angry
Don't do a thing, don't bother
Do something really useful and make everyone happy
Go and sit down quietly in Parliament.

— 99 Posse

Any political party committed to maintaining the institutions of the political system within which it operates cannot but share and apply the values of that system practically.

Such a simple statement takes on a specific meaning in modern Italy: because the whole postwar system has functioned on institutional corruption, patronage and nepotism, none of the minor or potentially progressive forces, either within or outside government, can be immune to the system's values.

Destroying this ethos, and its toleration not only of illegality but also of organised crime, means overthrowing this system and replacing it with something really democratic. Yet the political debate between various parties revolves around the question of how to manage the system and maintain its intrinsic values (including its links with organised crime), not how to destroy it.

The level of corruption and illegality that has historically been tolerated within state institutions makes any notion of piecemeal reform a pipedream. It comes as no surprise, therefore, that the

Table 7: Crimes and indictments in Campania,1989

	No. of crimes	No. of indictments	No. of unprosecuted crimes
Theft	102,436	4,427	99,315
Armed robbery	8,856	935	8,274

Table 8: Crimes in Campania and number of cases in which legal proceedings had begun, 1989

	No. of crimes reported	Legal action begun	No. of unsolved crimes
Theft	119,073	2,373	116,700
Armed robbery	15,889	347	15,542
Extortion	814	145	669

toleration of illegality and organised crime shows up most sharply within the legal system, the very institution entrusted with preserving legality.

WATCHING THE DETECTIVES, 1: CRIMINAL INVESTIGATIONS

What concerns most ordinary people is whether the police and judiciary are actually managing to solve crime, and the statistics clearly show that they are not. A close analysis unmistakably shows their inefficiency. In the years 1988–90 the percentage of unsolved crimes as a whole rose from 67 per cent to 84 per cent. The total lack of investigative ability is shown by the national clear-up rate for theft: 3.2 per cent in 1988 and 2 per cent in 1990.[1] Tables 7 and 8[2] illustrate in greater detail the inability of the Campanian police in particular to make any impact on lawbreaking.

The main underlying reason for the failure of the police to apprehend lawbreakers and obtain convictions is the alienation of most ordinary people from institutions of the state, as the Head of the Naples Flying Squad once admitted:

We receive some anonymous phone calls, but nothing more
. . . it is impossible to find a witness, even one, who will point
their finger and say: it was he who came into my shop and
demanded protection money. In Naples investigations hardly
ever end in the capture of a criminal, given that nobody helps
us to find the evidence that would justify an arrest.[3]

But, as he goes on to acknowledge, the police's failure to
complete investigations successfully is the result of a long-
standing popular scepticism:

a section of the population does not love us, they do not see
the police as the incarnation of the state and the defenders of
freedom and people's rights. In those desolate areas it is
Camorra bosses and not policemen in uniform who are
figures of authority. In Forcella, whoever suffers a wrong or
an act of violence doesn't turn to the police but to the
Giuliano family.[4]

Magistrates too have on occasion acknowledged that it is mass
distrust of institutions that makes investigative work almost
impossible:

there is a lack of confidence in the judicial system and in the
state in general. There is a belief that the ordinary police and
the finance police do not function very well, that in the field
of casual employment safety regulations are ignored, that
health and safety inspectors do not exist, that public offices in
general – and the financial ones in particular – are insufficient
and inadequate.[5]

In short, it is the very inefficiency and corruption of the institutions that antagonizes people. However, hostility towards
authority and the legal system also has an economic basis, as
Table 9 illustrates.

While the unemployed charged with relatively minor crimes are
sent to jail on remand, they see senior politicians accused of
serious crimes, such as the Christian Democrat Giulio Andreotti,
who served seven terms as prime minister and now faces trial
for membership of the Mafia, and notice that he, for instance, is
still at liberty and sitting in the Upper House of Parliament. The
stark reality of Parliamentary hypocrisy emerged between 1992
and 1994: on one the hand, there were ritual denunciations of

Table 9: Economic status of those convicted in Campania, 1989[6]

	Employed	Unemployed*
Contraband	106	278
Possession of arms	178	360
Extortion	45	111
Murder	124	234
Producing, selling and buying drugs	189	493

Note: * These figures include students, housewives and pensioners.

corruption and calls for strong moves against organised crime; on the other hand, politicians of all major parties were often protected since Parliament generally voted not to lift MPs' parliamentary immunity from prosecution.

In June 1994 Silvio Berlusconi's new government tried to continue this tradition by passing a decree which facilitated the release from jail of politicians facing trial, but the decree was hastily withdrawn in the face of widespread and vocal public outrage.

All this should be compared with the situation of Italy's 'ordinary' prison population: at national level, 60 per cent of all inmates are people held on remand awaiting trial, while in Campania the number of prisoners on remand in September 1993 was 67 per cent of the total prison population.[7] In this context one will soon understand why a demonstration by wives of presumed or convicted *camorristi* outside Naples' law courts featured placards with slogans such as 'The real *"camorristi"* are the politicians. Their problems get solved, and ours?'[8]

The police occasionally admit that the real problem is not a lack of resources: 'All police forces reported that in terms of the fight against the phenomenon [of organised crime] they were adequately staffed both in a quantitative and qualitative sense; indeed sometimes they even had more staff than had been planned.'[9] What is lacking is public support for the police and the judiciary; in other words, many people see the police and the judiciary as part of a system that encourages organised crime.

And it is not surprising that people should have these views: the exposure of members of the police force with Camorra connections is a weekly, if not daily, event in Campania, and the links encompass all levels of police activity.

For example, in 1990 a *carabinieri* major was convicted of acting as a spy for Camorra gangs, informing them of both phone taps and who was under observation. For his services he received at least $12,000 and a new Fiat Regata from one gang alone.[10]

A gang of six police drug pushers was discovered on the island of Ischia in July 1993. When the houses of the six were searched, investigating policemen found rolls of banknotes, jewellery, guns with serial numbers removed, documents of stolen cars and cassettes containing compromising phone calls. The policemen forced discotheque and night club owners to buy cocaine and heroin from them rather than from conventional criminals.[11]

Several policemen were arrested in March 1994 and charged with corruption and membership of the Stolder gang. One of them specialised in medical supervision, and when a gang leader was under arrest in hospital he allegedly allowed him to hold meetings with other members of his gang. Another policeman is accused of providing an escort for a gang leader, while four members of the Flying Squad are accused of corruption. Apparently Stolder's wife paid them a retainer of $400 a week.[12]

Moreover, recent evidence suggests that there is direct collusion between top policemen and *camorristi*. The event which brings this into focus occurred at 7.36 p.m. on 10 February 1990.[13] On that day Criminalpol, the police intelligence unit, recorded a telephone conversation between Carmine Alfieri's cousin Francesco and Marzio Sepe, one of Alfieri's closest allies, in which Sepe tells Alfieri: 'We're all going to meet up at the Roccarainola restaurant in Caserta; Don Geppino and the President will be there too.' It is clear from the context and the names mentioned that Carmine Alfieri, the Camorra's most powerful boss, was to be there too. The 'President' was probably Luigi Riccio, Mayor of San Paolo Belsito, a town close to Nola, and a member of Antonio Gava's DC faction.

Many policemen prepared to leave immediately and started forming teams, but then an order came through from Matteo Cinque, head of Criminalpol from 1990 to 1991 and head of the Flying Squad from 1987 to 1989: 'Stop; we haven't got enough men, it's not even worth telling magistrates.' This puzzling attitude, given that it was a rare chance to capture the Camorra's most powerful leader, can be explained, according to the accusations now facing Cinque, 'by a reluctance to reveal in sensational fashion the links between the Nola Camorra and some corrupt local politicians who belonged to the same party and faction as Antonio Gava, at the time Minister of the Interior'.

Three days later police found out about another meeting due to be held between Francesco Alfieri and local DC politicians belonging to Gava's faction. The area was studied, and police were moved into the area, but nobody arrived at the meeting. The conclusion of the investigating magistrate is that 'a tip-off was made, in all probability from within the ranks of Criminalpol'.

It may not be the case, however, that the tip-off came from such a high level, as recent evidence has pointed to Alfieri's gang also having created a lower level of police informers. A *carabinieri* marshal in Pomigliano received $4,000 a month for the information he passed on to the gang, while two other *carabinieri* in Pomigliano and a policeman in Nola divided up a total monthly payment of $8,000.[14]

An event similar to those above is likely to occur in Campania at least on a weekly basis: in essence the very people entrusted with stamping out illegality are often breaking the law themselves, even at the highest level.

WATCHING THE DETECTIVES, 2: JUDGING THE JUDGES

There is a fundamental difference between the legal systems of Anglo-Saxon and Continental European countries in the way they investigate crimes and obtain prosecutions. In Italy, although the police deal directly with issues of public order and the documenting and assessment of crimes reported, for major investigations they work largely under the direction of the judiciary.

Historically there have been many examples of low-level police corruption and collusion with criminals, but it is only in the 1990s that the same pattern has been revealed at the level of the judiciary. By late 1993 there were twenty magistrates in Campania facing either criminal charges or internal disciplinary procedures, and an examination of the alleged activities of just two magistrates gives an indication of the extent to which collusion with the Camorra appears to have pervaded the judicial system.

The judge facing the most serious charges is Alfonso Lamberti, currently held in jail on charges of criminal association, corruption, extortion and possession of explosives.

It is thought that his systematic involvement with the Camorra came about as a result of personal tragedy: the murder of his 12-year-old daughter Simonetta in 1989. After that he earned the nickname 'handcuffs' at the Salerno court where he was based for the frequency with which he issued arrest warrants, although it is widely believed that these measures were almost exclusively directed against the gang he believed was responsible for his daughter's death. Later, he apparently asked Alfieri's gang to murder the presumed killer of his daughter and celebrated his death with a champagne meal with Alfieri.[15]

However, it is his period as president of the inspection branch of the court of Naples (which deals with the supervision of convicted and remand prisoners) that has given rise to greater concern. It is presumed that he granted favours to Camorra prisoners – the inspection branch also has powers to revoke 'internal exile' in towns far away from Naples and Campania – and that he ordered the restitution of goods seized by police as illicit gains.[16] Lamberti is also accused of making deals with Giorgio Nocaro's gang in Ponticelli, some of whose members allegedly came to see him with an offer of $40,000 for releasing goods that had been seized. Lamberti is said to have replied, 'Either $120,000 or nothing; here things are split three ways'. Whatever the truth of such accusations, what is beyond doubt is that Lamberti signed an order in November 1988 for the release of the Nocaro gang's assets.[17]

Another allegation concerns his intervention on behalf of two men whose assets had been seized as a result of various investigations. He managed to get both the seizure and the house arrest that went with it reversed during an appeal trial. It appears that this manoeuvre, started at Alfieri's instigation, was rewarded with $120,000 and two gold Rolex watches.[18] During his deposition to the Anti-Mafia Commission Pasquale Galasso described the judge in the following terms: 'Lamberti was another magistrate in our hands. We had a direct link to Lamberti, we could meet him whenever we wanted, and I remember that more than once he, Alfieri, Lamberti's cousin and I all had meetings.'[19]

Armando Cono Lancuba is facing similar charges, particularly concerning his role as an appeal court judge who passed a series of 'light sentences'. One notable case was the appeal trial over the August 1984 Torre Annunziata massacre, the worst ever gangland murder in Italy.

In the first instance Carmine Alfieri and others had been convicted of having organised the murders and given life sentences.[20] Yet on appeal the same people were acquitted, and without entering into detailed arguments concerning evidence, this was viewed at the time as a particularly surprising decision, given Alfieri's criminal record.[21] This is how Pasquale Galasso describes the help both he and Carmine Alfieri received from Cono Lancuba: 'on appeal [Carmine] was acquitted thanks to the intervention, once again, of some politicians, whose interests were taken care of by Lancuba. He advised us on how to bring our influence to bear and how to present our written evidence.'[22]

This pattern of first conviction and then acquittal or commutation on appeal is perhaps the most worrying aspect of such 'light' sentences or acquittals. Harsh sentences at the main trial create the perception in the public's mind that criminals are being convicted and put behind bars. Once public interest wanes and a few years pass, the sentences are then either drastically reduced or simply overturned on appeal. Even though the release of a notorious criminal may cause disquiet in some quarters, the fact that criminals have been in jail for a few years leads most people to believe that they are no longer dangerous.

Cono Lancuba was also the appeal court judge who decided to return to Pasquale Galasso $24 million worth of assets that had previously been impounded with the intention of permanent confiscation. Apart from these cases and several charges of corruption, Cono Lancuba is also accused of being Alfieri's 'judicial counsellor' as well as of Camorra membership. As to his reward for his services, it has been established that at the very least he was allowed to stay rent-free in a luxury flat in Positano every summer and was also given fur coats as gifts for his wife.[23] In addition, Alfieri bought him a legal office in central Naples.[24]

Prior to these events he had been criticised for many of his activities, such as the fact that he was one of the magistrates employed as inspectors of building sites following the 1980 earthquake. And for many years he was in charge of perhaps the most vital and delicate office in the Naples law courts: the declarations office.[25] It is here that accusations and tip-offs are made and police, *carabinieri* and finance police reports are sent. All information is then filtered and assessed, and passed on to the Federal Prosecutor for a decision.

Cono Lancuba was also Deputy Federal Prosecutor during the investigations concerning the Cirillo affair and is now thought to have tried to cover up the fact that the Christian Democrats negotiated with Raffaele Cutolo. Amongst his alleged manoeuvres in this context were: privately advising witnesses not to mention certain facts, rewriting certain passages of an indictment written by another magistrate and forging a letter supposedly written by Judge Carlo Alemi.[26]

Supergrass Salvatore Migliorino has stated that, when he was facing a trial for extortion at the Torre Annunziata fish market, once he paid $55,000 to a go-between who took the money to Cono Lancuba, 'the trial went really well – it was never spoken about again' – i.e. all charges were dropped.[27]

However, this is not to say that all judges are corrupt and linked to the Camorra, far from it. Investigating magistrates are probably the people most at risk from assassination, they work in inadequate conditions and in the majority of cases are dedicated to their job. The point is that, while a majority might well be honest, a powerful minority are not, and these dishonest ones have even more powerful political friends.

Furthermore, senior judges are also senior members of the Italian state. As a group they have for decades turned a blind eye to the rampant corruption and bribery among politicians and the business community, as well as to politicians' links with organised crime. In the final analysis they are an integral part of that system, and it is in their own interests to defend it. In other words, magistrates are part of a ruling class, and even Pasquale Galasso, who was outside this grouping, was able to identify the common positions they shared:

> at the bottom of it all, there is a strong sense of friendship between Gava and Lancuba, or Gava, Scotti and Lancuba, or Gava, Scotti, Lancuba and Bargi and others; it was a bit of a magic circle. Over time, between 1986 and 87, I then found

out that other people were part of this group: journalists, representatives of various institutions.[28]

As to the judiciary's relations with politicians, it is the widespread toleration and practice of illegality by politicians themselves that leads the judiciary to be selective in the application of the law, as any campaign for consistent judicial values would entail a head-on collision with the judiciary's political overseers. Consequently the administration of justice, too, is far from equal: an unemployed seller of contraband cigarettes is far more likely to spend time in jail than a gang leader accused of murder or drug trafficking.

But as has been the case with politicians defending their interests as a group when faced with requests to remove parliamentary immunity, so too will the judiciary defend its own power and privilege. During his term as Naples' federal prosecutor, Alfredo Sant'Elia once explained why he asked a deputy prosecutor to reduce the seven-year sentence demanded for a regional councillor facing charges of extortion. Sant'Elia began by telling his subordinate that the accused was

> a person of senior social extraction, so I gave him the same explanation I normally gave when I was at the bench myself. The physical and moral suffering which is inflicted on a prisoner of a higher social extraction is far greater than that of a common prisoner or a common criminal, because I believe that if any of us were to be so unlucky as to end up in Regina Coeli or Poggioreale, our suffering would be totally different from that endured by somebody born in the backstreets of Trastevere or Via Toledo.[29]

Not surprisingly, even the most senior members of the judiciary have now been forced to admit the real extent of problems. The current federal prosecutor, Agostino Cordova, is very pessimistic about cleaning things up, as he believes that, while in the *Tangentopoli* scandals of the North it was 'only' the top levels of power which were corrupt, in the South there is structural corruption as well as individual corruption at the highest level.

If Cordova, the government's senior legal representative in Naples, can publicly outline the area under his jurisdiction in the following terms, then the idea of the system reforming itself appears naive in the extreme:

a territory totally penetrated by the Camorra and political-administrative poisoning, which implies above all – and this is an aspect that has been completely ignored – the poisoning of the bureaucracy. The various individuals under investigation, who have managed senior government responsibilities, have placed their followers throughout all structures of the state and public bodies; these people have remained at their posts as nobody has identified them. If these polluted structures remain intact it is an illusion to believe that the situation will change, as the old perverted system will remain along with the same secret power groups, but with different faces.[30]

The end of Christian Democrat rule and the election of the Berlusconi government have done nothing to change his pessimistic outlook:

the Merloni law, which would have guaranteed transparency as regards public sector contracts, has been suspended. Accusations against supergrasses need to be added to this, but with the use of an appropriate level of caution – they have nevertheless been very important in our investigations. Then there have been the arguments over article 41a, a law that puts the most dangerous jailed Mafiosi in strict isolation.[31]

This is why the slogan of the left-wing council elected in Naples in late 1993, 'legality and efficiency', is likely to prove hollow; the more powerful forces in favour of managed illegality are almost certain to knock it off course.

THE FAILURE OF THE PCI/PDS[32]

It is important to examine the recent history of the Neapolitan communists because, throughout the period of the Italian 'First Republic' – the Christian-Democrat-dominated governments of 1945–94 – they were, and still remain, the strongest opposition force.

In November 1993 they regained control of Naples city council after ten years in opposition, electing Antonio Bassolino as mayor. They previously ran the council, under the leadership of Maurizio Valenzi, in the crucial years of 1975–83, the period of massive Camorra expansion due to contraband cigarettes, drugs and earthquake reconstruction contracts.

The history of Valenzi's council, whose election saw dancing in the streets, is a useful illustration of the futility of trying to effect lasting change through the existing system. At the heart of the experience of this administration, likely to be repeated under Bassolino, is a fatal flaw: a keen willingness to govern with elements who view corruption, clientelism and links with *camorristi* as the most normal things in the world.

The power of the forces that Valenzi now recognises he had to contend with during the earthquake reconstruction period is staggering:

> After the earthquake, organised crime began finding political friends in the opposition, in the construction business, in the city's infrastructure. With their political friends, they held up the money for the reconstruction until after the election of 1983, so we were seen to fail, and they to succeed.
>
> Contracts would disappear up north and come back as subcontracts to *camorristi*. We realised that we had no real control.
>
> Now, they simply pick candidates off the lists; they offer to get them votes in return for contracts and favours. And it's not just the politicians – it works right across the system. There is a trial, so they need lawyers. You go in a lawyer, you come out a *camorrista*.[33]

Most of the period of the Valenzi council coincided with the PCI's 'historic compromise' with the Christian Democrats, a policy which led to profound demoralisation within the party and eventually to significant levels of corruption.[34] Although the PCI never governed directly with the DC in Naples, the whole party was nevertheless orientated towards the maximum accommodation possible.

One of the immediate consequences of the historic compromise was a haemorrhage in party membership: in the period from 1976 to 1981 the PCI lost 33,825 members in the South (i.e. total southern membership fell from 372,595 to 338,760, a 10 per cent fall in five years), with the highest regional losses occurring in Puglia, Sicily and Calabria.[35] Interestingly enough, Achille Occhetto, until June 1994 leader of the PDS, had responsibility for the South at that time.

Consequently, at their February 1982 southern conference, party leader Enrico Berlinguer, as well as Occhetto, called for the PCI to become a 'party of struggle' and to forget about becoming a 'party of government'. But despite the authority of their leadership

> Berlinguer's strategy, and the strategy of most of the party's national leadership, was not at all popular amongst some sectors of the PCI; this was particularly so amongst party members active in local administration in the South. Berlinguer and Occhetto were reproached for proposing 'a far too rigid political orientation, exclusively based upon struggle and not upon proposals for government'.[36]

Communists who, after such a long time in opposition, had finally tasted power were unwilling to break comfortable working alliances and risk their position over a serious political clash with the Christian Democrats. And the Neapolitan communists, whose vote had held up better than the communist vote in most other areas in the South, were amongst the strongest critics of Berlinguer's new strategy.

In other words, communist militants had given in to the temptations of power and privilege. As the years progressed, some senior communists were gradually sucked deeper and deeper into the shady and corrupt world inhabited by Christian Democrats and Socialists, and significant numbers ended their political careers sharing their values.

Antonio Pastore, the PCI's administrative secretary in Naples from 1975 to 1991, was arrested in April 1993 and is currently facing charges of having solicited and obtained bi-monthly bribes for the party from companies building the new Naples underground line. The agreement, which was to benefit all major parties, appears to have been made prior to 1980, even before the Camorra's systematic rise to power – at the very time when 'the party of clean hands', the PCI, was controlling the city council. Apparently $720,000 per year were paid to the main parties: the DC and PSI divided up 40 per cent, while the PCI took 40 per cent on its own.[37] For the PCI this meant $288,000 per year.

Both Pastore and Berardo Impegno – for most of the 1980s a senior councillor within the communist opposition group on the city council and provincial party secretary – who apparently acted in tandem, are accused of taking a kickback of $200,000 for building work related to the 1990 World Cup. Part of the agreement between the PCI and companies hoping to win construction contracts was that communist councillors guaranteed their appearance in council meetings in order to make them quorate. In other words, they were being paid appearance money, both in the sense of their physical presence and their apparent opposition to certain decisions.[38]

Impegno also appears to have been the leader of a group of PCI councillors and party bureaucrats who took $400,000 for themselves between 1988 and 1992, as a result of the plan to privatise rubbish collection outlined in the previous chapter. The money was given in order to guarantee a 'soft' opposition to privatisation when it was debated in the council and in the appropriate committee.[39]

Impegno, now in jail as a result of his parliamentary immunity being removed following the March 1994 elections, is also accused of taking an $80,000 bribe in 1991 from a major builder, who needed the full approval of Naples city council for the construction of 140 houses at Soccavo worth $18.4 million. The Christian Democrat deputy mayor allegedly told the builder: 'My dear fellow, you either give them something or they will hold up construction until you die.' The investigating magistrate eloquently wrote in his indictment:

> This matter testifies to the enslavement of public administration to corrupt politicians, and shows how both differences and battles between political parties, and the disputes between the ruling group and the opposition, are merely a facade which hypocritically masks premeditated decisions and precise agreements over the division of illegal gains.[40]

This particular payment was only one in a series which were paid to four other major parties.

There are many other senior figures of the PDS who have either been convicted or are facing serious charges. The point here is not to assign individual blame but to illustrate the atmosphere within the party. None of these individuals could have made these decisions without many other senior party members being aware of their actions. Ultimately it is a collective and not an individual issue.

Essentially, the difference between PCI/PDS and Christian

Democrat leaders is one of the degree of power. As the PCI/PDS has been locked out of the national power system, and has therefore always been dependent on national finance for its local administrations, it has controlled far fewer resources and so had far fewer opportunities to engage in illegality and acts of corruption. Yet its track record both in local and national politics can only suggest that greater power will lead to greater corruption, including closer links with the Camorra.

Despite these traumatic experiences, the PDS seems destined to repeat many of the contradictions of the historic compromise period. This tendency was brought into focus again in April 1994, when the majority of the PDS suddenly cobbled together a new regional government with members of the ex-DC, so as to form a ruling group of 33 councillors out of 60, in which ex-DC councillors have the majority.

The surprising thing about such a move is that five months earlier a left-wing alliance had been formed at the city council, and to create this new regional ruling group the majority of the PDS had to break with the rest of the left. The crucial political fact is that this ruling group was only elected thanks to ten ex-DC councillors who are under investigation for a variety of crimes.[41] It was also a petty deal: when it was elected, the council only had another ten months to run. And despite the fact that the PDS already enjoys a clear majority on the city council, there have also been suggestions to enlarge the ruling group to include former Christian Democrats.[42]

Until the mid-1970s the PCI could claim with justification that it was 'the party of clean hands', and it often engaged in serious opposition against the Christian Democrat system of government. Today the PDS has lost both of these qualities, and indeed is prepared to salvage the dregs of the Christian Democrats, responsible for so much corruption and links with the Camorra, thereby giving them a new lease of life. Considering the party's degeneration over the last twenty years, it is not surprising that the average age of PDS members is very high nowadays, namely over 60, and that those under 25 represent just 3 per cent of the Naples membership.[43]

The PDS also has had its fair share of councils disbanded for presumed Camorra infiltration: the Pagani council had a PDS mayor, while PDS councillors were part of the ruling group in the disbanded councils of Ercolano, Nocera and Sessa Aurunca.[44]

Even Pasquale Galasso, in his small home town of Poggiomarino, could notice a certain social ambivalence of supposedly 'communist' councillors: 'They are good professional people who I have always admired. I used to go to university with some of them.'[45]

However, this is not to say that the PDS is the same as all the other major parties, far from it. The PCI/PDS has clearly been distinct as regards the low proportion of cases in which its members have been accused of links with the Camorra. Although all politicians run the risk of intimidation, the PDS is the only party to be harassed by the Camorra when it engages in public activities. Intimidation was particularly noticeable during the 1992 election campaign: the PDS branch in Mariglianella was destroyed, the walls of the Pozzuoli branch were covered with threatening graffiti and the pasting up of election posters was often hampered; a PDS meeting at Casal di Principe near Aversa was also disrupted by the father of a known Camorra leader and several of his associates, who told those present to 'talk about yourselves and not about us', and warned them, 'it would be better for you if you minded your own business'.[46]

Nevertheless, the PDS leadership remains thoroughly committed to defending existing institutions and power blocs, or in other words, a ruling class which has always had close links with the Camorra: from ordinary police officers to senior officials, from court ushers to senior judges, from council clerks to government ministers and from small businesses to international conglomerates, the PDS essentially wants to maintain the current system of power.

The appointment of new managers of council utilities is a useful illustration of the intention of the new PDS council in Naples to follow conventional economic policy. The new manager of the council-owned milk board is a former bank manager, while the municipally owned bus and train fleet will be managed by an economics professor.[47] Following a familiar script of left-wing parties enacting policies normally associated with the right, Mayor Bassolino's first act was to write to his workforce demanding 'a profound change in terms of working methods, efficiency and productivity'. And as part of financial restrictions on the new council, Bassolino is planning to place in 'external mobility' – a euphemism for sacking – 1,729 council workers, 9 per cent of the total workforce.[48]

But the PDS rank and file, as well as their many working-class supporters, have interests diametrically opposed to a system dominated by the ruling class and the Camorra: it is in their interests to destroy the present system and create a new one based on political and economic equality.

Some people may say this is a dream, yet it is both a necessary and a feasible dream, and infinitely preferable to the very real nightmare that most people have experienced in Naples and Campania throughout this century. We shall therefore briefly examine one specific period of mass resistance and make some more general observations.

MASS·RESISTANCE

The case for the importance of mass resistance to the Camorra relies on two main arguments: the first is that it is the most efficient method to counter Camorra intimidation. While it is easy to threaten individuals, the continued mass harassment or general social isolation of even low-level Camorra activities are forms of resistance on which Camorra gangs cannot bring direct pressure to bear. Strike action against Camorra infiltration of a workplace, or local harassment of drug pushers or even contraband cigarette sellers, would be concrete steps not only towards combating the Camorra, but crucially towards socially isolating Camorra activity.

The second argument is broader but strategically linked to the first: it is ordinary people who suffer most from the dominance of the Camorra, and who therefore have the greatest interest in establishing a new political system in which organised crime is not supported by state institutions. Indeed, ordinary people have been systematically deceived by those institutions, which have historically perpetuated a socioeconomic environment of mass unemployment, illegality and violence. In more than a hundred years, no attempts at 'reform' have substantially resolved the problems afflicting Naples and Campania. None of the major political parties has been prepared to overthrow the existing system of capitalism, the only way in which the dominance of illegality and criminality can be brought to an end.

Yet, despite frequent racist stereotyping, Campania also has a long and impressive history of mass movements against both the existing political system and organised crime in particular.

Perhaps the most important period was that of the early 1980s, when it became clear that the Camorra was attempting to gain control of reconstruction contracts and gain influence over many local councils. In late 1982 groups of students began to organise systematic protests against the Camorra: in early November several dozen held a demonstration during a funeral at Acerra, and two weeks later 5,000 marched in Ottaviano – the home town of Raffaele Cutolo – then at the height of his power.

On 24 November another 5,000 students took to the streets in Torre del Greco, this time supported by trade unionists and a delegation of students from Palermo; shops also closed as a sign of solidarity. A few miles to the north, at Afragola, hundreds of students crowded into a library to debate how to fight the Camorra.[49]

Three days later another demonstration of 5,000, mainly made up of students but also including workers, was organised by women's committees in Castellammare.[50] Two weeks later students, teachers and other workers marched from Nocera to Pagani, while on the other side of Vesuvius two simultaneous marches were organised, one from Afragola and one from a factory threatened with closure at Casavatore, which met up at Casoria in a rally of 10,000. In a particularly important development, building unions organised a simultaneous half-day strike in the same area against Camorra infiltration of sites engaged in earthquake reconstruction work.[51]

The following week Cutolo's home town of Ottaviano witnessed a second, larger demonstration of students and workers, whose main demand was 'jobs to beat the Camorra'.[52]

After Christmas, activity moved to Naples, where shopowners organised a two-day strike against Camorra protection rackets, an action which turned the city into a ghost town.[53] The high point of this whole campaign occurred two weeks later, with a massive national demonstration of at least 100,000 in Naples, backed up by a two-hour general strike. The march was a mile and a half long, took 90 minutes to pass and included significant delegations from all the Italian regions as well as numerous contingents of blue- and white-collar workers, unemployed and women's organisations.[54]

The demands raised by this movement consisted of perfectly feasible and appropriate proposals, and revealed an incisive political understanding; for example, one of the banners carried on the demonstration read: 'The Cirillo affair taught us that the Mafia and the Camorra are inside the state.' This slogan summed up the contradiction that remains at the heart of any strategy aimed at defeating the Camorra: the very institutions called upon to defeat organised crime both tolerate and encourage it.

This is why such an impressive movement – only one brief example of the mass working-class actions that frequently engulf Campania,[55] and which contradict the stereotyed image of Neapolitans as passive and resigned to the Camorra – eventually met with defeat. The politicians called upon to take action, indeed some of the very politicians who received a delegation from the February 1983 demonstration, were discovered ten years later to have been in league with the Camorra even then.

This is not to say that demands should not be made of the institutions and leading politicians; rather, the duplicity and resistance of these forces should be taken into account in creating a long-term strategy. A radically different approach is needed to combat the Camorra, one which is outlined in greater detail in the concluding chapter.

Conclusion

'Ha dda passà 'a nuttata'[1]

Words are easy, words are cheap.

— Yothu Yindi

THE 'POLITICAL CAMORRA': THE BIRTH OF A NEW CAMPANIAN MAFIA?

We have already noted the emergence of three distinct forms of modern Camorra: Raffaele Cutolo's 'mass Camorra', Lorenzo Nuvoletta's 'business Camorra' and Carmine Alfieri's 'political Camorra'.

The most recent form of Camorra is 'political' in the sense that the Alfieri gang's main source of profits were probably public sector contracts awarded by politicians, rather than the activities, such as drug trafficking, construction work, extortion and trade in contraband cigarettes, favoured by Cutolo and Nuvoletta.

However, the 'political' form of Camorra has also been innovatory in its attempt to forge a federation between gangs in order to overcome the mutual suspicion and bloodletting which has normally prevailed.

The attempt to create greater agreement between gangs began in the mid-1980s, when the 'maxi-blitzes' of 1983–84 were a thing of the past, and when Cutolo's NCO had clearly been destroyed. The fact that by then most reconstruction contracts had been assigned also led to a reduction in friction.

The end of the Bardellino–Nuvoletta war, which had culminated in the Torre Annunziata massacre of August 1984, ushered in a few years of relative peace. But following the slaughter of Gionta's gang in Torre Annunziata, and the murder of Ciro Nuvoletta two months earlier, the balance of power was shifting increasingly in favour of Carmine Alfieri.

Alfieri wanted to set up a unitary vertical structure within Campania to replace the traditional unregulated 'horizontal' system in which no one gang ever attempts to give orders to the others. However, he had learnt from Cutolo not to try to impose an oppressive monolithic structure, and it seems that he first floated the idea at a summit meeting in Mario Iovine's luxury hotel just outside Nice; those taking part were Gennaro Licciardi, Nunzio De Falco and Iovine.

Gennaro Licciardi was the key player in this strategy, as within the city of Naples he had built up respect and notoriety over the years for his ability to act as a mediator between various gangs.[2] While Alfieri's gang dominated the area around Nola, the major gangs within Naples at this time were led by Gennaro Licciardi, by Edoardo Contini in the Arenaccia, the Giulianos in Forcella and by the Lo Russos in Secondigliano. However, the dividing lines between territories were sometimes quite fluid, and control of some spheres of operation extended far beyond a particular gang's area; furthermore, gangs would often cooperate on operations that required large amounts of capital or human resources. Nevertheless, the plan was that Licciardi would control Naples and Alfieri the Provinces.[3]

It is beyond doubt that Alfieri's grouping was the dominant element in this tentative alliance. It is clear that between 1984 and 1989 he managed – through a toleration of local, lower-level autonomy – to gain control of a huge area surrounding Vesuvius. It ran from his home town of Nola in the north-east to San Sebastiano in the north-west, down to Castellammare di Stabia in the south-west and Pagani in the south-east.[4] The various local gangs in this alliance included Michele D'Alessandro's in Castellammare, Mario Fabbrocino's gang based in San Giuseppe Vesuviano and the surrounding towns, the Galassos in Poggiomarino and the Nuvolettas from Marano.

The relative calm of the late 1980s suggests that a higher degree of agreement between gangs had been achieved. A key element in this coordinated strategy was to keep Camorra activity out of the public eye. For example, instead of bombing building sites as an intimidatory warning, two people would be sent on a scooter to fire warning shots at workers; this was perhaps even more frightening than an overnight bombing, but did not normally lead to media attention. One reason for the decrease in the murder rate was that the number of kneecappings rose to over 200 in the Province of Naples alone during 1988,[5] indicating a deliberate policy of not drawing attention to Camorra activity and rivalry.

Pasquale Galasso has confirmed this strategy, but has also revealed different levels of 'Camorra':

> Things were getting out of hand, so people thought it would be useful to create a coalition of the most violent groups, the ones which were more rooted in local areas, so that all those little vendettas and wars could be brought to an end and peace could be established. This is convenient for the more powerful Camorra groups given their linkages and agreements with other institutional and political circles . . .
>
> When there's no war, when nothing's happening, you can work peacefully. Certain relationships can be made stronger, and all our movements take place smoothly, the police have no need to harass us and we aren't distracted by worries.[6]

The success of this strategy was such that by 1990 investigators had reached the conclusion that Alfieri had created

> a kind of anti-state, made up of its own laws and regulations, such as to guarantee for the organisation the uncontested use of typical criminal activities and other activities associated with Mafia methods. Furthermore, all of this took place mainly through the conditioning of, and often the open complicity of, public administrators and officials.[7]

However, the plan soon began to unravel for a variety of reasons, the most immediate being the revelations of a number of supergrasses, beginning with the professional killer Pasquale Frajese in March 1990. It was these supergrasses who initially destroyed Alfieri's grand design, in that between 1991 and 1992 most major Camorra gang leaders were captured by the police: Carmine Alfieri, Michele D'Alessandro, Valentino Gionta, Gennaro Licciardi, Ciro Mariano and Lorenzo Nuvoletta. It would appear that they were captured largely as a result of tip-offs, although there was also an element of investigative skill in some cases.

The instability caused by these arrests led to a number of notable massacres during 1992: five people were killed in Acerra on May Day, another five in Secondigliano seventeen days later, with another four murders in Mugnano, near Marano, in September.

With the divisions clearly illustrated by these massacres, the growing number of supergrasses and the arrest of the Camorra's top leaders, the judiciary began to make significant progress in preventing the formation of a federal Camorra. This was revealed in October 1992, when eight arrest warrants were issued with the accusation that a 'New Campanian Mafia' (NCM) had been created. Gennaro Licciardi was one of those charged; and one of the specific accusations was that the NCM 'cupola', or high committee of various gang leaders, had taken a collective decision upon a couple of murders in May 1990.[8]

Another key reason for the collapse of this more federal structure was widespread political instability within Italy. The fall of the Berlin Wall in 1989 had removed the main justification for keeping the PCI out of government, which in turn led to a loss of credibility for the Christian Democrats. The stability and permanence of the old political system were cast into doubt, and so the relations between politicians and *camorristi* entered a state of flux, which still seems to prevail today. The instability deepened in 1992 with the beginning of the *Tangentopoli* scandal in Milan, and the old Christian Democrat order was finally overturned in the March 1994 elections.

In assessing why Carmine Alfieri was unable to create a stable federation of Camorra gangs before his arrest in 1992, one must not underestimate the underlying general importance of the social and political structure of Campania. As the American academic James Walston has argued, while in the provincial towns 'gangsters might control the local council . . . in the city and region as a whole there is too great a heterogeneity for one social group to gain control'.[9] And he adds: 'Neapolitan society is too fragmented, as indeed one would expect a city of two million people to be, to allow a single figure (or group) to control the whole or even a fractional part of the whole.'[10]

However, there are also subjective reasons for the lack of a unified structure and a single leader, as a senior investigator has argued:

the reality of the Camorra is that there has never been one, and probably there could never be one ... for a certain period this was the dream of Raffaele Cutolo, i.e. becoming the undisputed leader of the entire Camorra, but his evil dream was shattered by the New Family alliance ...

If we were to define criminal organisations as made up of logical, rational and sensible people – people who are building for the future – and who are therefore able to give something up to enable them to create this future, then we would never have had outrageous actions that have led to either the defeat or the weakening of criminal organisations.

For example, we wouldn't have seen Judge Falcone killed, or Borsellino, because they were very negative moments for the Mafia. We wouldn't have had the massacre of Torre Annunziata or many of the other massacres perpetrated in Naples, which have definitely been negative moments for them.[11]

None of these limits on greater Camorra unity, not to mention possibly the most important one of all – the tradition of mistrust and independence which has historically characterised Camorra gangs – makes the sum total of Camorra gangs any less dangerous. Compared with the Mafia, the Camorra has more of a 'horizontal' than a 'vertical' structure, so individual gangs act by and large independently of one another. On the whole, this makes the Camorra more resilient when top leaders are arrested, or when a gang war erupts. In Pasquale Galasso's words, 'Campania can get even worse because you could cut into a Camorra group, but another ten could emerge from it.'[12]

This tendency is described in greater detail by the Anti-Mafia Commission:

The Mafia is separated from society; its hierarchical structure makes it an organisation that immerses itself in social life without being part of it.

On the contrary, the Camorra, with over a hundred gangs, its speedy substitution of leaders and rapid processes of disintegration and reconstitution, its use of social desperation, is capable of reproducing itself wherever an illegal avenue gives a young person the impression of being able to build a future.

For the great number of the young and very young who

can be manoeuvred by Camorra bosses, legality has never represented either dignity or a future. They have never managed to identify with legality; on the contrary, all they have seen is the crisis of institutions which should have preserved, defended and administered legality.[13]

The current uncertainty does not allow for categorical predictions about the future strength of the Camorra. The arrest in 1991–92 of the gang leaders who had become dominant during the 1980s has led many to believe that the Camorra is facing defeat, but such judgements are premature. Another reason for optimism is that the current high number of supergrasses will inflict severe blows on the major Camorra gangs. Furthermore, Gennaro Licciardi, Lorenzo Nuvoletta and Michele Zaza all died in mid-1994. Although these developments are undoubtedly important, the conditions which gave rise to the Camorra are just as strong now as when Alfieri, Cutolo and the Nuvolettas began their rise in the 1970s.

The level of unemployment, the basic economic condition from which criminal activities arise, is if anything worse than the 1970s. In January 1994 the national unemployment rate was 11.3 per cent; but this average masks very wide regional variations: 7.2 per cent in the North and 18.8 per cent in the South. In Campania the rate was even higher: the figure of 20.9 per cent, a 2 per cent rise during 1993, was the highest level ever recorded.[14] Optimists also tend to overlook the fact that the phenomenon of supergrasses represents nothing new in the Camorra's recent history.[15]

Pasquale Galasso's decision to collaborate with investigators in mid-1992, followed by Umberto Ammaturo's in 1993 and Carmine Alfieri's in early 1994, seemed to indicate a downward trend in the Camorra's power. But since the economic conditions which favour the Camorra remain largely unchanged, an upward trend may well follow. The crucial problem is that the economic and social conditions which enable Camorra gangs to reproduce themselves are not being changed to any significant extent. An ex-*camorrista* from an area where, he estimates, 90 per cent of the population earn their living illegally noted: 'It's enough that these 90 per cent are put into a different situation – and this is what they really want – they want legality, they want to lead a normal life, to go off to work in the morning and not have anything to do with guns, violence or prison.'[16]

Indeed, Silvio Berlusconi's 'new' government is travelling a very old and familiar road. Within a few weeks of its election in March 1994 the 'Merloni law' was cancelled, a law which placed stricter controls on the awarding of public sector contracts, most of which had in any case been blocked for the previous two years due to judicial investigations. In September an amnesty on illegal building was announced, a key area of criminal investment; indeed, it is a market estimated to have seen $44 billion of investment in the South since 1985, 75 per cent of the national total.[17] Furthermore, the massive cuts in public sector spending currently planned by the Berlusconi government will hit the South disproportionately hard and thereby perpetuate the conditions which lead to the regeneration of organised crime.

Even though Galasso's revelations have led to the arrest and incrimination of dozens of senior politicians, magistrates and bureaucrats, the Camorra goes on. New leaders such as Marzio Sepe or Giuseppe Autorino may be taking over Alfieri's empire, or alternatively he may be succeeded by longer established bosses such as Mario Fabbrocino.

Although the current political uncertainty makes any accurate predictions about the future of the Camorra impossible, as a guide for the future it is useful to examine why so many strategies have failed to prevent its resurgence in the past.

FAILED ECONOMIC ATTEMPTS TO CURB THE CAMORRA IN THE PAST

As we have seen in Chapter 1, during a period of significant industrialisation in the early part of this century, and the subsequent growth of a working class, the Camorra entered into decline. In other words, real economic development can make a difference in reducing the appeal of criminal activities.

However, following the hiatus of the interwar Fascist period, the major postwar innovation throughout the South was the establishment of the Southern Development Fund in the early 1950s. In the short term this was aimed at alleviating the immediate economic hardships the southern population had to endure, and over the long term, at closing the huge economic gap between the North and the South.

By the 1960s it had become clear that the targets which had been set were not being reached, and it was hoped that a law passed in 1971 – which restructured the financing of the Fund through a new policy of 'intervention through projects' – would overcome many of the problems. Some of the new proposals involved plans to end pollution in the Bay of Naples, intensive meat production and better internal communications within Campania. In retrospect it can be seen that the improved communications and meat production achieved have also led to the reinforcement of political clientelism and the growth of the Camorra, and the Bay of Naples remains as polluted as ever.

By the 1980s the whole Fund had become a public scandal as it was clear that it had achieved very few of its objectives, and it was therefore wound up. It is estimated that the almost inconceivable figure of $320 billion has been spent on fixed capital investment in the South over a forty-year period, with the money mainly set aside for public works programmes, infrastructure and industry.[18] Yet more than anything else this expenditure has reinforced regional differences and bolstered a corrupt political system, the exact opposite of what its original supporters had intended.

Judge Giovanni Falcone also noted the real consequences of major public spending in the South:

> We have reached the point where any economic intervention on the part of the state only runs the risk of offering the Mafia further opportunities for speculation, and of widening the economic gap between North and South. The same is true of State subsidies . . .
>
> It is all too clear that investment initiatives are driven by politically motivated choices with short-term, typically pre-electoral aims, whose horizons stretch only a few months or weeks ahead: for the political parties, the South is nothing more than a reservoir of votes.[19]

The same tendency can be seen again in two further specific events: following an outbreak of cholera in Naples in 1973, millions were spent on water and sewage plants, yet once again the sea remained as polluted as ever. More recently there has been the scandal of the billions that disappeared from earthquake reconstruction funds during the 1980s. Of the $40 billion spent on earthquake reconstruction, an estimated $20 billion went to 'create an entirely new social class of millionaires in the region', $6.4 billion went 'straight into the pockets of the Camorra' and

$4 billion went to politicians in bribes. The remaining $9.6 billion, i.e. a mere 24 per cent of the total amount, were actually spent on people's needs.[20]

However, it would be a mistake to respond to all this by accepting one of the key economic slogans of the political right in Britain and the US – 'you can't solve problems by throwing money at them'. The real problem in Campania and the rest of the South has never been that money was simply thrown into the wind; more often than not it has been pocketed by corrupt politicians and businessmen, or alternatively passed on to the Camorra or the Mafia. The crucial issue as regards economic development – whether in Italy, Britain or the US for that matter – is the political control of public finances, not that money well spent is unable to make a positive difference.

The fundamental purpose of public expenditure should be, in the long term, to create the conditions for independent economic development. Yet Campanian politicians have used finances in such a way as to retard development and make people even more dependent on state handouts. Organised crime also holds back development, as it is largely parasitical on public sector contracts and generally invests in either non-productive or labour-intensive industries.

The problem therefore has never been a lack of money, but a political system unwilling to create economic growth. Consequently, the $22.5 billion of EC structural funds set aside for the development of Southern Italy in the 1994–9 period[21] are likely to be largely wasted. As we shall see below, real economic and social development of the area would jeopardise the rule of the local ruling class.

Having analysed the difficulties associated with economic development, we shall now turn to the issue of crime repression, another area commonly held to be fundamental to any strategy of defeating organised crime.

THE FAILURE OF REPRESSION

In 1963 Italy was outraged by the massacre of seven policemen in the Sicilian town of Ciaculli. All parties united in condemning the attack, and after many years of resistance the Christian Democrats finally agreed to the institution of a permanent parliamentary committee, the Anti-Mafia Commission. Over the last thirty years it has published fifty-five hefty volumes of testimony and evidence. However, as one Mafia expert has commented, 'One has the impression that this institution has been used as a gym in which government forces allowed the left-wing opposition to land anti-Mafia punches on them, as long as they were thrown in a vacuum.'[22] The Commission's first report took fifteen years to produce, and even then there was one majority and one minority report from both the left and the right.

During its first decade the Commission largely analysed the Mafia as a mainly Sicilian phenomenon. It was only in the 1970s that organised crime became a serious problem in other regions of the South, as well as having ramifications overseas and within the ranks of government in Rome.

The growth of the Mafia of the 1970s forced politicians to move beyond the mere analysis represented by the Anti-Mafia Commission and to take more concrete measures to tackle organised crime. The Mafia had by now not only managed to dominate and increase the international heroin trade but had also left behind a series of 'illustrious corpses', primarily policemen, politicians and journalists. The most prominent victim of this period was General Carlo Dalla Chiesa, who had played a major role in defeating the Red Brigades in the 1970s.

Despite the fact that he was given unprecedented powers and enjoyed considerable public support, he was murdered in a car bomb attack in September 1982, just three months after arriving in Sicily. Public outrage exploded at a similar level to that which greeted the death of Judges Falcone and Borsellino ten years later, and a new investigative judicial structure was immediately created, the High Commission against the Mafia.

However, it became clear during the 1980s that the High Commission was being used by the government as a means to deflect public criticism, as a kind of shock absorber for the Christian Democrats. Indeed, Giovanni Falcone wrote shortly before his death: 'Ministers of the Interior and the government as a whole have been able to blame the institution for anything that hasn't worked and attribute to it responsibility for every failure.'[23] Even when the High Commission was given greater powers in November 1988, there was no improvement in its activities, as a minority parliamentary Anti-Mafia Commission report noted: 'After more than a year since the passing of these reforms, compared with the considerable extension in the High Commission's powers, there has not been a corresponding increase in anti-Mafia action.'[24]

Nine days after the murder of Dalla Chiesa, i.e. at the same time as the High Commission began its work, the 'La Torre' law (named after an MP murdered shortly before Dalla Chiesa) was passed. For the first time this introduced the specific crime of Mafia membership, as well as the right to seize illegal assets, but it was quickly seen that this innovation did not produce any great changes either. After two years of operation in Campania, 4,024 checks had been made on assets and bank accounts, leading to 515 requests for seizure of goods. Yet permission for seizure was only granted in 55 cases, and from these seizures no goods were permanently confiscated.[25]

A further spate of laws was passed in 1991: in March Parliament introduced measures giving greater protection to supergrasses, in May it passed a law that required greater openness in the tendering of public contracts, and in December an anti-extortion law was passed. In the same month the DIA (the National Anti-Mafia Coordination) was formed; it largely superseded the High Commission and, like an Italian version of the FBI, was designed to coordinate all three police forces.

In July 1991 the police were given greater powers to dissolve councils believed to be infiltrated by criminal organisations and to call fresh elections 18 months after dissolution. Yet the fact that *all* councillors are thrown out of office simply produces greater cynicism and does not help people to distinguish between politicians who are honest and those who are suspected of criminality.

But, as with so many of these laws, such measures amount to no more than window dressing, in the sense that they only deal with the symptoms rather than the cause of corruption. The arrival of one honest Extraordinary Commissioner cannot drastically change the way in which medium-sized towns have been run for several years, so it is not surprising to learn that 'the Extraordinary Commissioners have in many cases taken on total power without, however, radically changing things, as was requested'.[26]

In February 1994 a new law came into force against the buying and selling of contraband cigarettes. Transgressors who buy illegal cigarettes will have to pay a $65 fine, while street sellers risk up to four years in jail. It is unlikely that the law will ever be rigorously enforced due to the social tension it would create; but even if it were, the people who today earn their living in this manner would simply be forced to move on to other activities, with predictably negative consequences. Once again, tackling the symptoms of crime will have no long-term benefit if the causes of crime are not eradicated.

The only effect that many of these laws have had is to crowd Italian jails with remand prisoners. The fact that the prison population nearly doubled in three years – from 26,150 in 1990 to 49,471 in 1993 – has done nothing to stop the reproduction of criminal organisations.[27] Indeed, those closer to the ground have a more accurate picture of what imprisonment may mean, as the Naples police chief once said: 'The majority of crimes which happen outside are today organised from inside jails.'[28]

Apart from the criticisms of individual laws – Parliament has passed thirty-five laws relating to organised crime since 1975[29] – their general effect on the development of the Camorra is perhaps the most telling comment on the futility of repression. In 1983, around the time of the 'maxi-blitz' against Cutolo's NCO, it was estimated that there were about a dozen Camorra 'families'. By 1987 the number had risen to twenty-six, in the following year a report of the Naples Flying Squad put their number at thirty-two, and by 1993 it was estimated there were 111 identifiable gangs.[30]

There is a strange irony to the fact that it is ex-*camorristi* who are able to recognise, albeit in a distorted fashion, the brutal truth of 'law and order' campaigns: 'Through this instrument – the struggle against the Camorra and the Mafia – they create Camorra and Mafia. They create and use it for anti-democratic goals.'[31]

CRIMINAL MISTAKES

If attempts at economic improvement have failed due to the vested interests of the local ruling class, and repression has failed for the same reason, but also because masses of desperate people are forced to risk death and imprisonment, then there clearly needs to be a fresh and broader approach.

The deep-rooted nature of organised crime in Campania calls for a far more radical solution than the user-friendly packaging and right-wing revivalism that characterised the election of Silvio Berlusconi's government in 1994.

It is therefore necessary to closely study alternative political forces, those people who have never governed at a national level – primarily the ex-communist PDS.

A frequent theme in its programme is the need to restore legality, as outlined by Vito Faenza, a campaigning Neapolitan journalist with the PDS daily *L'Unità*: 'If we want to defeat our "Neapolitan Cosa Nostra", legality must be restored in areas such as Aversa. It is the only direction to go in, but up till now nobody has gone down that road.'[32]

The creation of a climate of legality, or perhaps more precisely the freedom to engage in democratic debate and activity without fear of arbitrary intimidation, is undoubtedly a fundamental first step towards defeating the Camorra. However, the whole tradition of the state structure in the South, as the current PDS shadow minister for the South, Isaia Sales, has pointed out, has always relied on a rather flexible notion of legality:

> variations in the level of legality have served as an instrument of social control in the South. This unusual political adaptation of the concept of legality has meant that for long periods the South did not socially explode but instead imploded along criminal channels.[33]

A reforming government would find itself immersed in this tradition of ambiguous and shifting legalities; besides, demands for 'legality' do not allow the PDS to present itself as a real alternative to any of the other parties – and the very mention of 'legality' brings a sarcastic smile to the lips of most southerners. Yet in many senses the PDS is not an alternative, as it is fully committed to maintaining the existing state structure. Although its positions are often distorted by the right, the strong defence by the PDS of the current constitution often makes it appear conservative.

In any case, it cannot be denied that if the PDS were to win power it would peacefully enter into the state machinery and rely on the existing judiciary, police forces and state bureaucracy to carry out its plans for combating organised crime. But this would do nothing to resolve a contradiction that has been repeatedly highlighted: 'Even though they are laws of the land, the men who manage these democratic laws are anti-democratic.'[34]

In other words, a PDS government would probably lead to just more of the same. This failure, represented in microcosm by the PCI/PDS in Naples during the 1980s, would occur despite the party's genuine commitment to the creation of legality and the reduction of social and economic inequalities – their crucial strategic mistake is the belief that real political and economic power lies in Parliament.

In economic terms, if big business were to view government reforms in a bad light it could use a variety of tactics to bring politicians back into line: companies could go on investment strike nationally and invest overseas; they could destabilise the currency through speculation and pressure on interest rates; they could refuse to provide credit to government organisations or to place orders with them. The problem for politicians in all these circumstances, as was seen, for example, in the currency crisis that devastated the UK in September 1992, is that Parliament has no power to control these manoeuvres.

The same can be said for the machinery of state. If certain reforms were perceived as damaging to the interests of the state bureaucracy or the judiciary, they could either be circumvented or delayed for long periods by provoking administrative chaos or simply refusing to obey instructions. If, for example, senior investigators were to refuse to investigate the foreign bank accounts of senior politicians or businesspeople on the pretext that the request had a political rather than a judicial basis, then there would be no other body capable of taking on that task.

This scenario presumes, however, that the PDS would be prepared to engage in a head-on collision with the Italian ruling class, a notion which would viewed as abhorrent by any PDS leader.

WHY THE INSTITUTIONS CANNOT BEAT THE CAMORRA

What is striking about the Camorra is that, in the space of twenty years, an organisation which was believed to be on the verge of extinction has instead grown to rival the Mafia in terms of its power and influence.

Over these two decades the more powerful gangs have

become semi-autonomous from local politicians and are no longer purely parasitical in the way they accumulate wealth. Their control over significant economic resources has meant that the traditional patron–client relationship with politicians has in some cases been overturned. Many politicians, judges, businesses and even parties have sponsored Camorra's interests within their field of influence, thus becoming lobbyists for Camorra interests, which, however, do not extend to total control of the political system.

Although the Mafia may still possess far more international power, and greater influence within national government, the Camorra can draw on far stronger social and economic roots than its Sicilian counterpart. It commands a higher level of mass social legitimacy due to its capacity to provide employment for tens of thousands of people. As one magistrate put it, 'In many areas of this region the Camorra is not viewed as a negative phenomenon to be fought, but as the expression of a justified revolt against a corrupt, distant and inefficient state.'[35]

The Camorra probably has an even closer relationship with the local ruling class than the Mafia, a hypothesis supported by the relative lack of 'illustrious corpses' left behind by Camorra gangs. In recent years there have been no spectacular assassinations in Campania that might be compared with the murders of Salvo Lima, Giovanni Falcone and Paolo Borsellino.

The local political traditions of extreme centralisation, bureaucracy and clientelism have always nurtured a network of local mediators and middlemen. These, in turn, have favoured the participation of organised criminals, first as a group of subaltern brokers hired to provide votes, and later as a semi-independent power base in its own right.

However, the advantages that politicians receive have always gone beyond the creation of an electoral base. It can easily be argued that organised crime functions as a vital, and perhaps even more efficient instrument of social control than the official representatives of law and order, as the fear it instils in the population, and the precarious or oppressive nature of employment in criminal enterprises, serve as useful shock absorbers for ruling politicians and powerful business interests.[36]

One only needs to imagine what a huge difference it would make if organised crime lost its dominance in the urban areas of the South: first, there would no longer be such widespread fear of speaking out against a whole series of injustices and second – and perhaps more importantly – it would transform people's expectations concerning employment.

Once violent intimidation and the atmosphere of illegality were removed from the workplace, workers would begin to organise and come to expect a whole series of changes as their automatic right: permanent employment contracts, the application of health and safety legislation, payment of overtime and shift work rates, trade union representation, regular pay increases and so on.[37] Masses of people would begin to resolve their material problems collectively, and by doing so, they would also begin to socially isolate individualistic and illegal approaches aimed at solving material difficulties.

The changes that the extinction of organised crime would bring to the South would therefore be extremely threatening to the ruling class: businesses would face higher wage bills as workers began to organise, and politicians would be selected or deselected on the basis of their programme rather than the favours they are presumed to be in a position to grant.

In short, for the southern ruling class organised crime has become a vital mechanism of maintaining its power and privilege. During his deposition before the Anti-Mafia Commission Pasquale Galasso spoke for many of his fellow Neapolitans when he challenged the MPs listening to him to undermine their own position by dealing with the social causes of organised crime. His statement also perhaps reveals some of the reasons which led him to cooperate with the police:

At the end of the 1970s I used to socialise and take part in political meetings. Everybody liked us; I met Gava and all those politicians.

Then at a certain point in my life I became a criminal and met them again, this time in meetings on the other side of a table – even a young bobby on the beat knows about this!

This is something that you don't want to deal with or perhaps you don't want to believe, also because you're split into so many corporations. Forgive me, these are my ideas, I want to unburden myself and bring them to your attention.

This is too much! Can't you see the state Naples is in? My contemporaries, people who studied with me and who now have degrees, who after thirty years of studying have to turn to their fathers every Friday and Saturday for a fiver because they're unemployed . . .

If you don't change this social reality, if you don't get at its roots, how do you think you're going to beat the Camorra? My own personal belief is that criminals will spontaneously disappear if each one of you plays their part.[38]

But the southern ruling class does not want to deal with the root problems within society, which lead people towards criminal activity, because this would place its own rule in jeopardy. It will therefore resist fundamental change and have no scruples about encouraging illegality and the growth of organised crime if this helps to defend its power and privileges. This is why any strategy for defeating organised crime has to involve the over-throw of the ruling class and their capitalist system through the creation of a completely different system.

A system of economic and social equality, in other words a socialist system, would vastly reduce the temptation of masses of people to embark on a life of crime. As a former *camorrista* bluntly put it: 'If you've got a job and I haven't, if you've got a house and I haven't, it's obvious I'm going to come and steal from you.'[39] The material desperation and long-term insecurity which many people experience in southern Italy makes a criminal choice inevitable for large numbers of people; the possibility of huge wealth compared with a normal miserable existence is a temptation difficult to resist.

Although they are a small minority in society, it is encourag-ing that notorious ex-*camorristi* or supergrasses have begun to understand how the existing capitalist system destroys the lives of so many ordinary people in the South. As Pasquale Galasso again has observed:

over the years I have understood that the whole sequence of murders which destroyed me and my family, and many others throughout Campania, is in the final analysis a part of these politicians' manoeuvres. They are prepared to run away and wait for the winner, with whom they will then make an alliance to manage elections and business affairs.[40]

And elsewhere he comments: 'My town, Poggiomarino, is a backwater, it is a town mistreated by these politicians and the government. There's nothing there, no industry, not even a tiny little factory of ten workers.'[41]

In terms of creating a political alternative to the present system, the fundamental problem with choosing a criminal career is not that current laws are not respected, but rather that poor people look for an individual solution to their common situation of poverty. Any political strategy aimed at ending organised crime and the political system it is part of, and which involves masses of people, clearly needs to resolve this weakness.

Even the realisation of the need to become politically active implies a monumental improvement in traditional political awareness; in the words of Nunzio Giuliano: 'Those who have ruled the South have always had the intention of never creating mass awareness; they have always wanted to perpetuate, at all costs, a low level of culture or even ignorance.'[42]

In order for political, economic and ideological changes to take place, the southern masses, together with their counterparts in the North, need to organise themselves collectively into a party that is prepared to lead the way towards these changes.

What is beyond doubt is that the opposition parties are unwilling to take on this role, while the parties and politicians who have been or who are now in government, would stand in the way of such changes. Just as the Christian Democrats started to collude with organised crime from 1945 onwards, so did the Socialist Party following its rise to power in 1963, and so will the present government. The track record and traditions of Italian political life illustrate that any solution to the problems posed by the Camorra cannot come from government and its state machinery: they are very much part of the problem rather than part of the solution.

The wealth of evidence concerning the links between organised crime and the political and economic elite can only lead to one conclusion: any political strategy that leaves the foundations of the existing system intact is a proposal which accommodates to and favours organised crime.

Notes

INTRODUCTION

1 *Corriere della Sera*, 21 August 1993.
2 *Economist*, 5 February 1994.
3 Currency conversion throughout is based on a rate of L. 1,250 to the US dollar and the figures quoted in the original sources have not been adjusted for inflation or fluctuation over time.
4 Even before his election victory in March 1994 it was clear that Silvio Berlusconi's Forza Italia movement, like Bossi's Northern League, did not represent a fundamentally different political tradition.
  Berlusconi had been a member of the powerful but secret P2 Freemason lodge in the early 1980s, and throughout that decade expanded his media empire thanks to his close relationship with Socialist Party leader Bettino Craxi, one of the major protagonists of the *Tangentopoli* scandals. Old habits resurfaced in July 1994 when the government passed a decree which would have allowed the release from custody of most of the major politicians facing trial; however, the government had to hastily withdraw the decree due to widespread protests.
5 See D. Gambetta's review of L. Ricolfi, *L'ultimo parlamento: Sulla fine della prima repubblica* (Nuova Italia Scientifica, Rome, 1993) in *L'Indice*, July 1994.
6 Anti-Mafia Commission report on the Camorra approved on 21 December 1993, published in book form by *L'Unità* in February 1994 and entitled *Rapporto sulla camorra*, p. 15. Hereafter referred to as *Rapporto sulla camorra*.
7 Ibid., p. 16.
8 Ibid., p. 17.
9 Ibid., p. 166.
10 Ibid., p. 17.
11 EURISPES, 'Rapporto Italia '94', cited in *Panorama*, 28 January 1994. A report published in 1991, based on police statistics, estimated the Camorra's annual turnover at $10 billion, roughly equivalent to Italy's public debt at that time, or alternatively, to the value of

goods traded between Italy and the UK; see *Fortune* (Italian edition), July/August 1991.
12 *Il Manifesto*, 10 May 1994.
13 *Sun*, 18 June 1983.
14 *Daily Mail*, 11 June 1991.
15 *Guardian*, 29 March 1993. The chaos which daily pervades the city makes it quite unique – indeed, many Italians do not consider Naples to be part of Italy. It is perhaps the only city in the world where the city council's appointment of a 'Normality Committee', charged with creating greater order and respect for laws and regulations, seems the most normal thing in the world.
16 *Il Manifesto*, 13 February 1994.
17 *Rapporto sulla camorra*, p. 10.
18 Ibid., p. 20.

1 THE ORIGINS OF THE CAMORRA AND THE MAFIA

1 See M. Short, *Murder Inc.: The Story of Organized Crime* (Thames/Methuen, London, 1984), p. 19.
2 See I. Sales, *La camorra, le camorre* (2nd edn, Editori Riuniti, Rome, 1993), p. 26.
3 Ibid., p. 65. For a discussion of the origin of the word itself, see G. L. Messina, *L'etimologia di mafia, camorra e 'ndrangheta* (Bonanno Editore, Arcireale, 1990).
4 See G. D'Agostino, *Per una storia di Napoli capitale* (Liguori, Naples, 1988), p. 131.
5 Sales, *La camorra*, 32.
6 See J. A. Davis, 'Oligarchia capitalistica e immobilismo economico a Napoli 1815–60', *Studi Storici*, 1975.
7 Sales, *La camorra*, pp. 35–6.
8 M. Monnier, *La camorra: Notizie storiche raccolte e documentate* (Argo, Lecce, 1994), p. 121. This is a reprint of a book first published in 1863; written by a Swiss academic who lived in Naples from 1855–64, it is one of the best contemporary accounts of the Camorra's early growth.
9 Sales, *La camorra*, p. 72.
10 D'Agostino, *Storia di Napoli*, p. 146.
11 Monnier, *La camorra*, p. 47.
12 Ibid., p. 127.
13 Ibid., p. 128.
14 Ibid., pp. 112–3.
15 Ibid., p. 115.
16 Ibid., p. 118.
17 See D. Demarco, 'L'economia degli stati italiani prima dell'unità', *Rassegna storica del Risorgimento* 44, 1957.
18 Monnier, *La camorra*, p. 84.

19 Ibid., pp. 129–30.
20 'A curse upon this liberty'. This is a phrase from a song of one of the bandit groups that roamed the southern countryside after unification and refers to the lack of freedom under the new Italian government.
21 L. Romano, *Memorie politiche* (Naples, 1873), p. 50.
22 See H. Acton, *The last Bourbons of Naples* (Methuen, London, 1961), pp. 485–90.
23 Monnier, *La camorra*, p. 138.
24 Ibid., p. 140.
25 M. Marmo, 'La camorra e lo stato liberale', in F. Barbagallo (ed.), *Camorra e criminalità organizzata in Campania* (Liguori, Naples, 1988), p. 19.
26 See Demarco, 'Economia degli stati italiani'.
27 Cited in N. Dell'Erba, *Le origini del socialismo a Napoli (1870–92)* (Franco Angeli, Milan, 1979), p. 22.
28 Cited in P. Ricci, *Le origini della camorra* (Edizioni Sintesi, Naples, 1989), pp. 94–5.
29 See Dell'Erba, *Origini del socialismo*, pp. 7, 9.
30 Cited in Sales, *La camorra*, pp. 100–1.
31 E. Ciccotti, *Come divenni e come cessai di essere deputato di Vicaria* (Naples, 1909), p. 63.
32 See Sales, *La camorra*, p. 107.
33 Figures cited in G. Aragno, *Socialismo e sindacalismo rivoluzionario a Napoli in età giolittiana* (Bulzoni Editore, Rome, 1980), p. 93.
34 *Guappo* is a Neapolitan word generally used to denote a senior member of a criminal gang, often prepared to use violence. Like *guappa ria* it can also refer to an individual's attitude.
35 See R. Minna, *Breve storia della Mafia* (Editori Riuniti, Rome, 1984), pp. 17, 25.
36 See A. Blok, *The Mafia of a Sicilian Village, 1860–1960* (Waveland Press, Prospect Heights, Ill., 1978), pp. 89–102.
37 Minna, *Breve storia*, p. 30.
38 Ibid., p. 32.
39 Cited in R. Catanzaro, *Il delitto come impresa: Storia sociale della mafia* (Liviana Editrice, Padua, 1988), p. 99.
40 Sales, *La camorra*, p. 37.

2 THE POSTWAR DEVELOPMENT OF THE CAMORRA

1 See P. Ginsborg, *A History of Contemporary Italy: Society and Politics 1943–88* (Penguin, Harmondsworth, 1990), p. 37.
2 G. D'Agostino, *Per una storia di Napoli capitale* (Liguori, Naples, 1988), p. 184.
3 The Risorgimento was the movement which led to the unification of Italy in the last century; with hindsight it seems ironic that the main supporters of unification, chiefly Count Cavour and the

ruling House of Savoy in Piedmont, apparently only intended to unite northern and central Italy; it was an expeditionary force led by Giuseppe Garibaldi that eventually forced their hand into uniting the whole peninsula.

Trasformismo is a political term normally used to describe the process of co-optation between 1860 and Mussolini's seizure of power in 1922 that transformed a radical opposition into a harmless parliamentary force.

4 See the tables in G. D'Agostino, 'La politica in Campania nel quarantennio repubblicano', in P. Macry and P. Villani (eds), *Storia d'Italia: Le regioni dall'Unità ad oggi: La Campania* (Einaudi, Turin, 1990), pp. 1075–84.

5 See R. Minna, *Breve storia della Mafia* (Editori Riuniti, Rome, 1984), pp. 49–50.

6 Ibid., p. 50. See also the relevant sections of R. Campbell, *The Luciano Project: The Secret Wartime Collaboration of the Mafia and the U.S. Navy* (McGraw-Hill, New York, 1977).

7 M. Pantaleone, *The Mafia and Politics* (Chatto & Windus, London, 1966), pp. 60–61.

8 Minna, *Breve storia*, p. 50.

9 This included two Ministers and dozens of parliamentary deputies, generals, admirals and others; it was a kind of state within a state, pledged to help fellow members above everything else.

10 Cited in T. Cliff and D. Gluckstein, *The Labour Party: A Marxist History* (Bookmarks, London, 1988), pp. 196–7.

11 R. Catanzaro, *Men of Respect: A Social History of the Sicilian Mafia* (The Free Press, New York, 1992), p. 115.

12 G. Di Fiore, *Potere camorrista: Quattro secoli di malanapoli* (Guida Editore, Naples, 1993), p. 134.

13 P. Maas, *The Valachi Papers* (Panther, St Albans, 1970), p. 139.

14 Pantaleone, *Mafia and Politics*, p. 64.

15 Ginsborg, *History of Italy*, p. 37.

16 Pantaleone, *Mafia and Politics*, p. 63.

17 A leading postwar Mafioso, cited in C. Sterling, *The Mafia: The Long Reach of the International Sicilian Mafia* (Grafton, London, 1991), p. 68.

18 Pantaleone, *Mafia and Politics*, p. 64.

19 Ibid., pp. 64–5.

20 Ibid., p. 65. The original Italian edition, *Mafia e politica (1943–62)*, was published by Einaudi in 1962.

21 Minna, *Breve storia*, p. 51.

22 Cited in Sterling, *The Mafia*, p. 95.

23 Ibid., p. 97.

24 This is a legal measure, the compulsory relocation of people considered to be potentially dangerous within their current area of residence to another part of the country, where they are required to periodically register with the police.

25 'La malavita organizzata in Campania', *Nord e Sud* 18, April/June 1982, p. 15.

26 G. Fabiani and S. Vellante, 'L'evoluzione delle strutture agricole 1921–71', in F. Barbagallo (ed.), *Storia della Campania*, vol. 2 (Guida Editori, Naples, 1978), p. 464,

27 Ibid., p. 456.

28 Statistics taken from F. Barbagallo, 'Sviluppo e sottosviluppo agli inizi del Novecento', in F. Barbagallo (ed.), *Storia della Campania*, vol. 2 (Guida Editori, Naples, 1978), pp. 395, 397.

29 Ibid., p. 406.

30 Contemporary newspaper statistics, cited in P. Allum, *Politics and Society in Post-war Naples* (Cambridge University Press, London 1973), p. 106.

31 Ibid., p. 82.

32 N. Ajello, 'La camorra vestita di grigio', *L'Espresso*, 15 November 1964.

33 C. Cederna, *Giovanni Leone: La carriera di un presidente* (Feltrinelli, Milan, 1978), p. 130.

34 G. Tutino, 'Camorra 1957', *Nord e Sud* 35, December 1957, p. 88.

35 C. Guarino, 'La camorra', in *Napoli dopo un secolo* (Edizioni Scientifiche Italiane, Naples, 1961), p. 553.

These complaints raise the issue of developing a successful strategy for defeating organised crime, a debate which was to become far more important during the 1980s. The problem with calls for 'letting the police do their job' is that they ignore the political control that is normally exercised over the police in any parliamentary democracy. Although the secret services are often beyond parliamentary control and senior policemen enjoy considerable operational autonomy in times of serious social unrest, such as riots and major strikes, this clearly does not apply in a long-term campaign against a well-entrenched criminal organisation. In this case, any increase in police staffing, operations or powers will almost invariably be initiated and supervised by politicians, the very politicians who are now suspected of being in league with organised crime. Furthermore, such calls for increased police powers also presume that the police are immune to criminal infiltration or blackmail.

The problem of the Camorra has not become so deep-seated in Naples because of a lack of police power; indeed, police forces in the rest of northern and central Italy have largely managed to control organised crime using exactly the same powers that have failed in the South. The specific problem of the Naples area has been that long-term poverty has made membership of a criminal organisation an attractive prospect for large numbers of people.

36 See Sterling, *The Mafia*, p. 93.

37 *Nord e Sud* 18, 1982, p. 12.

38 Ibid.

39 E. Mazzetti, 'Il "caso Campania" nell'evoluzione territoriale del Mezzogiorno', *Nord e Sud* 19/20, July/December 1982, p. 105.

40 Ibid., p. 113.

41 Ibid., p. 111.

42 Ibid.
43 Ibid., p. 113.
44 G. Montroni, 'Popolazione e insediamenti in Campania (1861–1981)', in P. Macry and P. Villani (eds), *Storia d'Italia: Le regioni dall'Unità ad oggi: La Campania* (Einaudi, Turin, 1990), p. 250.
45 Allum, *Politics and Society*, p. 154.
46 Ibid., p. 160.
47 Mazzetti, 'Il "caso Campania"', p. 109.
48 P. Villani, 'L'eredità storica e la società rurale', in P. Macry and P. Villani (eds), *Storia d'Italia: Le regioni dall'Unità ad oggi: La Campania* (Einaudi, Turin, 1990), p. 88–9.
49 P. Cotugno, E. Pugliese and E. Rebeggiani, 'Mercato del lavoro e occupazione nel secondo dopoguerra', in P. Macry and P. Villani (eds), *Storia d'Italia: Le regioni dall'Unità ad oggi: La Campania* (Einaudi, Turin, 1990), p. 1173.
50 A communique released by the PCI branch nearest the docks on 22 March 1960, cited in C. Guarino, 'La camorra', p. 547.
51 See Sterling, *The Mafia*, pp. 190–1.
52 *Nord e Sud* 18, 1982, p. 15.
53 Di Fiore, *Potere camorrista*, p. 150.
54 N. Chieppa, 'Dal contrabbando alla camorra e dal colera al terremoto', *Osservatorio sulla Camorra* 4, May 1985, pp. 59–60.
55 Cited in I. Sales, *La camorra, le camorre* (2nd edn, Editori Riuniti, Rome, 1993), p. 152.
56 See Chieppa, 'Dal contrabbando alla camorra', p. 59.
57 *Nord e Sud* 18, 1982, p. 16.
58 Cited in Sterling, *The Mafia*, p. 201.
59 Di Fiore, *Potere camorrista*, p. 165.
60 *Nord e Sud* n.18, 1982, pp. 16–17.
61 For further details, see 'Sentenza-ordinanza n. 1140/81 contro Sabato Saviani e 261 altri', Tribunale Penale di Napoli, 21 January 1983, pp. 87–91 (hereafter 'Sentenza contro Saviani').
62 R. Cutolo, *Poesie e pensieri* (Berisio, Naples, 1980), p. 56.
63 Nord e Sud 18, 1982, p. 17.
64 See 'Sentenza contro Saviani', pp. 82–4.
65 Cutolo, *Poesie*, p. 89.
66 'Sentenza n. 80/88 contro Cutolo Raffaele e 17 altri', Corte di Assise di Napoli, 4 November 1988, pp. 364–5.
67 Statistics compiled by ISTAT, the government's statistical office, cited in D. Sassoon, *Contemporary Italy: Politics, Economy and Society since 1945* (Longman, Harlow, 1986), p. 214.
68 ISTAT figures, cited in ibid., p. 112.
69 Statistics cited in Sales, *La camorra*, p. 166.
70 L. Rossi, *Camorra: Un mese ad Ottaviano* (Mondadori, Milan, 1983), pp. 32–3.
71 Statistics cited in Sales, *La camorra*, p. 164.
72 'Sentenza-ordinanza n. 1935/84 contro Amendola Giuseppe e altri', Tribunale Penale di Napoli, 28 March 1985, p. 15 (hereafter 'Sentenza contro Amendola').

73 Ibid., p. 14.
74 Ibid., p. 16.
75 Sales, *La camorra*, p. 192. These figures can be compared with the 'roaring twenties' (1922–32) in Chicago, when 'only' 680 were murdered.
76 *Nord e Sud* 18, 1982, p. 17.
77 S. De Gregorio, *I nemici di Cutolo* (Pironti, Naples, 1983), p. 12.
78 'Sentenza contro Saviani', p. 109.
79 De Gregorio, *Cutolo*, p. 16.
80 Statistics cited in Sales, *La camorra*, p. 252.
81 Di Fiore, *Potere camorrista*, p. 176.
82 Commissione Parlamentare di inchiesta sul fenomeno della mafia e sulle associazioni criminali similari, *Audizione di Salvatore Migliorino, 12 novembre 1993* (Camera dei Deputati, Rome, 1993), p. 3090.
83 'Sentenza contro Amendola', p. 25.
84 F. Feo, *Uomini e affari della camorra* (Edizioni Sintesi, Naples, 1989), p. 55.

3 THE 'ADMINISTRATIVE ECONOMY' AND THE 1980 EARTHQUAKE

1 The recollection of the communist Mayor of Naples from 1975–83, Maurizio Valenzi, in A. Wanderlingh, *Maurizio Valenzi, un romanzo civile* (Edizioni Sintesi, Naples, 1988), pp. 21–2.
2 I. Sales, *La camorra, le camorre* (2nd edn, Editori Riuniti, Rome, 1993), p. 151.
3 See P. Allum, *Politics and Society in Post-war Naples* (Cambridge University Press, London, 1973), pp. 297–307, for a description of the Gavas' rise to power.
4 F. Barbagallo, *Mezzogiorno e questione meridionale 1860–1980* (Guida, Naples, 1980), p. 84.
5 Allum, *Politics amd Society*, p. 322.
6 Interview with Maurizio Valenzi by the author, 8 December 1992.
7 I. Talia, 'Il decentramento urbano ed industriale in Campania', *Nord e Sud* 19/20, July/December 1982, p. 122.
8 G. D'Agostino, 'La politica in Campania nel quarantennio repubblicano', in P. Macry and P. Villani (eds), *Storia d'Italia: Le regioni dall'Unità ad oggi: La Campania* (Einaudi, Turin, 1990), p. 1059.
9 See M. Clark, *Modern Italy 1871–1982* (Longman, London, 1984), pp. 391–2.
10 Barbagallo, *Mezzogiorno*, pp. 90–1.
11 Sales, *La camorra*, p. 205.
12 Ibid., p. 209.
13 Ibid., p. 207.
14 M. Cammelli, 'Governo locale e sistema amministrativo nel Mezzogiorno', *Il Mulino* 329, May/June 1990, p. 435.
15 Ibid., p. 436. Apart from the expense of maintaining public parks,

Naples has so little green space compared with other cities: 1.2 m²
per inhabitant. This can be compared with 10.9 m² per inhabitant
in Rome, 24.0 m² in London and 50.0 m² in Hamburg. See *Il
Manifesto*, 1 May 1994.

16 Interview with Franco Malvano by the author, 3 December 1992.
Malvano was head of the Naples Flying Squad from 1982–6, and is
currently the city's Deputy Police Chief. Following the disbanding
of Marano council for presumed Camorra infiltration, he was also
appointed Special Police Commissioner with government responsibilities for Marano in October 1991, as three civilian commissioners
had resigned in fear.

17 Sales, *La camorra*, p. 150.

18 Cammelli, 'Governo locale', p. 433.

19 D'Agostino, 'La politica in Campania', pp. 1059–60.

20 G. Di Fiore, *Potere camorrista: Quattro secoli di malanapoli* (Guida,
Naples, 1993), p. 191.

21 A. Becchi Collidà, 'L'evoluzione della legislazione post-terremoto',
in *L'affare terremoto* (Comitato regionale del PCI campano, Naples,
1989). Some local councils were added to the list of those which
had suffered damage as late as 1987.

22 Ibid., p. 29.

23 I. Sales, A. Lamberti, A. Dottorini, A. Leone, 'Il commissariato
regionale alla ricostruzione', in *L'affare terremoto* (Comitato regionale
del PCI campano, Naples, 1989), p. 76.

24 See EURISPES, *Rapporto Italia '94* (Koinè, Rome, 1994), p. 638.

25 Sales, Lamberti, Dottorini and Leone, 'Il commissariato regionale',
p. 77.

26 Ibid., pp. 78–9.

27 *Il Manifesto*, 9 October 1984.

28 *L'Unità*, 11 October 1982.

29 *Il Manifesto*, 9 October 1984.

30 'Lo Stato "collaudatore"' in *L'affare terremoto*, (Comitato regionale
del PCI campano, Naples, 1989), p. 119.

31 Ibid., p. 118.

32 Ibid., p. 126.

33 Ibid., p. 123.

34 A letter dated 27 October 1980, sent by the Prefect of Avellino to
the Scalfaro Parliamentary Commission of Inquiry, copy in author's
possession.

35 *La Repubblica*, 23 November 1990

36 PCI historian Francesco Barbagallo, writing in *La Voce della Campania*, April 1989.

37 *La Voce della Campania*, January 1991.

38 Vito Di Virgilio, owner of a small building company in Potenza,
cited in *Panorama*, 14 February 1993. Yet many of these very
businesses had not complained when *they initially offered* bribes to
politicians, which was generally how the system started, in order
that competing firms could be shut out of the market.

39 *Panorama*, 4 February 1994.

4 THE 'BUSINESS CAMORRA' OF THE NUVOLETTA GANG

1 The documentation in question is Judge Paolo Mancuso's 'Sentenza-ordinanza n. 1873/84 contro Nuvoletta Lorenzo e 29 altri', Tribunale Penale di Napoli, 29 July 1989 (hereafter 'Sentenza contro Nuvoletta').

2 C. Sterling, *The Mafia: The Long Reach of the International Sicilian Mafia* (Grafton, London, 1991), pp. 141–2.

3 S. De Gregorio, *I nemici di Cutolo* (Tullio Pironti, Naples, 1983), p. 89.

4 'La malavita organizzata in Campania', *Nord e Sud* 18, April/June 1982, p. 23.

5 Cited in De Gregorio, *I nemici*, p. 88.

6 Ibid., p. 73.

7 'La malavita organizzata', p. 14.

8 See *carabinieri* report n. 455/1 of 22 July 1981, cited in 'La malavita organizzata in Campania', *Nord e Sud* 18, April/June 1982, p. 24. See also De Gregorio, *I nemici*, p. 86.

9 'La malavita organizzata', p. 14.

10 See C. Stajano (ed.), *Mafia: L'atto di accusa dei giudici di Palermo* (Editori Riuniti, Rome, 1986), pp. 28, 93.

11 As recounted to P. Arlacchi in *Gli uomini del disonore* (Mondadori, Milan, 1992), p. 134.

12 Commissione Parlamentare di inchiesta sul fenomeno della mafia e sulle associazioni criminali similari, *Audizione di Pasquale Galasso 13 luglio 1993* (Camera dei Deputati, Rome, 1993), pp. 2241–2.

   Galasso goes on to claim that Nuvoletta's protection was provided by Christian Democrat politician Antonio Gava. Riina, Provenzano and Bagarella were all senior members of the Sicilian Mafia.

13 'Sentenza contro Nuvoletta', p. 115.

14 *La Voce della Campania*, March 1987.

15 These statistics are taken from a finance police report dated 18 December 1985, cited in 'Sentenza contro Nuvoletta', p. 115.

16 Ibid., p. 181.

17 Ibid., p. 119.

18 Ibid., p. 273.

19 Ibid., p. 279.

20 Ibid., p. 276.

21 Ibid., p. 279.

22 *La Voce della Campania*, January 1991, and 'Sentenza contro Nuvoletta', p. 138.

23 *La Voce della Campania*, April 1988.

24 See *Il Mattino*, 25 August 1983. Relatively little has been written about the role of organised labour in opposing the Camorra. This is unfortunate, as it is potentially the most effective method of opposition.

25 Cited in *Il Manifesto*, 28 November 1984.
26 Statement cited in 'Sentenza contro Nuvoletta', p. 127.
27 Ibid., p. 122.
28 Ibid.
29 Cited in V. Faenza, 'La camorra nelle amministrazioni comunali', in F. Barbagallo and I. Sales (eds), *Rapporto 1990 sulla camorra* (L'Unità, Rome, 1990), p. 133.
30 Ibid.
31 *La Repubblica*, 31 May 1991.
32 Statistics cited in Faenza, 'La camorra', p. 133.
33 Interview with Franco Malvano by the author, 3 December 1992.
    While allowing for a certain amount of exaggeration, the frequent irrelevancy of official political affiliation is also confirmed, from the opposite end of the spectrum, by supergrass Salvatore Migliorino. When asked about the political affiliation of the mayor of Torre Annunziata, with whom Migliorino had dealings for many years, he answered, 'He appears to be a socialist'; he then described two councillors as 'between Christian Democracy and the Socialist Party' and another politician thus: 'I don't know whether he was a Republican or Social Democrat, I can't really remember.' See Commissione Parlamentare di inchiesta sul fenomeno della mafia e sulle associazioni criminali similari, *Audizione di Salvatore Migliorino 12 novembre 1993* (Camera dei Deputati, Rome, 1993), pp. 3102, 3137.
34 *La Voce della Campania*, September 1989.
35 *L'Unità*, 3 May 1990.
36 *La Voce della Campania*, October 1992.
37 *Il Manifesto*, 26 January 1993.
38 *Il Manifesto*, 9 October 1984.
39 'Sentenza contro Nuvoletta', p. 32.
40 Cited in ibid., p. 21.
41 Stajano, *Mafia*, p. 87.
42 See 'Sentenza-ordinanza n. 1935/84 contro Amendola Giuseppe e altri', Tribunale Penale di Napoli, 28 March 1985, pp. 148–52.
43 *L'Unità*, 31 May 1990.
44 *Il Manifesto*, 9 October 1984.
45 *La Voce della Campania*, March 1987.
46 *L'Unità*, 31 May 1990.
47 'Sentenza contro Nuvoletta', p. 182.
48 'Mandato di cattura n. 104/86 contro Di Somma Raffaele e 5 altri', Tribunale Civile e Penale di Napoli, 9 April 1986, p. 25. See also F. Barbagallo and I. Sales, (eds), *Rapporto 1990 sulla camorra* (L'Unità, Rome, 1990), pp. 162–3.
49 'Mandato di cattura n. 104–86', p. 5.
50 Ibid., p. 6.
51 Ibid., p. 15.
52 F. Feo, *Uomini e affari della camorra* (Edizioni Sintesi, Naples, 1989), p. 68.

53 Ibid., p. 71.
54 Ibid., p. 72.
55 *Il Manifesto*, 11 October 1992.
56 Ibid., p. 31. See also Feo, *Uomini e affari*, pp. 55–60.
57 Interview with Francesco Cirillo conducted by the author, 2 February 1994. Cirillo is head of the Naples office of the Direzione Investigativa Antimafia, or Anti-Mafia Investigative Commission, a kind of Italian FBI created in October 1991.
58 Cited in D. Ceglie, 'Camorra e cemento', in V. Faenza (ed.), *Cosa Nostra Napoletana: Rapporto 1992 sulla camorra*. (Publiprint, Trento, 1993), p. 70.

5 THE CIRILLO AFFAIR

1 *L'Unità*, 4 August 1988.
2 Cited in G. Di Fiore, *Potere camorrista: Quattro secoli di malanapoli* (Guida, Naples, 1993), pp. 220–2. Nonno was later convicted of libel.
3 The film, a fictional account of Cutolo's criminal career, was entitled *Il camorrista* and starred Ben Gazzara in the title role. Cirillo, renamed Mesillo in the film, probably took exception to the following dialogue set in a prison, in which a leading politician appealed to Cutolo, using his real-life nickname, 'the Professor': 'Councillor Mesillo does not have a strong character; he has been in politics for thirty years in Campania and knows many things. If he should give in to the terrorists' blackmail, confidence in the institutions would be severely compromised. So Professor, my party is asking you to take action to save the councillor's life.' Although no legal action was taken against it, the film has virtually disappeared from cinema and home video screens; it was shown on television for the first time in March 1994. See the fascinating account in *Narcomafie*, October 1993.
4 Cited in 'Sentenza-ordinanza contro Cutolo Raffaele e altri', Tribunale di Napoli, 28 July 1988. The quotation from the Red Brigades' communiqué in fact comes from a shorter, edited version of 250 pages, rather than the 1,500 pages of the original sentence: see V. Vasile (ed.), *L'affare Cirillo: L'atto di accusa del giudice Carlo Alemi* (Editori Riuniti, Rome, 1989), p. 8.
5 'Sentenza n. 11219 contro Fabbrocino Mario e 94 altri', Tribunale Civile e Penale di Napoli, 29 August 1983, p. 23
6 *L'Unità*, 2 August 1988, citing an October 1984 Parliamentary Committee report on information and security written by Senator Libero Gualtieri. See also I. Sales, 'Ciro Cirillo', in N. Tranfaglia (ed.), *Cirillo, Ligato & Lima: Tre storie di mafia e politica* (Laterza, Bari and Rome, 1994), p. 47.
7 Cited in an Anti-Mafia Commission report on the Camorra approved on 21 December 1993, published in book form by *L'Unità*

and entitled *Rapporto sulla camorra* (Rome, 1994), p. 125. Hereafter referred to as *Rapporto sulla camorra*.

8 Cited in Vasile, *L'affare Cirillo*, p. 47.

9 'Sentenza-ordinanza n. 1140/81 contro Sabato Saviani e 261 altri', Tribunale Penale di Napoli, 21 January 1983, p. 49.

10 M. Figurato, *Patto Inconfessabile: Politica, crimine e affari dopo il caso Cirillo a Napoli* (Pironti, Naples, 1993), p. 48.

11 Ibid., p. 41.

12 See *Il Manifesto*, 22 September 1994.

13 Vasile, *L'affare Cirillo*, pp. 183–92.

14 Ibid., p. 98.

15 Ibid., p. 99.

16 See Sales, 'Ciro Cirillo', pp. 69–73, for a detailed reconstruction of the likely amount and contributors to the ransom payment.

17 See *Rapporto sulla camorra*, p. 140, and U. Santino and G. La Furia, *L'impresa mafiosa: Dall'Italia agli Stati Uniti* (Franco Angeli, Milan, 1990), p. 330.

18 Vasile, *L'affare Cirillo*, p. 218.

19 *La Repubblica*, 23 May 1989.

20 Vasile, *L'affare Cirillo*, p. 165.

21 *Oggi*, 12 August 1981.

22 Vasile, *L'affare Cirillo*, p. 7.

23 *Rapporto sulla camorra*, p. 147.

24 Vasile, *L'affare Cirillo*, pp. 239–40.

25 Ibid., p. 244.

26 F. Tarsitano and S. Pastore, *Il caso Cirillo: Parola d'ordine: Inquinare* (Tribunale di Napoli, Naples, 1990), pp. 88–9.

27 Vasile, *L'affare Cirillo*, p. 139, emphasis in the original.

28 *La Voce della Campania*, April 1988.

29 Ibid.

30 Vasile, *L'affare Cirillo*, pp. 158–9.

31 *La Repubblica*, 2 July 1993.

32 *L'Unità*, 7 February 1994.

33 Pasquale Galasso's revelations are likely to be more important for an understanding of the Camorra than Tommaso Buscetta's have been for understanding the Mafia. When Buscetta decided to cooperate with the authorities he had been living abroad for several years, away from the nerve centres of power. Galasso had been in the eye of the storm until his arrest, and had arguably played a more important role within the Camorra than Buscetta had within the Mafia.

   The fact that he has confessed to over twenty murders, and indicated to police where many of his victims were buried, makes it highly unlikely that Galasso might have any motive to invent his involvement in other crimes, such as those connected to the Cirillo affair. His credibility is also accepted by investigating magistrates, who are currently preparing a series of trials against major Neapolitan politicians based on his statements.

   We shall discuss Carmine Alfieri's gang, of which Galasso was a leading member, in later chapters.

34 Commissione Parlamentare di inchiesta sul fenomeno della mafia e sulle associazioni criminali similari, *Audizione di Pasquale Galasso 13 luglio 1993* (Camera dei Deputati, Rome, 1993), p. 2313.
35 Ibid., pp. 2314–15.
36 Cited in Vasile, *L'affare Cirillo*, p. 26.
37 The Oxford Dictionary defines symbiosis as 'an association of two different living organisms attached to each other or one within the other, usually to their mutual advantage.' It is a concept frequently used by Camorra supergrass Pasquale Galasso.
38 Tarsitano and Pastore, *Il caso Cirillo*, p. 50.
39 Cited originally in 'Richiesta di autorizzazione a procedere nei confronti di Antonio Gava, Raffaele Mastrantuono, Vincenzo Meo, Paolo Cirino Pomicino e Alfredo Vito', Direzione Distrettuale Antimafia, Naples, 6 April 1993. The same document has been published in book form by M. Coscia (ed.), *Il patto scellerato: Potere e politica di un regime mafioso* (Crescenzi Allendorf, Rome, 1993), p. 197.
40 Coscia, *Il patto scellerato*, p. 242. Salvatore Alfieri, Carmine's brother, was murdered five months after Cirillo's release, in December 1981.
41 *Audizione di Pasquale Galasso 13 luglio 1993*, p. 2264. The Dorotea faction was formed in the 1950s and was, roughly speaking, a centrist faction within the DC.
42 *Rapporto sulla camorra*, p. 145.
43 Coscia, *Il patto scellerato*, p. 248.

6 HOW THE CAMORRA WORKS

1 *Panorama*, 14 January 1994.
2 See A. Lamberti, 'La camorra: Struttura, dimensioni e caratteristiche dei fenomeni di criminalità organizzata in Campania negli anni 90', *Osservatorio sulla Camorra* 2, June 1992, pp. 15–22.
3 N. Tranfaglia, *La mafia come metodo nell'Italia contemporanea* (Laterza, Rome and Bari, 1991), p. 99.
4 F. Feo, *Uomini e affari della camorra* (Edizioni Sintesi, Naples, 1989), p. 193.
5 Anti-Mafia Commission report on the Camorra approved on 21 December 1993, published in book form by *L'Unità* in February 1994 and entitled *Rapporto sulla camorra*; see also page 77. Hereafter referred to as *Rapporto sulla camorra*.
6 The use of the masculine pronoun here and elsewhere is deliberate. While female activity within Camorra gangs certainly exists, at a higher level than within the Mafia, there are, apart from Raffaele Cutolo's sister Rosetta and Pupetta Maresca, no significant examples of women becoming major gang leaders; indeed, both these women's 'criminal careers' were probably mapped out by their brother and husband/lover respectively.
7 Commissione Parlamentare di inchiesta sul fenomeno della mafia e

sulle associazioni criminali similari, *Audizione di Pasquale Galasso 13 luglio 1993* (Camera dei Deputati, Rome, 1993), p. 2233.
8 Ibid., p. 2236.
9 Cited in F. Imposimato, 'Da camorra a mafia', in V. Faenza (ed.), *Cosa Nostra napoletana. Rapporto 1992 sulla camorra* (Publiprint, Trento, 1993), p. 34.
10 *La Repubblica*, 25 February 1992.
11 *La Repubblica*, 5 December 1991.
12 Feo, *Uomini e affari*, p. 145.
13 Ibid., p. 146.
14 *Fortune*, (Italian edition), July/August 1991.
15 Interview with Francesco Cirillo conducted by the author, 2 February 1994. Cirillo is head of the Naples office of the Direzione Investigativa Antimafia, or Anti-Mafia Investigative Commission, a kind of Italian FBI created in October 1991.
16 It is difficult not to believe this hypothesis. In the 1986–7 season the Naples team had performed brilliantly, and they continued to do so the following year – five games before the end of the season they were four points clear of their rivals Milan. Then they suddenly collapsed, Maradona even refused to play in one match, and the team fell apart, winning just one point in five games and so allowing Milan to win the League.

   Furthermore, there is considerable circumstantial evidence to link Maradona to the Camorra: he was photographed socialising with some of the Giuliano brothers on more than one occasion, he had relationships with women closely linked to Camorra clans, and developed a cocaine habit which eventually led to his rapid departure from Naples as a result of a ban on playing and the obligation to face a trial.
17 *The Independent*, 29 December 1993.
18 Cited in M. Coscia (ed.), *Il patto scellerato: Potere e politica di un regime mafioso* (Crescenzi Allendorf, Rome, 1993), pp. 218–19.
19 Cited in ibid., p. 236.
20 Ibid., p. 237.
21 *European*, 7 September 1990. See also G. Di Fiore, *Il palazzo dei misteri* (Il Mattino, Naples, 1991), p. 90.
22 *La Repubblica*, 6 October 1991. An even more sordid fact concerning the same contract has since come to light. According to the managers of the companies that won the new contracts, before signing, council politicians had demanded the right to choose the new workers. Three months later three councillors – the Socialists Di Donato and Mastrantuono and the Christian Democrat Vito – began demanding kickbacks totalling $1 million. See *Il Manifesto*, 16 March 1993.
23 *Il Messagero*, 17 January 1993.
24 *Il Manifesto*, 25 September 1992.
25 *Rapporto sulla camorra*, p. 158.
26 *Observer*, 13 February 1994.
27 Cited in J. Haycraft, *The Italian Labyrinth: Italy in the 1980s* (Secker

& Warburg, London, 1985), pp. 199–200. The Agnelli referred to is Gianni Agnelli, president of the Turin-based car multinational.

28 *La Repubblica*, 17 November 1991.

29 *La Repubblica*, 22 December 1991. The Lockheed scandal broke in 1976, when it emerged that the American aircraft company had been paying bribes to politicians in several major countries in order to gain contracts; one minister, Mario Tanassi, was briefly sent to jail the following year. The first petrol scandal occurred in 1974, when it was discovered that major petrol companies were secretly financing parties in return for favourable legislation, while the second petrol scandal, in 1980, saw the involvement of politicians, finance police and petrol companies in tax frauds worth $1.6 billion. Zaza's outburst now carries even more weight when one considers that it came three months before the all-encompassing *Tangentopoli* scandal began to emerge in Milan.

30 *La Repubblica*, 3 March 1992.

31 G. Ruotolo, *La quarta mafia: Storie di mafia in Puglia* (Pironti, Naples, 1994), pp. 147–8. See also, *Rapporto sulla camorra*, p. 24.

32 *Il Manifesto*, 19 December 1991.

33 Commissione Parlamentare di inchiesta sul fenomeno della mafia e sulle associazioni criminali similari, *Audizione di Salvatore Migliorino 12 novembre 1993* (Camera dei Deputati, Rome, 1993), p. 3136.

34 *Il Manifesto*, 20 December 1991.

35 *Narcomafie*, February 1994.

36 Cited in A. Becchi and M. Turvani, *Proibito? Il mercato mondiale della droga* (Donzelli, Rome, 1993), p. 121.

37 A. Lamberti, 'Le trasformazioni strutturali della camorra', in F. Barbagallo and I. Sales (eds), *Rapporto 1990 sulla camorra* (L'Unità, Rome, 1990), p. 103.

38 Lamberti, 'La camorra', p. 21.

39 A. Cipriani, *Mafia: Il riciclaggio del denaro sporco* (Napoleone, Rome, 1989), p. 23, and Feo, *Uomini e affari*, pp. 157–8.

40 Cipriani, *Mafia*, p. 24.

41 *Il Manifesto*, 29/30 September 1992.

42 Lamberti, 'La camorra', p. 34.

43 Gianfranco Donadio, an investigating magistrate at the Salerno Law Courts who specialises in money laundering investigations, writing in *La Voce della Campania*, May 1993.

44 *Rapporto sulla camorra*, p. 81.

45 See Coscia, *Il patto scellerato*, pp. 267–72.

46 *La Repubblica*, 9 November 1991.

47 Cipriani, *Mafia*, pp. 55–6.

48 As regards Italian organised crime in the US, the fact that Sicilian migration to North America in the early part of this century was far higher than Campanian migration, gave many Sicilian-based Mafiosi a bolt-hole to run to during the Fascist period. This large expat community then became a launching pad during the Allied invasion of Sicily in 1943. The smaller number of Neapolitans

residing in the US has always meant that the Sicilians have dominated Italian organised crime in the US.

49 See *The Times*, 12 November 1991, and the *Sunday Times*, 2
January 1994.
50 Interview with Robert Elliott, detective at the Organized Crime
Unit, US National Criminal Intelligence Service, conducted by the
author, 4 February 1993.
51 *Guardian*, 14 March 1992.
52 See *La Repubblica*, 13 January 1991.
53 *Il Manifesto*, 2 July 1992.
54 *Guardian*, 11 January 1994.
55 Feo, *Uomini e affari*, p. 91.
56 Ibid., p. 95.
57 See C. Sterling, *The Mafia: The Long Reach of the International
Sicilian Mafia* (Grafton, London, 1990), pp. 335–7.
58 Feo, *Uomini e affari*, pp. 89–90.
59 *Guardian*, 26 July 1991.
60 *Panorama*, 7 July 1991.
61 S. Cervasio and A. M. Chiariello, 'I grandi latitanti', in V. Faenza
(ed.), *Cosa Nostra napoletana: Rapporto 1992 sulla camorra* (Publiprint, Trento, 1993), pp. 93–4. For further details of Ammaturo's
South American cocaine deals, see Feo, *Uomini e affari*, pp. 159–60.
62 *Il Giornale di Napoli*, 13 March 1992.
63 *Il Manifesto*, 5 July 1992.
64 A report written by Leonid Fituni, Director of the Centre for
Global and Strategic Studies at the Moscow Academy of Science,
reproduced in *Narcomafie*, November 1993.
65 *Guardian*, 14 March 1992.
66 *Independent*, 3 February 1993.
67 *Il Mattino*, 6 February 1994.
68 Interview with Francesco Cirillo conducted by the author, 2 February 1994.

7 CRIMINAL POLITICS

1 The 1901 report of Giuseppe Saredo's Commission of Inquiry into
Naples, cited in an Anti-Mafia Commission report on the Camorra
approved on 21 December 1993, published in book form by
L'Unità in February 1994 and entitled *Rapporto sulla camorra*,
p. 96 (hereafter referred to as *Rapporto sulla camorra*).
2 G. Di Fiore, *Potere camorrista: Quattro secoli di malanapoli* (Guida,
Naples, 1993), p. 191.
3 *Rinascita*, 20 January 1984.
4 Amato Lamberti, interviewed in *La Repubblica*, 31 May 1991.
5 *Il Manifesto*, 23 September 1992. This small example raises a very
important issue in terms of mass popular resistance to the Camorra:
the effectiveness of genuine mass action is complicated by the fact
that gangs sometimes deliberately organise and encourage mass
actions for their own interests.

Politicians can also be directly involved in mass protests which are not what they seem. Ex-DC Senator Francesco Patriarca is currently accused of organising a series of demonstrations in Gragnano during the early 1980s with the Rosanova gang, which were part of a campaign to obtain public sector contracts; see *Il Manifesto*, 4 July 1993.

6 I. Sales, 'Gli enti locali tra illegalità ed inefficienza', in *Enti locali in Campania: Radiografia di un malessere* (Editrice Sintesi, Naples, 1985), p. 11.

7 Ibid., p. 12.

8 Ibid., p. 14.

9 See *La Repubblica*, 13 April 1990, and *Il Manifesto*, 18 April 1990.

10 Judge Paolo Mancuso, interviewed in *La Repubblica*, 14 April 1990.

11 Ibid.

12 G. Di Fiore, *Il palazzo dei misteri* (Il Mattino, Naples, 1991), p. 139.

13 Ibid.

14 Ibid., p. 140.

15 Ibid., p. 56.

16 *La Repubblica*, 5 December 1991. Masciari later faced charges relating to a $5 million bank account he was unable to find an explanation for; magistrates suspect it derives from bribes paid for a fast-tram line planned but never built, and for works connected with the 1990 World Cup; see *Il Manifesto*, 27 February 1993. After two years on the run he finally turned himself in in March 1993 to face a series of charges, including membership of the Camorra.

17 *Guardian*, 14 September 1990.

18 *La Repubblica*, 4 June 1992.

19 *Rapporto sulla camorra*, pp. 91–2.

20 *Il Manifesto*, 30 March 1993.

21 Statement made to the Anti-Mafia Commission, cited in *Rapporto sulla camorra*, p. 95. Tagliamonte was mayor from April to July 1993.

22 *Rapporto sulla camorra*, p. 199, note.

23 Ibid., p. 93.

24 'Ordinanza di custodia cautelare in carcere n. 638/93 contro Carmine Alfieri e 22 altri', Tribunale di Napoli, 3 November 1993, p. 131 (hereafter referred to as 'Ordinanza contro Carmine Alfieri').

Interestingly enough, the town is named after an Egyptian saint who, apart from proposing a semi-hermitic lifestyle, is often represented in popular tradition as fighting against demons; he is also a protector of animals, particularly domestic ones.

25 Ibid., p. 132.

26 Ibid., p. 223.

27 Ibid., p. 226.

28 Ibid., p. 137.

29 Ibid., p. 140.

30 Ibid., p. 138.

31 Ibid., p. 144.

32 Ibid., p. 150.

33 Ibid., p. 192.
34 Ibid., pp. 268–9.
35 Ibid., pp. 270–1
36 *Rapporto sulla camorra*, p. 168.
37 'Ordinanza contro Carmine Alfieri', p. 185.
38 Ibid., p. 196
39 'Sentenza-Ordinanza n. 148/88 contro Catello De Riso, Ciro D'Auria, Bernardo Santonicola, Gaetano Mercurio e Diodato D'Auria', Tribunale di Napoli, 20 April 1989, p. 8.
40 Ibid., p. 12.
41 'Ordinanza contro Carmine Alfieri', p. 191.
42 Ibid., p. 193.
43 *Rapporto sulla camorra*, p. 171.
44 'Ordinanza contro Carmine Alfieri', p. 170.
45 *Roma*, 7 August 1993.
46 Minister of the Interior report dated 26 August 1993, reproduced in *Gazzetta Ufficiale della Repubblica Italiana*, 6 September 1993.
47 Reproduced in the *Gazzetta Ufficiale della Repubblica Italiana*, 6 September 1993.
48 See R. D. Putnam, *Making Democracy Work: Civic Traditions in Modern Italy* (Princeton University Press, Princeton, 1993), p. 211, note.
49 S. Minolfi and F. Soverina, *L'incerta frontiera: Saggio sui consiglieri comunali a Napoli 1946–92* (E.S.I., Naples, 1993), p. 52.
50 Putnam, *Making Democracy Work*, p. 27.
51 See ibid., pp. 73, 201–4.
52 ISTAT, *Le regioni in cifre* (ISTAT, Rome, 1993), p. 24.
53 Patriarca also faces charges of illegally favouring the application for a cleaning contract by a company owned by his nephew, worth $320,000 annually between 1983–90. See *Il Mattino*, 8 April 1993.
54 The most detailed account of USL 35 is G. Martano, 'L'Usl malata', in V. Faenza (ed.), *Cosa Nostra napoletana. Rapporto 1992 sulla camorra* (Publiprint, Trento, 1993), pp. 115–22.
55 *Avvenimenti*, 3 February 1993. Primary schools in Castellammare also recently found themselves without school dinners, due to Camorra intimidation aimed at winning the contract for supplying the food. See *Il Giornale di Napoli*, 18 November 1994.
56 *Il Manifesto*, 18 April 1990. There is also a photograph taken in 1980, which shows Gava together with Alfieri and Galasso at the opening of a local school. See *Il Manifesto*, 22 September 1994.
57 See M. Figurato, *Patto inconfessabile: Politica, crimine e affari dopo il caso Cirillo a Napoli* (Pironti, Naples, 1993), p. 28, and M. Coscia (ed.), *Il patto scellerato – Potere e politica di un regime mafioso* (Crescenzi Allendorf, Rome, 1993), p. 207.
58 *L'Espresso*, 25 September 1983.
59 *Il Mattino*, 8 January 1994.
60 Figurato, *Patto inconfessabile*, pp. 14–15.
61 S. Messina, *Nomenklatura* (Mondadori, Milan, 1992), p. 54.
62 Coscia, *Il patto scellerato*, p. 312.

63 *La Repubblica*, 23 April 1994; emphasis in the original.
64 *L'Espresso*, 30 September 1994.
65 Cited in 'Ordinanza contro Carmine Alfieri', pp. 134–5.
66 Interview with Francesco Cirillo conducted by the author, 2 February 1994. Cirillo is head of the Naples office of the *Direzione Investigativa Antimafia*, or Anti-Mafia Investigative Commission, a kind of Italian FBI created in October 1991.
67 Commissione Parlamentare di inchiesta sul fenomeno della mafia e sulle associazioni criminali similari, *Audizione di Pasquale Galasso 17 settembre 1993* (Camera dei Deputati, Rome, 1993), pp. 2748–9.
68 Cited in Messina, *Nomenklatura*, p. 53.
69 See V. Faenza, 'La camorra nelle amministrazioni comunali', in F. Barbagallo and I. Sales (eds), *Rapporto 1990 sulla camorra* (L'Unità, Rome, 1990), pp. 126-7, for a review of some of the other methods used.
70 See G. D'Agostino, 'Voto e camorra', in F. Barbagallo (ed.), *Camorra e criminalità in Campania* (Liguori, Naples, 1988), pp. 86–91, for a discussion of electoral trends influenced by the Camorra. See also F. Imposimato, 'Potere politico e criminalità', in F. Barbagallo and I. Sales (eds), *Rapporto 1990 sulla camorra* (L'Unità, Rome, 1990), pp. 63–70, for a slightly more impressionistic view.
71 Commissione Parlamentare di inchiesta sul fenomeno della mafia e sulle associazioni criminali similari, *Audizione di Pasquale Galasso 13 luglio 1993* (Camera dei Deputati, Rome, 1993), pp. 2277–8.
72 Cited in Coscia, *Il patto scellerato*, p. 215.
73 Ibid., p. 275.
74 *La Repubblica*, 23 April 1993.
75 Isaia Sales, writing in *La Voce della Campania*, May 1992.

8 WHO WILL STOP THE CAMORRA?

1 V. Sgroi, *Relazione sull'amministrazione della Giustizia nell'anno 1991*, (Stamperia Reale, Rome, 1992), p. 66.
2 These tables are extrapolated from the *statistiche giudiziarie* of the government's statistical office, ISTAT. The discrepancies in some of the figures are due to the fact that legal procedings initiated in a given year often relate to crimes committed in previous years.
3 *La Repubblica*, 4 April 1990.
4 Ibid.
5 Senato della Repubblica–Camera dei Deputati, X. Legislatura, Commissione Antimafia, Doc. XXIII, n. 9 (Tipografia del Senato, Rome, 1989), pp. 38–9.
6 ISTAT, *Statistiche giudiziarie*. Despite the absence of powerful criminal gangs, the same unemployment-related economic hardship causes a similar, if not more marked, trend in Britain; in 1993 70 per cent of convicted offenders were unemployed.
7 Prisons Department statistics, cited in *Narcomafie*, March 1994. According to official statistics there were 29 suicides and 531 attempted suicides in Italian jails in 1992, together with 8,385

individual hunger strikes. Such desperate action is provoked not only by the long period spent held on remand, but also by overcrowding. The trend worsened in the first half of 1993: 26 suicides in the first six months alone, 260 attempted suicides, and 5,324 hunger strikes. See EURISPES, *Rapporto Italia '94* (Koinè, Rome, 1994), p. 735. The situation is now so dramatic that in August 1994 the 'Victims of Injustice Association' organised a three-day work and hunger strike, and could subsequently claim that 70 per cent of inmates had supported the action; see *Il Mattino*, 17 August 1994.

Things are no better in British jails: 221 suicides between 1990 and 1994, and an average of 3,000 acts of self-mutilation per year.

8 *Il Manifesto*, 27 April 1994.
9 Senato della Repubblica–Camera dei Deputati, X. Legislatura, Commissione Antimafia, Doc. XXIII, n. 9 (Tipografia del Senato, Rome, 1989), pp. 17–18.
10 *La Repubblica*, 3 April 1990.
11 *Il Manifesto*, 13/14 July 1993.
12 *Il Manifesto*, 22 March 1994.
13 This account is taken from *La Repubblica*, 20 April 1994, and *Il Manifesto*, 21 April 1994.
14 *Il Mattino*, 27 September 1994.
15 G. Locatelli, *Mazzette e manette: Dizionario di politici e imprenditori beccati a Napoli e a Milano* (Pironti, Naples, 1993), p. 108.
16 *Il Manifesto*, 21 May 1993.
17 *Il Manifesto* and *Il Mattino*, 22 May 1993.
18 *Il Mattino*, 29 May 1993.
19 Commissione Parlamentare di inchiesta sul fenomeno della mafia e sulle associazioni criminali similari, *Audizione di Pasquale Galasso 17 settembre 1993* (Camera dei Deputati, Rome, 1993), p. 2735.
20 See M. Coscia (ed.), *Il patto scellerato: Potere e politica di un regime mafioso* (Crescenzi Allendorf, Rome, 1993), p. 208.
21 Ibid., pp. 209–10.
22 *Audizione di Pasquale Galasso 17 settembre 1993*, p. 2737.
23 *Independent*, 12 March 1994. This has been confirmed by ex-DC senator and lawyer Dino Bargi, who admitted to being the contact between Galasso and Cono Lancuba. He also stated that 'the three of us' – i.e. a *camorrista*, a lawyer and a judge – 'passed many evenings together' in a house at Positano. See *Il Manifesto*, 13 March 1994.
24 Commissione Parlamentare di inchiesta sul fenomeno della mafia e sulle associazioni criminali similari, *Audizione di Pasquale Galasso 13 luglio 1993* (Camera dei Deputati, Rome, 1993), p. 2314.
25 G. Di Fiore, *Il palazzo dei misteri* (Il Mattino, Naples, 1991), p. 14.
26 *Il Manifesto*, 9 March 1994.
27 Commissione Parlamentare di inchiesta sul fenomeno della mafia e sulle associazioni criminali similari, *Audizione di Salvatore Migliorino 12 novembre 1993* (Camera dei Deputati, Rome, 1993), p. 3118.
28 *Audizione di Pasquale Galasso 17 settembre 1993*, p. 2738.

29 The High Council of Magistrates plenary session of 9 April 1988. Cited in *Rapporto sulla camorra* (L'Unità, Rome, 1994), p. 98.

Regina Coeli and Poggioreale are the two main jails of Rome and Naples respectively, while the backstreets of Via Toledo are a particularly poor area of Naples.

30 *Panorama*, 14 January 1994.

31 *L'Espresso*, 21 October 1994.

32 The Italian Communist Party (PCI), founded in 1921, changed its name in 1991 to the Democratic Party of the Left (PDS). At the same time it also transformed its programme by adopting openly social-democratic policies, thus officially sanctioning a process which had been evolving over the preceding thirty years.

33 *Guardian*, 14 September 1990.

34 The 'historic compromise' was first formulated in late 1973 by PCI leader Enrico Berlinguer in response to the military coup in Chile. He argued that Salvador Allende's left-wing government had gone too far and had antagonised the right-wing opposition. For Berlinguer, therefore, '51 per cent [of the electorate] wasn't enough' for the left to govern, an alliance must be built with the centre or right parties at all costs, i.e. a 'historic compromise' must be made. The closest this policy came to actual practice was the PCI's promise not to 'no confidence' Giulio Andreotti's Christian Democrat government of 1976–9. In exchange the Christian Democrats frequently hinted that communists might join their government, but the agreement was dropped once the DC regained strength.

In many ways the 'historic compromise' was a more modern version of the 'Popular Front' policies followed by western communist parties during the 1930s. See T. Behan, '*Forward to 1921: The dissolution of the Italian Communist Party*', University of Reading Politics Department occasional paper no. 3, 1991.

35 A. Galdo, 'Il lottatore stanco', *Nord e Sud* 17, January/March 1982, p. 9.

36 Ibid., p. 13.

37 M. Figurato, *Patto inconfessabile: Politica, crimine e affari dopo il caso Cirillo a Napoli* (Pironti, Naples, 1993), p. 92.

38 *Il Mattino*, 8 April 1993.

39 *Il Giornale di Napoli* and *Il Manifesto*, 24 April 1993.

40 *Il Manifesto* and *La Repubblica*, 20 April 1993

41 *Il Manifesto*, 29 April 1994.

42 *Il Manifesto*, 10 May 1994. At the November 1994 local elections in Campania there were many joint tickets of the PDS and the Popular Party, the remnants of the Christian Democrats, for example, in the major town of Casoria.

43 *Il Manifesto*, 19 June 1992.

44 *Il Giornale di Napoli*, 26 January 1993.

45 *Audizione di Pasquale Galasso 13 luglio 1993*, p. 2283. The use of inverted commas here is intended to highlight the incongruity of professionals dedicating themselves to the cause of communism.

46 *Il Manifesto*, 3 and 26 April 1992.

47 *L'Espresso*, 18 February 1994.
48 *Panorama*, 31 December 1993.
49 *Il Mattino*, 25 November 1982.
50 *L'Unità*, 28 November 1982.
51 *L'Unità*, 10 December 1982, *Il Mattino* and *Paese Sera*, 11 December 1982.
52 *Paese Sera*, 18 December 1982.
53 *Guardian* and *Il Mattino*, 27 January 1983.
54 *Il Manifesto, Il Mattino, Paese Sera* and *La Repubblica*, 12 February 1983.
55 Until recently Naples had a significant industrial working class, mainly centred on the massive Bagnoli steelworks. See F. Mazzucca, *Il mare e la fornace* (Ediesse, Rome, 1983), and Istituto campano per la storia della Resistenza, *Italsider: Una fabbrica, una città* (Naples, 1983). Indeed it is no coincidence that the rise of the Camorra generally coincides with the decline of the industrial working class: not only has the level of unemployment and under-employment risen as a result of factory closures, the absence of organised labour has been a critical element in Naples from the early 1980s onwards. Nevertheless, general strikes are not infrequent; for example, October 1993 saw a strike and demonstration of 50,000 people, with more than twice as many marching a year later.
    Naples has also experienced the longest and probably largest movement of the unemployed of any major western city. The *movimento dei disoccupati organizzati* was formed in Castellammare in 1972, and although it has undergone many changes since then – the most disturbing being Camorra infiltration – demonstrations of thousands of unemployed are still regular events. Again, the most recent notable action occurred in October 1993, when the cathedral was occupied symbolically by hundreds of unemployed, who accused all civil institutions of abandoning them. See P. Basso, *Disoccupati e Stato: Il movimento dei disoccupati organizzati a Napoli (1975–81)* (Franco Angeli, Milan, 1981), and F. Ramondino (ed.), *Napoli: I disoccupati organizzati* (Feltrinelli, Milan, 1977).
    These traditions of mass resistance extend back through the century, and notably include the four-day insurrection of October 1943 which forced the Germans to withdraw from the city.

CONCLUSION: 'HA DDA PASSÀ 'A NUTTATA'

1 This phrase, in Neapolitan dialect, is one of the best-known sayings associated with the city's most famous actor and playwright, Eduardo De Filippo. Roughly translated, it means 'the bad times must come to an end'.
2 F. Feo, *Uomini e affari della camorra* (Edizioni Sintesi, Naples, 1989), p. 25.
3 F. Imposimato, 'Da camorra a mafia', in V. Faenza (ed.), *Cosa Nostra napoletana: Rapporto 1992 sulla camorra* (Publiprint, Trento, 1993), p. 32.

4 See M. Coscia (ed.), *Il patto scellerato: Potere e politica di un regime mafioso* (Crescenzi Allendorf, Rome, 1993), p. 210.

5 Feo, *Uomini e affari*, p. 34.

6 Commissione Parlamentare di inchiesta sul fenomeno della mafia e sulle associazioni criminali similari, *Audizione di Pasquale Galasso 13 luglio 1993* (Camera dei Deputati, Rome 1993), p. 2233.

7 See Coscia, *Il patto scellerato*, p. 211.

8 *Il Manifesto*, 22 October 1992.

9 J. Walston, 'See Naples and die: Organized crime in Campania', in R. J. Kelly (ed.), *Organized Crime: A Global Perspective* (Rowman & Littlefield, Lanham, Md., 1986), p. 143.

10 Ibid., p. 153.

11 Interview with Francesco Cirillo, head of the Naples office of the DIA, conducted by the author, 2 February 1994.

12 *Audizione di Pasquale Galasso 13 luglio 1993*, p. 2327.

13 Anti-Mafia Commission report on the Camorra approved on 21 December 1993, published in book form by *L'Unità* in February 1994 and entitled *Rapporto sulla camorra*, p. 185 (hereafter referred to as *Rapporto sulla camorra*).

14 *Il Manifesto*, 1 April and 1 May 1994.

15 Throughout the 1980s there was a succession of supergrasses, beginning with Pasquale Barra who, realising that Cutolo was prepared to let him be killed, decided to reveal details of NCO murders in order to gain greater protection. He was followed by Giovanni Pandico, one of the NCO's 'brains', whose accusations led to many of the arrests in the 1983 'maxi-blitz'; many of his allegations, however, were later proved to be unfounded. The third major NCO supergrass was Mario Incarnato, who confessed to a series of murders in late 1983. In the mid-1980s Giovanni Auriemma exposed the NCO's links with the secret services, while Pasquale D'Amico revealed Cutolo's links with Calabrian organisations.

16 Nunzio Giuliano is best described as a 'dissociate' *camorrista* rather than a supergrass. Over the last twenty years the Giuliano gang has always been amongst the top five Camorra gangs in the city of Naples, and is probably the longest-surviving gang in existence today. Their stronghold, Forcella, is an area of central Naples between the station and the cathedral.

Those who dissociate themselves from a Camorra gang let it be known both to the judiciary and to their former accomplices that their criminal activities are now over. Although this stance may lead to considerable judicial interest for several years and the risk of retribution from gang members, once this critical period is over, there is the possibility of full rehabilitation into society. Somebody who chooses to 'grass' on former gang members either has to build a new identity or live with the permanent risk of retribution.

Nunzio Giuliano's dissociation was prompted by the death of his eldest son Vittorio in October 1987 through a heroin overdose. Interviews conducted by the author, 21 and 25 January 1993.

17 See *Il Manifesto*, 23 September 1994.

18 Alberto Ziparo of Catania University, writing in *Il Manifesto*, 8 July 1993.
19 G. Falcone with M. Padovani, *Men of Honour: The Truth about the Mafia* (Warner Books, London, 1993), p. 135.
20 Earthquake expert Professor Rocco Caporale, cited in the *Guardian*, 16 October 1993.
21 *Il Manifesto*, 20 May 1994. Indeed, many experts are worried that the administration's inability to meet EC deadlines may even lead to the funds never being released; see *Il Mattino*, 18 November 1994.
22 Diego Gambetta, writing in *L'Indice*, December 1993.
23 Falcone, *Men of Honour*, p. 141.
24 'La relazione di minoranza nella Commissione Parlamentare Anti-mafia', published in book form as *Mafia e politica in Italia (1984–1990)* (Edizioni Associate, Rome, 1990), p. 79.
25 *Il Manifesto*, 9 October 1984.
26 G. Martano, 'Comuni senza governo', in V. Faenza (ed.), *Cosa Nostra napoletana: Rapporto 1992 sulla camorra* (Publiprint, Trento, 1993), p. 63. It is interesting to see how earlier laws have been modified: until 1977 the commitment for trial of a mayor or the head of a council committee was enough to lead to their suspension from office, yet as a result one council out of eight in Italy had its mayor suspended; the law was therefore changed to allow councillors to stay in office until convicted.
27 Government statistics, cited in *Il Manifesto*, 13 August 1993. The same tendency can be seen in the US: the rise in the prison population from 300,000 in 1980 to 1,400,000 in 1993 has done nothing to cut the crime rate; on the contrary, it has risen during this period.
      A similar trend, this time related to re-offending, can be noted in Britain. Sixty-five per cent of those convicted of burglary in 1987 who received prison sentences were reconvicted of either burglary or another crime within two years of their release. See the *Guardian*, 11 January 1994.
28 Vito Mattera, cited in G. Di Fiore, *Il palazzo dei misteri* (Il Mattino, Naples, 1991), pp. 119–20.
      It is interesting to compare the realistic views of Italian policemen and politicians on strategies to beat organised crime with those of their counterparts in Britain and the US. In Italy the discussion revolves around political honesty and material conditions; moral crusades about 'back to basics' and 'family values' are almost entirely absent from the debate. The strong traditional family structure in southern Italy, combined with the South's high level of crime, is clear evidence that it is not the lack of a 'traditional family life' that causes crime.
29 According to Agostino Cordova, Naples' Federal Prosecutor, interviewed in *Il Manifesto*, 21 November 1994.
30 *Rapporto sulla camorra*, p. 20.
31 Interview with Nunzio Giuliano conducted by the author, 21 January 1993.

32 V. Faenza, 'Cosa Nostra napoletana/1', in V. Faenza (ed.), *Cosa Nostra napoletana: Rapporto 1992 sulla camorra* (Publiprint, Trento, 1993), p. 24.

33 I. Sales, 'Introduzione', in V. Faenza (ed.), *Cosa Nostra napoletana: Rapporto 1992 sulla camorra* (Publiprint, Trento, 1993), p. 7.

34 Interview with Nunzio Giuliano.

35 Imposimato, 'Da camorra a mafia', p. 39. Imposimato is a magistrate specialising in fighting organised crime and has also recently become a consultant for the UN task force against the drugs trade.

36 The general climate of illegality tolerated and even encouraged by the ruling class is closely related to the existence of criminal gangs. Many people live in an environment characterised not only by powerful criminal gangs, but also by a general disrespect towards many day-to-day laws and regulations that is shared by both institutions and people in general. The existence of these two elements side by side naturally creates a political climate of fear, cynicism and passivity.

37 The question of the illegal or 'submerged economy' does not concern the South alone. See P. Mattera, *Off the Books: The Rise of the Underground Economy* (Pluto Press, London, 1985), pp. 84–97, for a broad discussion concerning the whole of Italy.

38 *Audizione di Pasquale Galasso 13 luglio 1993,* p. 2309.

39 Interview with Nunzio Giuliano.

40 Coscia, *Il patto scellerato*, p. 257.

41 *Audizione di Pasquale Galasso 13 luglio 1993*, p. 2278.

42 Interview with Nunzio Giuliano.

Index